Telling
the
Bible

To the Gang at Spring Harvest

BOB HARTMAN

Telling the Bible

Over 100 stories to read out loud

MONARCH
BOOKS

Oxford, UK & Grand Rapids, Michigan, USA

Published by Monarch Books
an imprint of
Lion Hudson plc
Wilkinson House, Jordan Hill Road,
Oxford OX2 8DR, England
Email: monarch@lionhudson.com
www.lionhudson.com/monarch

An earlier version of this material was previously published under the Lion
imprint as *Telling the Bible* and *Telling the Bible 2*

ISBN: 978-1-85424-774-2

First combined edition 2006

Acknowledgments
Unless otherwise stated, Scripture quotations are
taken from the Holy Bible, New International Version,
© 1973, 1978, 1984 by the International Bible Society.
Used by permission of Hodder & Stoughton Ltd.
All rights reserved.

A catalogue record for this book is available from the British Library.

Contents

Introduction

A couple of years ago, at a Christian festival, I was asked to read a passage from the Bible before the speaker got up to deliver the evening message. As I sat in my chalet, reading the text, the storyteller in me took over! I saw a line in the passage that made a good chorus – something simple and fun that everyone could repeat. So I reshaped the text with that in mind, and the crowd seemed to really enjoy it.

I was asked to do the same on the following few nights as well, and when I got home, I had a look at some of the other readings and short stories I had written over the years. Many of them were aimed at children or at all-age gatherings, but there were quite a few that had a lot more to say to adults. So I thought, Why not put them together into some kind of collection? Why not drop in a few suggestions for telling them as well – to make them easier to use? Why not see if others could find some use for them – in worship or in teaching or in small groups or even for personal meditation? And that's where *Telling the Bible* came from.

To be fair, *Telling (a bit of) the Bible* would probably be a more accurate title! There are only about 100 readings and stories here, so the book is not exhaustive by any means. As you will see, this volume is New Testament-heavy, with a particular bias for the works of Luke. That is because those were the passages I was dealing with and that's just how it turned out! What I can say is that I have tried to include readings for the major Christian holidays, and that most of them have been 'road-tested' – usually on the congregation at Bethesda Baptist Church in Trowbridge. In fact, many of these readings arose from my attempts to wrestle with the biblical passages, week by week, in a pastoral context.

As you will see, I deal with lots of different issues in the book. It's quite a personal book, in that sense. You might agree with my opinions on some things, and totally disagree with my opinions on others. So feel free to pick and choose. And also feel free to change, adapt and edit the material for your own particular situation. Because shaping and reshaping lies at the heart of all storytelling.

Finally, some of these readings will still seem more child-friendly than others, and you might feel happier using them primarily in Family Services. I do find, however, that when I tell them to the whole church – and am not specific about which age group they are for – that everyone accepts them just as they are. I also never ask the kids to come the front. If you make the reading for everybody, then everybody will listen! If you'd like more tips on storytelling techniques, you might like to pick up a copy of my book *Anyone Can Tell a Story*.

This is all a bit of an experiment – an experiment I have really enjoyed! I'm perfectly willing to accept the possibility that some people might not appreciate the kind of playing around with the texts that I have done here. But, I find that crawling into a text, asking questions and then coming out the other side, is the best way to discover what it's all about – to be surprised, challenged, moved and won over by what God has to say there. That has certainly been true for me. And as you use this book, as you 'tell' the Bible, I hope that it will be true for you as well.

Two Stories

With thanks to Yann Martel.

(Genesis 1:1, Matthew 5:3–10, John 15:13, Revelation 21:1–5)

Introduction

This is the first reading in this book, because it is, in many ways, the most important. And because it sets the stage for all that follows. The reading is based on a question asked by the main character in Yann Martel's prize-winning novel *Life of Pi*. The boy, Pi, has just survived a shipwreck and a long ordeal at sea, and he is required to give an account of his experiences to the agents of the company that has insured the boat. This account makes up the bulk of the book and it is, to say the least, incredible. The agents don't believe Pi and ask for a more realistic, sensible and down-to-earth explanation. And so he tells them another, quite ordinary and mundane, story. And that is the one they put in their report. Before their conversation ends, however, Pi asks them a question. THE question. The question that underlies the novel, and this reading as well. Of the two stories, he asks – the unbelievable story and the down-to-earth one – which one do you prefer? The insurance agents consider the question, and as one they answer – the first story, the unbelievable one. Pi's response is simple and profound. 'So it is with God,' he says. 'So it is with God.'

In the first century, in a pre-modern age, Christians told their story to a world that was filled with stories that sought to explain reality. They told their story and they lived their story, and, as unbelievable as it seemed, the world believed their story – preferred their story! – and the world was changed.

In the twenty-first century, in a post-modern age, we in the West find ourselves in a similar situation. Our world, too, is filled with stories – stories that seek to explain reality. None of them can be proved. (Not that anyone in a post-modern context is much interested in 'proof' anyway!) They are each based – even the most 'scientific' of them – on a set of presuppositions that have to be accepted by some kind of 'faith'. So the first question we need to ask is not 'Which story can you prove?', or even 'Which story do you believe?' The first question I think we need to ask, when it comes to introducing our story to our neighbours and family and workmates and friends, is Pi's question: 'Which story do you prefer?' Unbelievable as it may seem, which do you like better? And, in order to answer that question, they need to have some idea of what our story is about. And that is what this book is about, too. Telling the story. Telling the Bible. So they have the chance to make a choice. To decide, among all the explanations for this world and our lives and where we fit in and what it's all about, which of those stories they prefer.

> **TELLING TIPS: This is one to tell on your own. I have, in the past, worked with groups of actors on this one and turned it into a kind of sketch. I still did all the reading, but they mimed out the 'contrast' bits. They collided with each other randomly in the first section (and I think, at the end of that section, one dropped a chain and the other picked it up with an 'Oh, look! The Missing Link!'). In the second section, I think they just mimed creation. In the third section they mimed the 'kill or be killed part' with a pretend Matrix-y fight, and then finished by arguing about who was Number One (which finished off with a final pretend punch). In the fourth section, we continued the fighting metaphor, with one actor jumping in front of another to save him. In the fifth section, everyone just dropped dead to the floor, and in the sixth section, of course, they rose again! It's a little less serious this way, but it still makes the point!**

Here are two stories.
Which one do you prefer?

The first story begins like this:
Once upon a time, a very long time ago, there was a series of accidents. Energy and matter and molecules collided and somehow you are here today. Here by coincidence. Here by chance.

The second story starts this way:
In the beginning, God created the heavens and the earth. And you are here today, not by accident, but because he designed you, and loves you and wants to have a relationship with you.

Here are two stories.
Which one do you prefer?

The first story continues:
The fit live. The weak die. So kill or be killed. Survival is the name of the game. Look out for number one.

And here's how the second story goes:
Blessed are the meek. Blessed are the poor. Blessed are the peacemakers. Greater love has no one than this, that he lay down his life for his friends.

Here are two stories.
Which one do you prefer?

The first story finishes like this:
You die. The end.

And the second story? Actually, the second story has no end at all: *'For Jesus said, "I am the resurrection and the life. He who believes in me will live, even though he dies; and whoever lives and believes in me will never die."'*

Here are two stories.
Two stories to explain the world.
No one can prove which one is true.
No scientist, no philosopher, no politician, no priest.
It's up to you to choose.
So here are two stories.
Which one do you prefer?

Questions

1. I have included only two stories here. Two possible options. I chose to contrast these two in particular because the first story is the secular story which is so prevalent in the West (the context in which I spend most of my time), and the second is obviously the Christian story. What other stories might I have contrasted with the Christian story, if I lived in a different place? And then how would the contrasts differ?

2. When I was younger, I read a lot of books about Christian 'apologetics', which attempted to offer 'proofs' for the Christian faith. Yet, in this reading, I make the claim that the Christian story (along with the rest of the stories) can't be proved. And in the introduction I make the claim that, in a post-modern world, there's not much interest in 'proof' anyway. If it seems right or feels right, then it *is* right! How else do you explain belief in UFOs, Scientology (sorry, Chef!) and *The Da Vinci Code*? So, am I right? Is it all just down to personal preference? Or is there still a place for Christian apologetics and laying a credible foundation for Christian belief? And, if so, what is it?

3. What other contrasts could I have drawn between these two stories? Which story do you prefer? And why?

The Morning of the World

(Genesis 1–2)

Introduction

One of the first things I had published was a series of picture books that asked the question 'What was it like?' about six different Bible stories. The idea was to invite the reader into the story and ask some very simple questions: What did that smell like, or feel like, or look like? And then to offer some answers. Those books have been out of print for a few years now, but I think the stories still work really well. And since I'm a great fan of recycling anyway… here's the first of the lot!

> **TELLING TIPS: Give your crowd sounds to make for each of the key phrases:**
>
> **'It was clean.' (Make a happy 'Aaah!' sound.)**
> **'It was quiet.' (Make a 'Shhh' sound.)**
> **'Make some noise!' (Divide the crowd into four groups and have them do the birds, fish, insects and beasts in turn.)**
> **'Yawn from Adam.' (Everybody yawns.)**
>
> **Lead them in these noises early in the story, and then bring the animal noises back in at the end.**

What was it like on the morning of the world?
  It was clean.
  Clean as a baby, fresh from a bath.
  Clean as the tires on a brand new bicycle.
  Clean as a spring sunrise.
  Clean as a mountain snowfall.
  What was it like on the morning of the world?
  It was clean.

What was it like on the morning of the world?

It was quiet.

Every now and then, a breeze would catch hold of a leaf and send it crashing against its neighbour. Or a stream would bubble and bounce against its banks.

But otherwise it was quiet.

Quiet as a sleeping baby.

Quiet as a coasting bicycle.

Quiet as the rising sun.

Quiet as the falling snow.

What was it like on the morning of the world?

It was quiet.

Maybe too quiet.

What was it like on the morning of the world?

It was time to make some noise!

So God spoke – that was the first noise. And a zoo of noises followed.

Singing birds.

Splashing fish.

Buzzing insects.

Roaring beasts.

And then a yawn from the first man, Adam.

'I've got something noisy for you to do,' God said to Adam.

And he gave him a job. The best kind of job there is. A job that is more like a game. And the game was called 'Name the Animals'!

What was it like on the morning of the world?

It was time to make some noise.

Adam looked. Adam listened. Where to start?

And then an animal dropped a nut on his head.

The animal was grey. It had small pointed ears. Its bristly tail was as long as its body. And it sat on a branch and chattered at Adam as if it were scolding him.What did Adam name it? Nobody knows.

But when the people who lived in Greece first saw it and noticed that its tail was as long as it body, they called it 'squirrel' – which means 'shadow tail'.

Again Adam looked. Again Adam listened.

Then Adam spotted another animal, shuffling towards him through the undergrowth.

This animal was half the size of Adam. It was covered with bright orange fur. It walked on its feet, like Adam did. And on its knuckles, like Adam didn't.

But the most remarkable thing about this animal was its face – a face that looked a bit like Adam's face, in fact.

What did Adam name it? Nobody knows.

But when the people who lived in Malaysia first saw this animal, walking through the forest with its sad man face, they called it 'orang-utan' – which means 'man of the woods'.

Once more Adam looked. Once more Adam listened.

And he heard a munching, crunching sound.

Adam turned round, and behind him there stood a creature twice his height, chewing the bark off a tree. It was shaggy and brown. It had four long, knobbly legs. And sticking out of its head were two branches like a pair of open hands.

What did Adam name it? Nobody knows.

But when the people who lived in North America first saw this huge, shaggy animal, they called it 'moose', which means 'he strips off bark'.

So Adam named the animals.

Nobody knows what he called them.

Nobody knows how long it took.

But when he was finished, Adam looked at the world.

It was no longer clean. Birds' nests filled the trees. Rabbit holes dotted the ground. Fish littered the streams. And there was hardly a leaf anywhere that hadn't been chewed or chomped or nibbled on.

Then Adam listened to the world.

It was no longer quiet.

The air was full of cawing and squawking and singing. The ground was crawling with snorting and grunting and squeaking. The streams were rushing with jumping and splashing and diving. And the jungle rustled and snapped and shook.

What was it like on the morning of the world?

The world was no longer quiet. The world was no longer clean.

It was noisy. And it was messy.

So God gave Adam a name for it.
And the name God gave it was 'Good'.

Questions

1. What do you think it was like on the morning of the world?

2. What names would you have given to the three animals that appear in the story? Why not make a list of other animals and come up with your own names for them. What do you suppose is the significance of God giving Adam that job?

3. How can 'noisy' and 'messy' be 'good'? You might want to come up with some examples from your own experience!

Death and Regret

(Genesis 3)

Introduction

In a recently published survey that sought to explore the attitudes of non-Christians towards the church, the notion of 'dealing with one's sin' came very low on the list of reasons the respondents gave for considering the merits of Christianity. They did, however, recognise that people often hurt and abuse one another and that something needs to be done about that! Sin by another name is still sin. It's just a question of finding terms that people actually understand and to which they can relate. And that's why, in this reading, I chose to frame the fall and talk about sin in the context of regret. Because I think everyone understands the missed opportunity – to either do something good, or avoid hurting someone else.

That's why I like to use it in an evangelistic, or pre-evangelistic, context – to get the audience thinking about the nature, the reality and the consequences of sin. You might also find it useful during the Lenten season.

TELLING TIPS: There's no appropriate place for audience participation here, because this is a pretty serious reading and depends heavily on the intensity that the reader/storyteller brings to it. When I tell it, I always emphasise the more physical aspects of the text – the hacking, the looking at the hands, the shut eyes, the pounding of the fists against the temples. The key is that Adam and his struggle should be real to the audience – just as their own regret is real.

He hacked at the ground with his rough stone axe. He hacked at the weeds and at the bushes. He hacked till the sweat poured off his forehead and the calluses rose on his palms. He hacked until he could hear his heart pounding in his ears. But still the slithering thing slipped and squirmed away. So he sank down onto a stump and waited for his breath to return and his heart to stop racing. He wiped the sweat from his brow and stared at his hands. And that's when it all came back – the crushing memory of 'before', the pain of the paradise he'd lost.

It was like a bad bruise. It hurt to touch it, but touching it reminded him that it was there. Sometimes a smell would trigger it. Sometimes it would wake him in the night. Today, it was simply the sight of his hands.

Knuckles gnarled and cracked. Palms rough and swollen. Veins running down the backs like tree limbs.

Were these the hands, he wondered, that once tended the Garden? The hands that stroked the lion's mane and traced the zebra's stripes and danced across the rhino's wrinkled hide as he gave each one its name? Were these really the hands of Adam?

Sometimes it seemed impossible. Sometimes it seemed too good to have been true. And sometimes he wondered, How had it happened? How had he let it all slip between those rough and dirty fingers?

As if to answer the question, a voice called from across the rocky field.

Yes, he had blamed her once. Blamed her more than once. But he knew now that the fault was his, as well as hers.

Eve called again, and then walked slowly towards him. It was almost impossible to see her as she had once been. The years, and the children, and the endless toil it took just to survive had erased for ever the woman who had danced happily in the Garden.

He shut his eyes. He shut them tight. He shoved his fists into the sockets and for a second, just a second, there she was again. Flesh of his flesh. Bone of his bone. Lying beside him on the soft wet grass, at the dawn of their life together. He remembered touching her hair. And her lips. And tracing the shape of her face with his fingertips. And he remembered the prayer he had prayed. 'Thank you, Creator,' he had said, 'for this face and for this morning, and for all the mornings to come.'

'Adam!' the voice called again. 'Adam, why are you sitting there? Get back to work! We have a family to feed!'

Adam winced. There was still a trace of that other Eve in her voice. The same voice that had called out so many years ago – called out across the Garden, 'Adam, come quickly! There is someone I want you to meet!'

That voice was so sweet. The face so innocent and gentle. She skipped towards him, excited like a foal or a fawn. She took his hand (he could feel those fingers, still). And she led him, laughing, to the Knowledge Tree.

There was no reason to be alarmed. No cause for concern. Those words had no meaning then. All was trust and goodness and love. How could he have known? How could either of them have guessed that their new acquaintance would teach them the meaning of those words – and many more awful still.

The Serpent was a handsome creature. Confident. Articulate. Poised. There was venom in his words, but at the time, his arguments seemed reasonable.

'So the Creator forbids you to eat from the Knowledge Tree?' the Serpent had asked. 'He says that if you do, you will die? Well, what does he have to hide? That's what I want to know. And if he truly loves you, why would he want to keep anything from you? I suspect that he's afraid – afraid that if you eat from the tree, then you will know as much as he does! So why don't you taste the fruit and find out for yourselves?'

Even now, even after all the pain and the toil and the years away from the Garden, there was a part of Adam that still wanted to be convinced. Perhaps the Serpent was right – perhaps the Creator was just jealous of what he knew and did not want to share it. Was it so wrong to want to know? To know evil as well as good?

Adam looked up. His wife was staring at him, and the answer was there, in the lines on her face and in the sadness that never left her eyes. No amount of knowledge could make up for what those eyes had seen: their forced exile from the Garden, the angel with the fiery sword who was there to make sure they could never return, the desolate land they were condemned to till, the murder of one son by another...

Adam looked away and shook his head. His children had often asked him: What did the fruit taste like? Sweet like an apple? Sour like a lemon? How could he have told them the truth? Told them without seeming a fool? That it smelled of decay. That every bite was rotten. That it tasted like death. Death and regret.

Adam pounded his fists against his temples – as he had pounded them a thousand times before.

What if? What if? What if?

What if they had ignored the Serpent? What if they had obeyed the Creator? What if they had never tasted the fruit?

Would he still be wrestling the lion and running with the zebra? Would he still wake up each morning in the soft wet grass and trace his finger across Eve's forever beautiful face?

The thought was simply too much to bear. And so he picked up his axe again and began to hack at the earth. Eve grunted her approval and turned to walk away. But once she was out of sight, he listened again for the hissing one.

The Creator had made a promise – Adam remembered. The handsome one, the confident, articulate creature, would lose his limbs and crawl upon the ground. And one day – surely he was remembering this right – one day, Eve would bear a child who would crush that serpent's head!

But who was this child? And where was this child? All Adam could do was hope. Hope that the Creator's promise would come true. Hope that someone would some day destroy the Serpent. Hope and keep on hacking. Hacking at the ground. Hacking at the bushes. Hacking at the weeds. Because hacking was easier than yearning for what might have been. Because it was better than longing for the life he'd lost when he had to leave the Garden.

Questions

1. What do you regret? You might not want to share the answer out loud. But take a few minutes and make a list.

2. There's no way to turn back the clock on our regrets, but is there ever a way to put things right?

3. Adam is left hacking at the bushes. Where is the hope in this story?

The Edge of the River

(Exodus 2:1–10)

Introduction

Here's another one of those 'What was it like?' stories. It would work really well in an all-age service about Moses.

> **TELLING TIPS: Just as with 'The Morning of the World', teach your crowd sounds and actions to go along with Miriam's responses at the start of each section.**
>
> **'It was wet.' (Shake pretend water from hands or head.)**
> **'It was boring.' (Big Yawn or have everyone say 'BORING!')**
> **'It was looking bad.' (Say 'Uh-oh'.)**
> **'It was looking even worse.' (Make a bigger 'Uh-Oh'!)**
> **'It was looking better.' (Wipe forehead and say 'Phew!')**
> **'It was time to do something.' (Look at pretend watch – tap watch.)**
> **'It was time to wonder.' (Say 'Wow!')**

What was it like at the edge of the river?

It was wet.

Squishy toe wet.

Soggy bottom wet.

Hot-and-muggy sweaty wet.

The girl peered through the reeds. They sprouted thick and tall from the riverbank mud.

The girl peered out onto the river at a bobbing bulrush boat. She hoped that her brother was, at least, dry.

What was it like at the edge of the river?

It was wet.

What was it like at the edge of the river?

It was boring.

She was supposed to watch her brother. That's what her mother had said. She was supposed to make sure that nothing happened to him. She was supposed to just sit there and wait.

But for how long?

Till Pharaoh, king of Egypt, decided to stop killing all the baby Hebrew boys? Till her little brother started to outgrow his bulrush boat? Till his arms poked through the sides, and his legs poked through the end, and his head popped out of the top?

The girl laughed when she thought of that. It was nice to laugh for a change. Better than being bored.

Better than sitting leg-stiff still.

Better than staring, eyes tired and sore.

Better than nodding off, eyelids drooping and chin dropping onto her chest.

What was it like at the edge of the river?

It was boring.

What was it like at the edge of the river?

It was looking bad.

The girl's long wait was broken by the sound of voices.

The river bank reeds were broken by tramping feet.

And the hot sweat of boredom broke into a cold sweaty fear.

The girl crouched down as low as she could, so she could see without being seen.

What she saw were women.

What she saw were Egyptian women.

What she saw were Egyptian women walking alongside the river, right towards her baby brother in his bulrush boat!

If they find him, she thought, they'll kill him.

But what could she do?

She was too small to fight them. She was too slow to reach him and pull him back to shore. And there was no time to run for help.

What was it like at the edge of the river?

It was looking bad.

What was it like at the edge of the river?

It was looking even worse!

The baby started to cry. The women started to point. And then one of them waded out into the river, pulled the bulrush boat out of the water and carried it back to shore.

The other women gathered round and blocked the girl's view. Now she was more helpless than ever!

And then the girl remembered. She remembered the stories her mother had told her about God.

God, who had led Abraham to a special land.

God, who had protected Jacob from the anger of his brother.

God, who had saved Joseph from another pharaoh's prison.

Maybe, just maybe, she thought, God could save her baby brother, too.

'Please, God,' she prayed, 'don't let them hurt him.'

At last, the women moved away and the girl could see her little brother again.

He wasn't dead.

He wasn't hurt.

He wasn't even crying.

In fact, one of the women was holding him and hugging him and stroking his head.

What was it like at the edge of the river?

It was looking better!

What was it like at the edge of the river?

It was time to do something.

If those Egyptian women were not going to hurt her brother, then the girl wanted to know what they did intend to do with him. So she crept towards them, her head below the reeds and her ears wide open.

'I am Pharaoh's daughter,' she heard one of the women say. 'I can do what I please. And what pleases me is to adopt this Hebrew child as my own. What I need is some woman to feed him and care for him until he is old enough to come and live with me.'

Like a pheasant spooked by a dog, like a puppet on a stage, like a Jack-in-the-box (or better still, a Jill-in-the-box!), the girl popped up out of the reeds.

'I know a woman,' she said, 'who would be just perfect for that job. She doesn't live far from here, and I am sure that she would love and care for your baby as if he were her very own!'

What was it like at the edge of the river?

It was time to do something.

What was it like at the edge of the river?

It was time to wonder.

'All right,' said the Egyptian to the girl. 'Go and fetch this woman. Say that Pharaoh's daughter commands her to care for...' And, here, she paused. 'For little "Pulled Out". For I pulled him out of the water!'

The girl nodded, then turned and ran quickly home.

How wonderful! Her brother was safe!

More wonderful still – his own mother would be able to care for him!

But what a silly name. Little 'Pulled Out'.

What was the Egyptian word for that? Moses.

And then, the girl thought, maybe it wasn't so silly. Maybe her brother's new name was a wonder, too. For hadn't she prayed? And hadn't the God of her fathers heard her prayer and pulled little Moses out of trouble? Like he'd pulled Abraham and Jacob and Joseph out of trouble, all those years ago?

God had pulled them out to do something special with them. And so the girl wondered. Had God pulled out Moses to do something special with him, as well?

What was it like at the edge of the river?

It was time to wonder.

Questions

1. What do you think it was like at the edge of the river?

2. Talk about a time when God asked you to do something and you felt like Miriam did in this story – bored or worried or wet!

3. Why is it significant that Moses was raised in an Egyptian household by a Hebrew mother?

I Hear Them Crying

(Exodus 3)

Introduction

This is the first of a series of four Moses stories I performed at a Christian festival in 2003. I was asked to tell the stories not from Moses' point of view, but from God's – an interesting twist and a challenging task. And so, in this first story, we don't join Moses on the mountain, surprised by the burning bush; we crawl behind the bush and see the story unfold from God's perspective. I think it's important to share that with your crowd, because that point of view is critical to the particiation activity you will be asking them to contribute to the story. I think this reading (and the three that follow) would work nicely for adults as an introduction to a sermon series on Moses. They could also be used in all-age services, and in Sunday School – particularly for children aged eight and up.

TELLING TIPS: Divide the group into two. Have one group put their hands to their ears and join you in saying 'I hear them crying'. Have the other group shield their eyes as if they are looking for something, and join you in saying 'I see them suffering'. Start small and quiet with this, and, as the reading moves along, lead the group in making this louder and more intense.

If you are simply going to deal with the Moses story, you might want to finish before the alternative ending, but if you want to bring the point a bit closer to home, then fill in whatever current issues you think are appropriate and carry on until the end.

At the top of a mountain, behind the mask of a burning bush, God watched the old shepherd creep closer and closer.

He looked an unlikely choice. Unlikely like Abraham. Unlikely like Isaac. Unlikely like Jacob, before him.

But the old shepherd was God's choice. And now it was time to say hello.

'Moses!' God called. 'Don't come any closer. Take off your shoes. For I am the God of your ancestors, Abraham, Isaac and Jacob. And this is a special place.'

Terrified, the old shepherd did as he was told. He slipped off his sandals and covered his eyes. Who wouldn't?

And then God spoke again:

'My people are slaves in the land of Egypt.
I hear them crying, I see them suffering.
They work long hours for nothing at all.
I hear them crying, I see them suffering.
Their masters whip them, and beat them, and bruise them.
I hear them crying, I see them suffering.
Their children are taken and murdered in front of them.
I hear them crying, I see them suffering.
I care for my people, I hurt when they do.
I hear them crying, I see them suffering.
And now I have come down to save them.
For I hear them crying, I see them suffering.'

And then God paused. And then God waited. The bush burned dim and low, for God had something else to say. Something sure to send the old shepherd shaking. Something scarier than anything that had happened so far.

'And Moses,' God said at last. 'Moses, you are going to help me.'

(Possible ending)
There was an item in the paper about starving children.
I hear them crying, I see them suffering.
There was something on the TV about a deadly disease.
I hear them crying, I see them suffering.
They want to pass a law to kill even more unborn babies.
I hear them crying, I see them suffering.
The council won't give permission to house refugees.
I hear them crying, I see them suffering.
And Moses, I know you're an unlikely choice.
And Moses, I know that sometimes you're scared.

But Moses, the bush is burning – like God's passion for
   a world in need.
And the holy place is any place where those needs are met.

So Moses, won't you hear?
Moses, won't you see?
Moses, won't you care?
And Moses, when God comes to save,
Moses, won't you be his helper too?

Questions

1. Have you ever wondered whether or not God heard your crying or saw your suffering? What made you wonder?

2. What might it feel like to actually see and hear the world's suffering through God's eyes and ears?

3. Talk about a time when you felt that God was calling you to be Moses in a particular situation.

A Thousand Bricks a Day

(Exodus 5)

Introduction

I like this reading a lot, because I think it helps bring home, through the participation and repetition, the hopelessness the Israelites must have felt.

TELLING TIPS: Teach the chorus before you start, and help your group to really get into it.

A Pile of Straw – use two hands to make the shape of a pile.
A Lump of Clay – one hand throwing a lump of clay, as onto a potter's wheel.
A Thousand Bricks a Day – two hands building a brick wall, brick by brick.
The Grunt – at the end is essential, particularly for a younger audience.

The key is to get the idea of the drudgery across in the way you say it, but also to have a bit of fun with the actions.

A pile of straw,
a lump of clay,
a thousand bricks a day (grunt).

The people of God worked hard for their masters. Every day. All day. And if they did not make as many bricks as they were meant to, the slave-drivers would whip them and beat them and bruise them.

A pile of straw,
a lump of clay,
a thousand bricks a day (grunt).

God felt sorry for his people. So he spoke to his helper, Moses.

'I have decided to rescue my people,' he said. 'To lead them out of the land of Egypt. But we must take this one step at a time. Tell Pharaoh, the king of Egypt, that my people must go into the desert to worship me for three days.'

A pile of straw,
a lump of clay,
a thousand bricks a day (grunt).

So Moses did what God said. But when Pharaoh heard, he just laughed. 'The god of your people?' he chuckled. 'Sorry, I don't think we've met. And if I've never heard of such a god, why should I listen to him, or let you leave to worship him?'

'You're lazy, that's all. You and your people! Now get back to work!'

A pile of straw,
a lump of clay,
a thousand bricks a day (grunt).

But later that day, Pharaoh spoke to the slave-drivers.

'Our slaves have asked for a little holiday,' he sneered, 'to worship some god or other. Obviously, they have too much time on their hands. So I think we shall teach them a lesson.

'Up till now, we have given them the straw they need. But from now on, they will have to find their own straw. And they will still have to make the same number of bricks each day!'

A pile of straw,
a lump of clay,
a thousand bricks a day (grunt).

So the people of God went to find their own straw. They gathered what little they could from the fields. But with so much gathering to do, there was no way they could make as many bricks.

A pile of straw,
a lump of clay,
a thousand bricks a day (grunt).

And because they failed to meet their goals, the slave-drivers whipped them and beat them and bruised them even more.

'This is not fair!' they cried to Pharaoh.

'This is your fault!' they cried to Moses. 'You told us you came to help. But now you have made things worse!'

A pile of straw,
a lump of clay,
a thousand bricks a day (grunt).

So Moses went to God and told him what the people said.

'I know it looks bad now,' God answered. 'But trust me, Moses, when Pharaoh sees my power, everything will change.

'There is hope. There will be justice. And, one day soon, my people will no longer sing:

A pile of straw,
a lump of clay,
a thousand bricks a day (grunt).

Questions

1. Describe how you would have felt if you were an Israelite working in these kinds of conditions. Have you ever experienced anything close to this in your life?

2. Why do you think that Pharaoh was so dismissive of Moses and of God?

3. How do you think Moses felt about the promises God had made to him when the plan backfired?

But Pharaoh Would Not Listen

(Exodus 7–14)

Introduction

The trick with this reading is to create a sense of excitement (and even a little humour) as the plagues progress, while also communicating the seriousness of the story. The audience will follow your lead, so it's up to you to make that change of tone obvious – getting very solemn, in particular, as you do the actions about the death of the firstborn. You might even want to say 'And Pharaoh would not listen' at that point, with a touch of sadness and regret.

> **TELLING TIPS:** Because there are so many actions and sounds for this story, I have included the tips at the appropriate places in the text. Before you begin the story, you will need to teach your group the Pharaoh line ('Nyah, nyah, nyah, nyah, nyah!' – and make it really big – like a child in the playground!) and also the wave UP and wave DOWN for the end. Otherwise, tell them you will show them what to do along the way, and then give them time to do the actions/sounds themselves after you. It might be helpful to have an assistant or two up front, so the crowd can follow them – it will help with the timing and the enthusiasm, and with knowing when to bring each action to an end. Don't pull a volunteer from the crowd for this. Use someone you have had a chance to practise with!

'Moses,' God said, 'I want you to pass a message on for me. Go to see Pharaoh, the king of all Egypt. Tell him it's time to set my people free. And warn him that if he does not listen, some terrible things will happen.'

So Moses did as he was told. He went to see Pharaoh and passed on God's message.

But Pharaoh would not listen. (*Everyone cover their ears and shout 'Nyah, nyah, nyah, nyah, nyah!'*)

So God filled the rivers of Egypt with blood. (*Make waves with hands – ick!*)
God filled the houses of Egypt with frogs. (*Jump and/or make frog sounds.*)
God filled the skies of Egypt with gnats. (*Make a buzzing sound and wave arms about.*)
But Pharaoh would not listen. (*Everyone cover their ears and shout 'Nyah, nyah, nyah, nyah, nyah!'*)

So God struck the land of Egypt with flies. (*Slap arms and neck.*)
God struck the animals of Egypt and they died. (*Make sad Moo or Baa sound.*)
God struck the people of Egypt with sores. (*Stroke arms.*)
But Pharaoh would not listen. (*Everyone cover their ears and shout 'Nyah, nyah, nyah, nyah, nyah!'*)

So God sent hail to crush the crops of Egypt. (*Make falling/pelting sounds.*)
God sent locusts to eat up whatever was left. (*Make gobbling sounds.*)
God sent darkness to blot out the days of Egypt. (*Look around as if they can't see – hands in front, feeling.*)
But Pharaoh would not listen. (*Everyone cover their ears and shout 'Nyah, nyah, nyah, nyah, nyah!'*)

So God sent an angel to kill the sons of Egypt – the firstborn son in every house. (*Pretend to hold dying child in arms – solemn.*)
And when Pharaoh's son died along with the rest, finally Pharaoh listened. 'Go!' he said to Moses. 'Go and take your people with you.'

But as soon as they had gone, Pharaoh changed his mind.
Still he would not listen. (*Everyone cover their ears and shout 'Nyah, nyah, nyah, nyah, nyah!'*)
He leaped into his chariot and sent his army after them.
Soon the sea stretched out before God's people, and Pharaoh's army rushed, like a wave, behind them. What could they do?
'Raise your special walking stick,' God whispered to Moses.
And Moses listened. Moses listened! He did what God told him, and the

sea split in two before him (*Do a wave UP and hold it there*) – leaving a path right down the middle.

God's people hurried to the farther shore, the Egyptian army close behind. And when the last of God's people had reached the shore, God spoke again.

'Lower your stick now, Moses.'

And when Moses did, the waters rushed back again. (*Do the wave DOWN.*)

God's people were free at last. (*Cheer!*)

But the army of Egypt was swept away. Because God had spoken – and Pharaoh would not listen.

Questions

1. Talk about a time when God was trying to get your attention. How did you know it was him? How long did it take you to listen?

2. How do you think the average Egyptian must have felt during the course of these plagues?

3. In the end, it took the deaths of innocent firstborn children to set the Israelites free – a fact that is sad and horrifying. Are there resonances of this story elsewhere in the Bible that might help us to understand it more clearly?

I Will Be Your God

(Exodus 16–20)

Introduction

The themes of this story are 'celebration' and 'covenant'. God has rescued his people from slavery and now, as they celebrate their newfound freedom, they enter into a very specific relationship with him. The way you tell the story needs to reflect this – both the joy (which comes through the fun and funny bits) and also the commitment (as the crowd look at the cross near the end, and embrace each other in the chorus).

TELLING TIPS: The chorus can be done in a variety of ways, depending on your crowd. If folks know each other well, you can break them into pairs, with one member of the pair saying (with outstretched arms), 'I will be your God' and the other replying, 'We will be your people' and embracing the first person. You might like to have a pair at the front to model this, with you (or you and a partner) leading everyone else in saying the lines. The advantage of this is that it has a real tactile appeal – and speaks the message of the text into the body. If folks know each other less well, then you can divide the whole group into two groups – one side of the room and the other – then just have them face each other during the chorus and lead them in their lines. As a final option, you might like to say the first line and have the rest of the crowd respond.

As in the previous story, I have placed the rest of the actions in the body of the text. The easiest thing for the crowd would be for you to divide them into five groups and have each group do the actions in their respective sections. Or you could just teach the actions first and have everyone do everything. There's a greater chance that they'll forget that way – but you can have fun with that too! By the way, make sure that you have fun doing the actions. That's the best way to guarantee that they will as well. And I don't

Now that I have set you free, and saved you from your enemies…

I will be your God.
We will be your people!

I'll lead you through the desert to a land of milk and honey. I'll be a cloud by day (*Look up and say, 'Ooh, Puffy!'*), and a fire by night (*Make siren sounds*).

I will be your God.
We will be your people!

I'll feed you when you're hungry; you can count on me. Quail from the sky (*Flap wings and make bird sounds*) and manna from the earth (*You can go 'MMM!'*).

I will be your God.
We will be your people!

I'll lead you to fresh water; you can count on me. Water from a rock (*Make strong pose and grunt*) in the middle of a desert.

I will be your God.
We will be your people!

I'll help you build a tent. I'll give you all the plans. A special place to worship me (*Hold hands in the air*), a special place to meet with me (*Then turn to neighbour and hold upraised hands together to make the shape of a tent*).

I will be your God.
We will be your people!

And I'll give you rules to live by – to treat each other well. No thieving, no killing, no wanting your neighbour's donkey (*Hee-haw!*) or his wife (*Oo-la-la!*).

I will be your God.
We will be your people!

And together we will wait for a prophet just like Moses. Who will welcome (*Reader stretches arms wide in shape of a cross*) all the world to join with our community.

I will be your God.
We will be your people!

And lions (*Everyone roars*) and lambs (*Everyone baas*) will lie down together and the kingdom of heaven will come to earth.

I will be your God.
We will be your people!
I will be your God.
We will be your people!
I will be your God.
We will be your people!

Questions

1. Talk about the time when you first said to God that you wanted to be a part of his people.

2. Notice that the word 'we' keeps cropping up here. The relationship was between God and his people – not just each person. How is that different from the way we often see our relationship with God? And what could the church today learn from that difference?

3. It might be interesting to find parallels in the new covenant for the things God promised to supply to his people in the old. Can you think of any?

Down and Up

(Exodus 19)

Introduction

This started out as an Advent meditation – linking two examples of the 'coming' of God. You can use it that way, or simply as another way of dealing with the Moses story. It's short, so it might fit in nicely at the start of the service, before the congregation spends time worshipping in song.

TELLING TIPS: Divide the group into two, then lead one group in saying 'God came down' and the other group in saying 'Moses went up'. You can stick the 'and' in during the chorus! And, if you want, a simple 'down' motion (maybe two hands) and an 'up' motion (two hands reaching up) might accompany the words.

In the thunder and the lightning,
God came down.
In the shaking and the quaking,
God came down.
Through the fire and the cloud,
God came down.
To the top of the mountain,
God came down.

God came down and Moses went up.
God came down and Moses went up.

In the thunder and the lightning,
Moses went up.
In the shaking and the quaking,
Moses went up.

Through the fire and the cloud,
Moses went up.

To the top of the mountain,
Moses went up.

God came down and Moses went up.
God came down and Moses went up.

Powerful Deliverer – ordinary man.
God came down and Moses went up.

Awesome Creator – humble creature.
God came down and Moses went up.

Babe in a manger – shepherds on a hill.
God came down and Moses went up.

God with us – revealed to us.
God came down and Moses went up.

God came down and Moses went up.
God came down and Moses went up.
God came down and Moses went up.

Questions

1. This particular meeting of God and man was not peaceful and quiet, but noisy and frightening. Have you ever had that kind of experience of God? Can you share a little bit about what it was like?

2. When you think of the 'awesome-ness' of God, what is the first thing that comes to mind?

3. The text links the nativity with Moses' meeting with God on the mountain. What similarities (and differences, for that matter) do you see between those events?

Under the Thumb

(Judges 6)

Introduction

This is the first of four stories about Gideon. As with the Moses stories, these could be used before the sermon each week in a series about Gideon. This first story is not nearly so much fun as the rest (being oppressed by your neighbours isn't exactly a laugh a minute!) but it's important for what follows to make it clear how desperate the situation of the Israelites was and how badly they needed delivering.

TELLING TIPS: The text needs to be read/told with a slow, trudging rhythm that is meant to get across the sense of oppression felt by the Israelites. What I had in mind when I wrote it was the chanting of the soldiers of the Wicked Witch of the West in *The Wizard of Oz*. **(You remember – that 'o-wee-o' thing.) As a matter of fact, when I do the the story, I do the 'Midian', 'Gideon', 'Have pity on' lines to that rhythm, and even to the same tune. So I say/sing 'Midian' and then the crowd responds with 'Midian' in turn. I teach them the Midian thing and even get them trudging with me in time, and then warn them that the 'Midian' will change to other words and that they should just follow along. It's really important to practise this one ahead of time – just to get the rhythm right for yourself. And if you feel that everyone trudging and stomping will put you off, then just do the trudging yourself!**

Midian (Midian)
Midian (Midian)

The people of Israel turned their back on the Lord.
They worshipped idols, they ignored his word.

So God let their enemies overcome
and for seven long years they were under the thumb of…

Midian (Midian)
Midian (Midian)

They killed their cattle, donkeys and goats.
They burned up their barley, wheat and oats.
The people of Israel had to hide in caves
but even that couldn't keep them safe from…

Midian (Midian)
Midian (Midian)

Have pity on (Have pity on)
Have pity on (Have pity on)

'Please have pity on us!' cried the people of Israel.
We've done what's wrong. We've gone our own way.
We don't deserve it, but we long for your grace.
Send someone to save us, we pray, from…'

Midian (Midian)
Midian (Midian)

Gideon (Gideon)
Gideon (Gideon)

'Oh, Gideon!' called the angel of the Lord,
'God has something for you to do.
He's chosen you to fight against Midian.
You mighty warrior, he's waiting for you!'

Gideon? (Gideon?)
Gideon? (Gideon?)

'I'm Gideon, yes, but I'm no warrior.
You've made a mistake, you've got the wrong man.

Why do you think I'm hiding in this wine press?
I'm the weakest guy from the weakest clan!'

Gideon! (Gideon!)
Gideon! (Gideon!)

'There's no mistake,' said the angel of the Lord,
'I've written it down on the back of my hand.
"Find Gideon, the guy who's hiding in the wine press.
The perfect choice for God's perfect plan!"'

So Gideon (So Gideon)
Fought Midian (Fought Midian)

How's it turn out? That's the question.
We'll just have to wait and see.
But I'll give you a hint – promise not to tell –
It all comes down to God's grace and mercy.

For Gideon (For Gideon)
Not Midian. (Not Midian)
God had pity on (God had pity on)
His people – just like you and me. (His people – just like you and me.)

Questions

1. Talk about a time when you found yourself in difficulties because there was some area of your life in which, like the Israelites, you'd wandered away from God. Who was the 'judge' God sent to rescue you?

2. How did Gideon feel when the angel told him what God wanted him to do?

3. Talk about a time that God asked you to do something and you felt just like Gideon.

Under the Thumb (Again)

(Judges 6)

Introduction

All right, so there are five Gideon stories – not four, as I said. But this one is just an alternative rendering of the first story. I like them both in their own way, so I thought I'd let you choose!

> **TELLING TIPS: Divide your crowd into five groups and teach each group one set of the lines and actions below. You might want to give the Midianites deep growly voices and Gideon a trembly voice. Make the actions as much fun as you can and they'll have more fun with them too. And, yes, I know it's the tree at 'Ophrah', not 'Oprah', but it's just another chance to have a bit of fun!**

A. Israelites	*We follow God and then we stop; we're always doing the religion hop. (Hop.)*
B. Midianites	*Crush the crops so they can't make bread. Knock the donkeys on the head! (Pretend to knock a donkey on the head!)*
C. Gideon	*I'm Gideon, I'm not your man, I'm the weakest guy from the smallest clan. (Look nervous and frightened.)*
D. Angel	*God will be with you, Gideon. He'll give you victory over Midian. (Stretch out angel wings.)*

E. Oprah	*Today on Oprah, something new,*
	my mother married a kangaroo!
	(Hold up arms like branches.)

Things weren't going well for the people of Israel (A).

They had stopped worshipping God – God, who had brought them out of the land of Egypt – and they were worshipping false gods called Baals instead. So God let them get on with it, and without his help, they fell under the power of their enemy, the Midianites (B).

For seven long years, the Midianites (B) destroyed the crops and killed the animals of the people of Israel (A). It got so bad that the Israelites had to hide in caves. So, in the end, the people of Israel (A) decided to hop back to God again.

'Save us!' they cried. 'We don't deserve it, we know. But send someone to deliver us from the Midianites (B).'

Now, there was a man named Gideon (C) who was the weakest member of the smallest clan in the land. He was no soldier, and no hero either. But God chose him for the job and decided to help him. And that was all that mattered.

Gideon (C) was hiding in a wine press under the tree of Oprah (E). He was threshing wheat there, so the Midianites (B) wouldn't find him. He was scared. He was tired. His feet were turning purple. And that's when he had a visit from the angel of the Lord (D).

God would help Gideon. That was the gist of the message, anyway. The message of the angel (D). Under the tree of Oprah (E). And no one was more surprised than Gideon (C). Under the tree of Oprah (E).

How did it all turn out?

All I can say is that God's grace is amazing. As he showed the people of Israel (A) when he saved them from the Midianites (B) by talking to Gideon (C) through an angel (D). Under the tree of Oprah (E).

Questions

1. Talk about a time when you found yourself in difficulties because there was some area of your life in which, like the Israelites, you'd wandered away from God. And who was the 'judge' God sent to rescue you?

2. How did Gideon feel when the angel told him what God wanted him to do?

3. Talk about a time that God asked you to do something and you felt just like Gideon.

The Fleece on the Floor

(Judges 6)

Introduction

The important thing in this story is to communicate Gideon's uncertainty – reflected in the weakness of his support troops and in his need to ask for confirmation through the 'fleece' – not once, but twice!

> **TELLING TIPS: Divide your crowd into three groups and teach them the chorus. Manasseh should have a high, squeaky voice; Asher a nerd-like voice; and Zebulun and Naphtali (one group for both) an old man's voice. The idea is that they are not the ideal fighting force! In the second line, and in the same voice, Manasseh says 'We'll choke you'; Asher says, 'provoke you'; and the Zebulun and Naphtali group says, 'and try to poke you in the eye!'**
>
> **You also need a volunteer (wearing a fleece!) to play the fleece. This person sits on a chair, and several other volunteers sit on the floor. They are the ground. Give one of them a squirty bottle (or water pistol) filled with water (be careful whom you choose here!). That person squirts the fleece at the appropriate time in the story. Don't tell them at the start that the roles will soon be reversed. If they don't know the story, just let them be surprised! Give the squirty bottle to the 'fleece' person after Gideon begs for a second test – and let the revenge begin!**

The Midianites and their allies crossed the River Jordan and camped in the Valley of Jezreel. It looked as if they were about to take over for good.

So Gideon blew his trumpet and gathered soldiers from four of the tribes of Israel.

We're Manasseh / Asher / Zebulun and Naphtali
We'll choke you / provoke you / and try to poke you in the eye!

Now Gideon was no warrior, but even he could see that this was not a promising start. So he asked the Lord for some help.

'Lord,' he prayed, 'you said you would use me to save your people. But look what I have to work with!'

We're Manasseh / Asher / Zebulun and Naphtali
We'll choke you / provoke you / and try to poke you in the eye!

'If you really mean what you've said, if you're really going to help, could you possibly, maybe, give me a sign? Here's what I had in mind. I'll take a fleece, an ordinary fleece, and lay it on the threshing floor. And if, tomorrow morning, the fleece is wet but the ground around it is dry, then I'll know for sure that I can count on you.'

So Gideon laid the fleece on the floor (*Fleece person sits down*). And, sure enough, when he returned the next morning, the fleece was wet (*Shoot fleece with water bottle/pistol*), but the ground around it was dry!

Gideon felt much better. And then he had another look at his army.

We're Manasseh / Asher / Zebulun and Naphtali
We'll choke you / provoke you / and try to poke you in the eye!

So Gideon went back to the Lord.

'Lord,' he prayed, 'please don't be angry, but is there any chance that I could have just one more sign? How about this? I'll put the fleece on the ground again, and this time, could you keep the fleece dry and wet the ground around it?

So Gideon put the fleece on the ground, and sure enough, the next morning, the fleece was dry, but the ground around it was soaking wet. (*Fleece person sprays everyone else!*)

'Thank you, Lord,' prayed Gideon. 'Now I know that you will be with us, no matter how impossible this seems.'

And so Gideon, and his army…

We're Manasseh / Asher / Zebulun and Naphtali
We'll choke you / provoke you / and try to poke you in the eye!

... went off to face the Midianites.

Questions

1. Have you ever had to work together with people on a task when you felt they just weren't up to it? How did you handle that?

2. Talk about a time when you 'laid a fleece' before the Lord. What was the fleece? What was the answer? Did it help?

3. Some people think that laying out a fleece demonstrates a lack of faith in God. What do you think?

Too Many Soldiers!

(Judges 7)

Introduction

There's a lot of text in this story, with the odd bit of participation dropped in here and there, so it will require a very dramatic reading on your part. This is also the key story, in which God leads Gideon and his soldiers against the Midianites. So you need to reflect Gideon's increasing anxiety/frustration as God whittles down his army, Gideon's surprise at what he hears outside the enemy tent, and his jubilation at the defeat of the Midianites. So you can focus on the reading, it might be helpful to have a few assistants (who have practised with you ahead of time) to lead the crowd in their part.

TELLING TIPS: Divide the crowd into three groups (one very big group, one smaller group and one quite small group) and get them to stand. That's right – this starts off as a 'standing story'! Make the biggest group the 'frightened' soldiers and have them scream with fear as loudly as they can at the appropriate place in the story, and then sit down. Make the next biggest group the soldiers who stick their heads in the water and slurp it up. Just have them bow their heads forward, shake their heads back and forth and make a slurping sound. They sit down as well, eventually. And make the smallest group the soldiers who scoop the water and lap it like dogs. Have them cup their hands and lap pretend water from them and then go 'Woof'! They stay standing. You'll need to demonstrate all these actions before the story begins – make them lots of fun!

For the battle itself, there are three actions that everyone can do – or, if you wish, you can just teach them to the smallest group. For the trumpets, they simply need to blow pretend trumpets. For the torches, I have them sing 'Shine, Torches, Shine!' to the tune of 'Shine, Jesus, Shine!' If you don't know that, then simply have them shout 'Ta-da'. And as for the breaking jars, you can either have everyone make a smashing, crashing sound, or (and this is my preference) have them say 'Me-sa Jar-Jar' and then, smacking fists into palms, pretend that they're bopping him on the head. *Star Wars* fans will love you for this!

Oh, and everyone needs to shout, 'A sword for the Lord and Gideon!' I know this sounds like a lot of 'set up' – and it is. But it can be just as much fun as doing the story itself, and it will reinforce the important bits in the text. So enjoy!

So Gideon and his army set off to fight the Midianites.

'Right then, Lord,' said Gideon. 'We're ready. Well, as ready as we'll ever be.'

But God said, 'Hang on, Gideon. We've got a problem here. You have too many soldiers to fight the Midianites.'

'Too many?' cried Gideon. 'Too MANY?'

'That's right,' said the Lord. 'Too many. I don't want you becoming big-headed over this, you see. Passing out medals and handing out citations and bragging to me about how you beat the Midianites with your own strength. So here's what I want you to do. Tell anyone who's frightened that he is free to go home.'

So Gideon did what the Lord told him. And 22,000 frightened men (*scream AAAH!*) went home.

'All right then, Lord,' sighed Gideon. 'There are 10,000 soldiers left. Ten thousand brave men. Now we're ready to face the Midianites.'

'Hang on a minute,' said the Lord. 'There are still too many men.'

'Too many?' cried Gideon. 'TOO MANY!!'

'That's what I said,' said the Lord. 'Too many. We wouldn't want you getting too big for your britches now, would we? Putting on parades and building monuments because you thought you were big and strong and powerful. So here's what I want you to do. Take your army down to the river. Those who scoop up the water and lap it like dogs from their hands can stay. And those who kneel down and drink straight from the river will have to go.'

So Gideon did what the Lord told him. Some of the men lapped the water like dogs from their hands. (*Slurp and woof!*) But most of them kneeled down and stuck their heads in the river. (*Shake heads and slurp.*) And when it was all over, there were only three hundred soldiers left!

'All right, Lord,' trembled Gideon. 'I guess we're ready to fight the Midianites now. I'll just tell everybody to get their swords, and we'll be on our way.'

'Swords?' said the Lord. 'Who said anything about swords? Look, you can carry them on your belts if you want to, but that's not how you'll win this battle. You see, when this is over, I don't want you going on and on about how fierce you were, how noble and mighty and proud, and about how you don't need me any more. I've heard it all before. If you want to win this battle you'll have to do it my way. So I want you to give each man a trumpet, an empty jar and a torch. Got it? And we'll wait till night, when your enemy is asleep.'

'All right, Lord,' sighed Gideon. But he was less convinced than ever.

'Look', said the Lord. 'If you're still worried, sneak down to the Midianite camp. Listen to what they're saying. And I promise you'll like what you hear.'

So Gideon and his servant Purah sneaked down to the Midianite camp. There were thousands of Midianites, as thick as locusts, more numerous than the grains of sand on the shore. It was not a good start. But when Gideon put his ear to one of the tents, everything changed.

'I just had a dream,' trembled one of the Midianite soldiers. 'I dreamed that a huge loaf of barley bread came tumbling into our camp and struck our tent with such force that it collapsed around us!'

'Barley bread,' said the soldier's mate. 'Surely that bread is the sword of Gideon, and God will give him victory over our whole camp!'

'Yes!' said Gideon. (Well, rather more quietly than that!) Then he and Purah sneaked back to the army of Israel.

'God will give us the victory!' said Gideon to his men. 'I know that for sure now.' And he gave each soldier a trumpet and a jar with a torch inside.

'We'll break into three groups,' he explained. 'We'll creep down around the edge of the Midianite camp. When you hear my group blow our trumpets, then you blow your trumpets too. Smash your clay jars as well and let your torches shine!'

And that's exactly what they did. While the Midianite army slept, Gideon and his men crept down to the camp, and at Gideon's signal, they blew their trumpets (*blow trumpets*), smashed their jars (*crashing sound*) and let their torches shine (*sing 'Shine, torches, shine!'*). Then they shouted together, 'A sword for the Lord and for Gideon!' (*Do so.*)

The Midianite army woke up at once. They were sleepy and frightened. They had no idea what was happening. And in the midst of their confusion, they started attacking one another. They choked each other and provoked each other and poked each other in the eye! And all Gideon's men had to do was chase them away.

And that is how just a few hundred men defeated many thousands.

With trumpets (*blow trumpets*), and jars (*crashing sound*), and torches (*sing 'Shine, torches, shine!'*).

And the help of the Lord, of course!

Questions

1. How do you think Gideon felt as he watched his carefully gathered army slip away?

2. Is it possible to have too many resources for doing God's work? Talk about a situation in which that might be the case.

3. How do we strike a balance between dependence on God and dependence on our own skills and resources?

Oh, Poo!

(Judges 8)

Introduction

Yes, I got letters! Not in the first week of the big national church convention, or even the second. But by the third, a few parents (seven in all, I think) decided that their kids shouldn't be encouraged to say the 'P' word, so I was asked to change it. I have included the alternative (stinky) version as well – in case you want to avoid getting letters yourself. All I can say is that I still like the Poo-ey version better (and so, presumably, did the 20,000 people who didn't write letters!)

The reason for the 'poo', by the way, has to do with my friend Al, who always says 'Oh, poo!' when things go badly for him. And things certainly go badly for Gideon in this story. It's the bit of his life that hardly ever gets told, but even though it's sad, it's just as instructive as the rest.

> **TELLING TIPS: Divide the crowd into four groups – Ephraim, Succoth, Peniel and Israel – and teach each group their couplet before the story begins. Then have them join you at the appropriate time. Do the final couplet yourself.**

Gideon beat the Midianites, the enemies of his people, and it would be nice to think that he then lived happily ever after. But the Bible is not a fairy tale. And so, sadly, he didn't. In fact, he ran into trouble almost immediately.

Gideon's soldiers were hunting down what was left of the Midianite army, when they ran into a bunch of moaners from the tribe of Ephraim.

We're from Ephraim, we think you're poo!
We wanted to fight the battle too!

They felt left out because Gideon hadn't asked them to join his army, and they made a huge fuss, so he let them capture a couple of Midianite leaders called Oreb and Zeeb. Then he buttered them up with all kinds of compliments about how great their grapes were. It seemed to do the trick. But then he ran into the tribe of Succoth.

We're from Succoth, we think you're poo!
We're still afraid, so we won't help you!

All Gideon wanted was a little bread for his men. But the people of Succoth knew that he hadn't yet captured the Midianite kings, Zebah and Zalmunna. And they were afraid to help until those kings were well and truly out of the way. So Gideon moved on to the next tribe. But he got the same answer from the people of Peniel.

We're from Peniel, we won't help you!
The people of Succoth say you're poo!

This was ridiculous! Gideon had trusted God, he'd risked his life and he'd beaten the Midianites. But instead of being the conquering hero, everyone was criticizing him. And he was getting no help at all! So he went and found Zebah and Zalmunna himself and finally finished off those Midianite kings. Then he went back and punished the towns who wouldn't help him. And at last he sat down to rest.

His troubles, however, were still not over. For there soon came an offer from the people of Israel.

We're Israel, please be our king!
You're quite the opposite of a poo-ey thing!

Gideon sighed. Either the people didn't like him at all. Or they liked him far too much.

'No!' he explained. 'I won't be your king. And my son won't either. God is our king and he alone should rule over us.'

And then, sadly, Gideon stepped right in it!

'I'll tell you what, though,' he said. 'I wouldn't mind a bit of gold. How about you each give me an earring that you took from the Midianites when we defeated them?'

So that's what the people did. And because all the Midianites had worn earrings, they managed to collect quite a pile of gold. Twenty kilos at least! And what did Gideon do with it? He melted it down and turned it into an idol, which was, of course, worshipped by all the people!

Imagine that – after everything God had done! Even Gideon forgot him when things got tough.

As I said, it's not quite one of those happily-ever-after endings. But it doesn't have to be that way for us. Life's hard sometimes – sure. But God is still there – just as he was there for Gideon, if he had only kept on looking. Or to put it another way:

Hang on to God, he's there for you,
Even when life's completely poo!

Questions

1. Talk about a time when you felt that you did a good job at something and then received lots of criticism for it. How did you feel? How did you react?

2. Why do you think Gideon did not want to be king?

3. Can you think of a case where you (or someone else) did something really good and then immediately succumbed to some temptation on the heels of it? How does that happen? How can we deal with it?

Samson was a Strong Man

(Judges 13–16)

Introduction

I just love the story of Samson! And, given the space he gets relative to some of the rest of the Judges, the people of Israel must have loved him, too. What is surprising about that, of course, is that there is very little about Samson's character that one might call exemplary. On the other hand, maybe that's not so surprising at all. For perhaps the thing we find delightful about him is what we hope for ourselves – that God should find a way to use a less-than-perfect servant to do his will.

> **TELLING TIPS: There are two things you can have your group do. Divide the crowd into two. And this time you might want to do it by gender. Have the males (or group one) join you, with a deep and manly voice, when you say 'And his hair just kept on growing'. You might even have them run their hands down the sides of their heads as they say this – or even out from the sides of their heads – just to give the idea that the hair gets bigger! Have the females (or group two) join you, with a high and ladylike voice, when you do Delilah's line 'Samson, Oh, Samson!'**

Samson was a strong man.
    But he wasn't strong because he lifted weights.
    And he wasn't strong because he did lots of push-ups.
    And he wasn't strong because he had big muscles.

No, Samson was strong because his mother had promised God that he would never drink strong wine.
    That he would never, ever drink strong beer.
    And that he would never, ever, ever cut his hair.

And Samson had promised that, too.

Samson was strong because of God.

So, one day, God asked Samson to do a strong thing.

'The Philistines are hurting my people, Israel,' God said. 'And I want you to protect them.'

So that's what Samson did. Or at least tried to do. Because it's fair to say that what he really did was to make a great big nuisance of himself!

He killed a lion with his bare hands.

And his hair just kept on growing.

He caught 300 foxes, tied their tails together in pairs and jammed a fiery torch between the tails. (Do not try this at home!) Then he sent them running through the Philistines' fields to burn down all their crops.

And his hair just kept on growing.

He took the jawbone of a dead donkey and used it to kill a thousand Philistine soldiers.

And his hair just kept on growing.

And when the Philistines thought they had him surrounded, he tore the enormous doors off the city gates of Gaza and carried them to the top of a hill.

And his hair just kept on growing.

So the rulers of the Philistines went to have a chat with Samson's girlfriend, Delilah.

'If you can find the secret to his strength,' they said, 'each of us will give you a great big pile of silver!'

So Delilah tried. 'Samson, oh Samson,' she cooed. 'Please tell me the secret of your strength.'

Now Samson really fancied Delilah. It's even fair to say that he was in love with her. But he wasn't stupid. So he decided to play a little trick on her.

'Tie me up with seven fresh bowstrings,' he lied, 'and I will be as weak as any man.'

So that's what Delilah did. She hid some men in the next room, she tied up Samson with the fresh bow-strings. And then she cried, 'Samson, oh Samson, the Philistines are coming!'

The men burst through the door! Samson burst the bow-strings! He chased the men away.

And his hair just kept on growing.

'Samson, oh Samson,' Delilah pouted. 'You lied to me and made me look a fool. Tell me, tell me please, the true secret of your strength.'

Samson liked this game, so he told her another lie.

'Tie me up with new ropes – ropes that have never been used – and I will be as weak as any man.'

So that's what Delilah did. She hid some men in the next room again, and she tied up Samson with new ropes. And then she cried, 'Samson, oh Samson! The Philistines are coming!'

The men burst through the door. Samson burst the ropes as if they were threads. He chased the men away.

And his hair just kept on growing.

'Samson, oh Samson,' Delilah whined. 'You lied to me again, and made me look a bigger fool. Please, please, tell me the secret of your strength.'

Samson grinned. 'All right then,' he said. But it was just another lie. 'Take the seven braids of my hair and weave them into the cloth on your loom. And then I will be as weak as any man.'

So that's what Delilah did. She hid some more men in the next room. She wove Samson's seven long braids into the cloth on her loom. And then she cried, 'Samson, oh Samson, the Philistines are coming!'

The men burst through the door. Samson burst to his feet, loom and cloth and all. He chased the men away.

And his hair just kept on growing.

'Samson, oh Samson,' wept Delilah. 'You don't love me at all! This is the third time you've made me look a fool. Please, please, please, please, pretty please tell me the secret of your strength.' And she said this not once, not twice, but day after day after day.

Maybe it was the nagging. Maybe it was the tears. Maybe Samson was truly, deeply in love with Delilah. Or maybe Samson just forgot where his strength really came from. Maybe he thought it was all down to him – and not the God he'd made his promise to.

Whatever the reason, Samson finally told Delilah the truth.

'I made a promise once,' he said, 'that a razor would never touch my head. Cut my hair and I will be as weak as any man.'

So that's what Delilah did. She hid some men in the next room – the rulers of the Philistines this time. And when Samson fell asleep, she had one of the men cut off his seven long braids.

'Samson, oh Samson!' she cried. 'The Philistines are coming!'

Samson woke. 'I'll chase them away, just like before!' he boasted. But when the men burst through the door, Samson could do nothing. He really was as weak as any man.

So the Philistines grabbed him, poked out his eyes, bound him and carried him off to prison. They chained him to a great stone wheel, and day after day, he pushed the wheel to grind their corn.

And his hair just kept on growing.

Some time later, the Philistines decided to have a big party – to celebrate Samson's capture and to thank their god Dagon for delivering him into their hands. What they didn't count on was the true God coming to their party – the God of Israel. The God who had given Samson his strength and who still wanted to use him to protect his people.

Three thousand Philistines and more gathered in the temple on that day. The place was packed. And in the middle of the celebration, the rulers had Samson dragged into their midst. The people laughed and clapped when they saw him.

'Our god has beaten our enemy,' they cheered, 'the one who caused us so much trouble.'

And when they were done laughing, Samson was dragged to the side of the temple and stood among the pillars.

'You know I'm blind,' said Samson to the man who guarded him. 'Put me where I can feel the pillars, please, so I can lean against them.'

So that's what the servant did. He put Samson between the pillars – the pillars that supported the whole of the temple.

'Dear Lord,' prayed Samson, 'the only strength I ever had came from you. I remember that now, so I ask that you would remember me and give me that strength just one more time.'

And with his left hand on one pillar and his right hand on another, he began to push.

The pillars creaked. The pillars cracked. The pillars crumbled. The pillars collapsed. And when they did, the whole of the temple came crashing down with them. It crashed down on the people. It crashed down on the rulers. And it crashed down on Samson, too.

'Let me die with the Philistines!' cried Samson. And so he did, killing many more with his death than he had ever done in his life, and doing finally what God had asked him to do – protecting his people from their enemy.

Questions

1. Were Samson's early actions against the Philistines anything more than his making a great nuisance of himself?

2. Why do you think Samson kept trusting Delilah?

3. When I was a kid, I always thought Samson's story was a bit sad. What do you think? Talk about a time when you weren't 'at your best' but God was still able to use you for something.

A Tale of Two Families

(1 Samuel 1–2)

Introduction

A few years ago, I had to prepare a worship service based on the first couple of chapters of the first book of Samuel, and the difference between these two families – the opposite directions that resulted from changing circumstances – really jumped out at me. It's all down to that Overweight-Diva-Winding-Up-The-Wagner thing, isn't it? You just can't tell what's going to happen until the story ends. And because God is at work in this story, there's a lesson for us all about assuming too much, too soon.

TELLING TIPS: Either you can do this one on your own, or, to emphasise the difference between the stories, you might want to read one half and have someone else read the second half. And then split the last line between you.

Hannah

Hannah was barren. And in the time and the place that Hannah lived, to be barren was to be cursed.

But things are not always what they look like.

Situations are not always what they seem.

And God has a way of taking one thing and turning it into something completely different.

Hannah was married to Elkanah – a man of means who could afford a second wife – Peninnah. And Peninnah, as it happens, was not barren at all. She had a brood of children, whom she stood before Hannah, at every opportunity, to make her curse even worse.

Elkanah was a good man. He saw, he understood, he longed to ease Hannah's pain. So when the family trooped from their home in Ramah to the holy place at Shiloh each year, and when they sat down to eat a portion of the meat that had been offered as a sacrifice to God, Elkanah always made sure that Hannah got a double helping of that meat – a special treat – and, surely, the first recorded example of comfort eating.

In spite of all her children, however (and as a powerful argument for monogamy!), Peninnah was jealous of this simple act of kindness. And she did all she could to make that a curse, as well.

'It is God who has closed your womb,' she would tell Hannah, there, in the presence of God himself, in his own holy place. And she would do this, not once, not twice, but again and again and again, right up to the time of the feast. And poor Hannah would be so upset that she could not enjoy the treat her husband had planned for her. In fact, she could not eat at all.

'Eat, Hannah, eat!' Elkanah would say. He meant well, but (being a man!) he ended up saying all the things a husband should never say to his wife when she is so unhappy she can't eat.

'Why are you crying?

Why are you so upset?

You may not have any children – but you have me!'

One year, Hannah was so upset that she left the table altogether. She went to the door of the holy place, where Eli the priest was sitting. And there, through her tears, she offered up a prayer to God.

'Look at me, Lord, please! See my misery. Remember my condition. And give me a son, I pray. For if you do, then I will give him back to you, and dedicate him as your servant for all the days of his life.'

These words were hard words. So hard that she could not speak them out loud. Hannah's lips moved, her tears flowed, and the old priest Eli (another man!) assumed that she was drunk.

'Sober up, woman!' he said. 'This is neither the time nor the place. Take your bottle and go home!'

Hannah could not believe this. All she wanted was help, and here was another curse.

'Drunk?' she cried. 'Is that what you think? I'm not drunk! In fact, I can hardly drink or eat a thing! I'm here to pray – that's all – to pour out my grief and my troubles before the Lord.'

'I see,' said Eli, sorry not only for her sadness but for his mistake. 'Then go in peace. And may the God of Israel give you what you asked for.'

It was a blessing. A blessing, at last. Hard won, to be sure. But a blessing and not a curse.

So Hannah went.

And Hannah had something to eat.

And when she saw her husband, she smiled.

And when they returned to Ramah, she lay with him and conceived and gave birth to a son and called him Samuel – a name which means 'God heard me.'

And when Samuel was old enough, she took him back to Shiloh, back to the old priest Eli.

And though it sounds like the act of a crazy woman, or a woman who has had too much to drink, she left her only son there to serve in the holy place.

A blessing in return for a blessing.

A blessing, not a curse.

Eli

Eli was a priest – the son of the son of the son of the son (and a few more sons!) of Moses' own brother, Aaron. And at the time that Eli lived, to be a priest – a chosen mediator between God and man – was to be blessed.

But things are not always what they look like.

Situations are not always what they seem.

And sadly we all have a way of taking one thing and making it into something completely different.

Eli had two sons – Hophni and Phinehas.

And the Bible says it about as plainly as it can be said.

Eli's sons were wicked men; they had no regard for the Lord.

(Not the best of qualifications for the priesthood!)

They had a plan, these brothers – a clever scam – and it went something like this. When the people sacrificed their animals to God, just some of the meat was burned on the altar. Only the best bits were offered up to the Lord. To put it in contemporary terms, if you were offering God a Bourbon crème, he would get to lick out the stuff in the middle. If you were offering him a piece of cake, he would get the corner with all the icing and the big sugar rose. Well, at the time of our story, the best bits were the fatty bits. Those bits were offered to God. And the rest of the meat was put into a pot and boiled.

During this process one of the priest's servants was supposed to plunge a fork into the pot and fish out whatever piece of meat the fork found. This piece was given to the priests to eat – a potluck way of providing for their needs.

But Hophni and Phinehas were not satisfied with this potluck blessing. They were tired of their servants hooking the odd neck and hoof and kneebone along with the choicer cuts. And what is more, without regard for their obligation to God (or to the possibility of rising cholesterol and accompanying heart disease), they were keen to add a little more fat to their diet.

So they ordered their servants to approach the worshippers before the sacrifices were made.

'The priests do not want boiled meat,' they would say. 'They want to choose their piece now, while the meat is raw.'

And if the worshippers objected and said, 'Well at least let us burn the fat for God first,' then all sorts of nasty things were likely to happen to them.

Word of this spread among the people. And finally old Eli, who should have been keeping an eye on his sons, heard about it too.

To be fair, he told them off in no uncertain terms.

'If you sin against another man,' he said, 'God is there to intervene for you. But who will be there to help you when you sin against God himself?'

But Hophni and Phinehas were enjoying their position and its newly found privileges, and refused to change their ways.

So God sent a prophet to Eli, who gave him some unhappy news.

'You have been so blessed,' the prophet said. 'God has chosen you and your family to make offerings and burn incense and to be his priests. But now you have dishonoured him by taking for yourself what is rightfully his. And so the Lord says that there will no longer be old men in your family. Your sons will die together, on the same day, and the priesthood will be given to another.'

And that's exactly what happened. Hophni and Phinehas were killed in a battle with the Philistines over the Ark of the Covenant. Killed on the same day. And when he was given the news, old Eli was so shaken that he fell off his chair, broke his neck and died.

And what should have been a blessing – a blessing to the people, a blessing to God, a blessing to Eli and his sons – became a curse.

For while God is more than able to turn a curse into a blessing, only we can find a way to turn a blessing into a curse.

Questions

1. Talk about a time when you jumped to conclusions that were absolutely unfounded.

2. Talk about a time when you saw a curse turned into a blessing.

3. Talk about a time when you saw a blessing turned into a curse.

The Middle of the Night

(1 Samuel 3)

Introduction

Here's another one of those 'What was it like?' stories. Again, it's a nice way of helping your crowd crawl into the story with you before you preach or teach about Samuel's calling.

TELLING TIPS: As with the other stories in this series, the participation focuses on Samuel's 'what was it like' feelings and reactions. So teach your crowd the actions and sounds before the story begins, and then lead them in those actions at the appropriate times.

'It was hard to sleep.' (Have everyone yawn.)
'It was like a dream.' (Say 'Ooooh' in a sleepy, dreamy voice.)
'It was embarrassing.' (Say 'Oh dear!' in an embarrassed kind of way.)
'It was kind of creepy.' (Make a mildly scared noise. Maybe a little 'Yikes!')
'It was like a nightmare.' (Make a big scary noise, a big 'YIKES!' or a scream – 'AAAH!')
'It was amazing.' (Say 'Wow!')

Make sure you do both the 'Frightening' and the 'Amazing' sounds on the last line.

What was is like, in the middle of the night?

It was hard to sleep.

Lamplight bounced off the Ark of the Covenant – the big box where God was supposed to live – and tossed strange shadows on the thin tent walls.

Those shadows bounced around inside young Samuel's head and tossed strange pictures into his dreams. And the dreams kept him bouncing and tossing on his bed.

What was it like, in the middle of the night?

It was hard to sleep.

What was it like, in the middle of the night?

It was like a dream. 'Samuel!' called a voice. And the boy's eyes cracked open at the sound of his name. Was it a dream, or had he really heard it?

'Samuel!' called the voice again.

And the boy thought, It must be my master, Eli.

Old, weak and blind, Eli the priest often needed Samuel's help. So the boy climbed out of bed, adding his shadow to the shadows on the wall. And by the light of one flickering lamp, he stumbled towards old Eli's room.

What was it like, in the middle of the night?

It was like a dream.

What was it like, in the middle of the night?

It was embarrassing.

Samuel tapped Eli on the shoulder and whispered his name. The old man grunted and rolled over. Samuel tapped him harder. The old man grunted again. So Samuel grabbed his shoulder and shook him. And the old man coughed and woke and grabbed the boy's arm.

'Samuel? Is that you? What do you want?'

Samuel was confused. 'I don't want anything. You called me and here I am.'

The old man sighed and shut his eyes.

'I didn't call you. You must have been dreaming. Go back to bed.'

So Samuel went. But as he made his way past the Ark of the Covenant, he couldn't help feeling a little foolish for disturbing the old priest.

What was it like, in the middle of the night?

It was embarrassing.

What was it like, in the middle of the night?

It was getting kind of creepy.

The boy had hardly shut his eyes when he heard the voice call 'Samuel!' once again.

Surely it was Eli, this time. So Samuel raced back to his master.

'I'm here!' the boy shouted, surprising even himself with the volume.

Eli woke up. But he didn't ask who it was this time. He didn't even roll over. He just blinked his weak eyes and said ever so sternly, 'I did not call you. I do not need you. Go back to bed!'

So Samuel crept back to his room, shaking his head and fighting the shivers that were starting to climb up the middle of his back.

What was it like, in the middle of the night?

It was getting kind of creepy.

What was it like, in the middle of the night?

It was like a nightmare.

The boy jumped into bed and pulled the cover over his face. But the cover was thin, and through it he could still see the light from the flickering lamp. And the shadow of the Ark on the wall.

So he shut his eyes. He shut them tight. But shutting his eyes could not shut out his fear. Samuel could still hear his pounding heart and, when it finally came, the sound of that voice as well.

'Samuel! Samuel!' the voice called.

And Samuel knew what he had to do. He didn't care what the old priest said. Nothing was going to make him stay in that place. Nothing!

So he ran to Eli's room, not daring to look at anything along the way.

What was it like in the middle of the night?

It was like a nightmare!

When Samuel reached Eli's room, he found the old priest wide awake, sitting up in bed. He threw himself into Eli's arms and buried his head in the priest's chest.

Eli held him tight until he stopped shaking, but he said nothing at all. He just peered into the darkness with his weak old eyes. And then, suddenly, those eyes began to shine – as if they saw something, as if they recognized someone.

'Samuel,' he said gently, 'I did not call you. But I think I know who did. If I am not mistaken, it was the Lord God, himself.'

'You mean the one who lives in the box?' whispered Samuel.

Eli smiled. 'The Lord God does not live in the box,' he explained. 'The Lord God cannot fit into any box. But he gave us the box to remind us that he is always with us. And he told our ancestors to put things in the box to remind us that he cares for us and that he has spoken to us. He has not spoken for a long time, Samuel, but I believe that he wants to speak to you tonight.'

Samuel looked at Eli. 'So what should I do?'

'You must go back to your room and lie down,' said the priest, 'and if he calls you again, you must say, "Speak, Lord, for I am your servant, and I am ready to listen."'

What was it like in the middle of the night?

It was frightening – and amazing – all at the same time.

Samuel walked slowly back to his room. He kept one trembling hand against the wall, and the other he spread, like a fan, across his eyes, so he could just see through his fingers.

When Samuel looked into his room, everything seemed normal. But as soon as he entered it, everything began to change. The light from the flickering lamp grew brighter. The shadows got darker. And through the tent walls, above the Ark of the Covenant, Samuel saw the shape of a figure.

The figure was frightening, and Samuel wanted to shut his fingers. But the figure was strangely beautiful, too, so Samuel also wanted to look.

Then, in the same voice he'd heard before, the figure called Samuel's name.

'Speak, Lord,' whispered Samuel, trying hard to remember what Eli had told him. 'I am your servant, and I am ready to listen.'

So the Lord spoke – and that was the first of many times that he had a message for Samuel.

Samuel listened – and that was the first of many times that this prophet heard the voice of the Lord.

What was it like, in the middle of the night?

It was frightening – and amazing – all at the same time.

Questions

1. What do you think it was like in the middle of the night?

2. Talk about a time when you truly believed you heard the voice of God.

3. Talk about an experience in which you were both frightened and amazed. Have you ever experienced God that way? Do you think that we have forgotten about the 'frightening' aspect of God's power and presence? And, if so, why do you think that has happened?

Good Idea. God Idea.

(2 Samuel 7)

Introduction

I think this reading came out of a normal weekly preaching situation. The passage from Samuel was one of the readings for the week, and it seemed like a good idea (or maybe even a God idea!) to focus on the difference between what we dream up and what God has in mind for us.

> **TELLING TIPS:** I'm pretty sure I just read the text myself when I did it, but to further emphasise the 'Oh', you might want to ask your group to join you in saying it. Or even split the group in two and have one group do the 'calling' kind of 'Oh' as in 'Oh, Nathan' and the other group do the 'discovery' kind of 'Oh' as in 'Oh, I see'. And, to further emphasise the point (or maybe just beat it to death!), you could put 'Good Idea, God Idea' up on the screen at the end.

'Oh Nathan!' said King David to the prophet one day. 'I've got a good idea! I live in this very nice palace, with cedar walls and cedar sofas and every modern cedar convenience. But the Lord God has to make do with that tiny little tent we call a tabernacle. Why don't we build him a house?'

'Oh, what a good idea!' said the prophet Nathan to King David. 'You live in this very nice palace, with cedar floors and cedar panelling and that lovely cedar cooker. But the Lord God has to make do with that tatty little tent. Why don't you build him a house?'

But that night, the Lord God spoke to the prophet Nathan.

'Oh Nathan,' he said. 'I hear that the king has a good idea. He wants to build me a house. I don't mean to sound ungrateful, but I have just one question: When did I say I wanted a house?

'Compared to the king's cedar palace, my tent is indeed tiny, and getting

71

a little tatty too. But it has served me well for many years, and it let me move with my people – from the wilderness to this lovely promised land.'

'Oh,' said Nathan. 'Then what shall I tell the king?'

'Oh – I know,' said the Lord God. 'Tell him I have a better idea. Tell him that I don't need a house, but that I would like to build him one instead! Not a house of stone or brick or cedar, but a house of people. A family that will stretch through all generations. A kingdom that will never end!'

So God built David a house – a family to last the generations. Some of them lived in palaces. Some of them lived in tents. And one of them – David's great great great great great great great great grandson – was even born in a stable!

David's palace is dust. And so is the temple his son Solomon built. But the kingdom that God made goes on for ever and ever.

Good idea – God idea.

They look almost the same. But, OH, what a difference that one little letter can make!

Questions

1. So which of your brilliant ideas has God changed/adapted/scrapped for his own purposes?

2. How did that turn out?

3. David had the advantage of Nathan the prophet sharing God's good idea with him. Where do we go to find those God Ideas?

Elijah Number One

(1 Kings 17)

Introduction

I'm really interested in the connection between story and song, particularly in a worship context, and several readings in the book reflect this. I think that in a lot of 'contemporary' worship situations there has been an unfortunate and unnatural separation between 'the spoken word' and 'song' – as if they are two different 'territories'. It may well be that there is actually a kind of territorialism about this – the music is the band's area; the words are up to the preacher. There is, however, no good theological reason for this. In fact, the history of the church and of liturgy suggests that, more often than not, the two have usually worked together, hand in hand. And my own experience, as both a preacher and a worship leader, suggests the same. And hence this one attempt among many in the book to play around with ways of bringing the two together again.

TELLING TIPS: This reading is built around Robin Mark's song 'Days of Elijah', published by Daybreak Music Ltd. If your crowd knows the song, fine. If not, you'll need to teach them the song first – and I would suggest doing that a week or two before you do the reading, so it's in their heads.

You'll need a guitar, or at a pinch a keyboard, to keep the beat of the song in the background, playing the first line of the song over and over again, while you do the reading to the rhythm of the song. The song is in B flat, I think, but do it in whatever key works for you. And you might want to set the rhythm just a little slower than the song itself, to help you get all the words in! Try it and see what works for you. When you get to the 'chorus', just lead the crowd in singing the line 'These are the days of Elijah' twice. Again – the first line in the song.

The other thing I sometimes do is to have the crowd repeat the verse lines after me. So you go, 'There once was a prophet called Elijah' and then they say it back to you: 'There once was a prophet called Elijah.' In this case, you might want to put the verses up on a screen to help them get the words right. You'll be surprised how easily they catch on! At the very end of the story, I usually lead the crowd in the whole of the song itself, starting with the song's chorus 'Behold he comes...', and picking the speed up a little as well. It really does make what is already a powerful song even more effective, because the crowd has been considering at least one part of the song's context.

If you don't have any musical accompaniment, you can just read the story and have them say the chorus lines. It's still important to 'keep the beat', though!

Chorus:

These are the days of Elijah.
These are the days of Elijah.

There once was a prophet called Elijah,
And he told the king
That the rain would stop
'Cause the people had wandered from the Lord.

There once was a prophet called Elijah,
Who ran and hid
'Cause the king was angry,
And the ravens brought him bread and meat.

Chorus:

These are the days of Elijah.
These are the days of Elijah.

There once was a prophet called Elijah,
Who met a widow

And asked for bread,
Though her oil and wheat were nearly gone.

'Have faith,' said the prophet called Elijah.
And the more she used,
The more she had,
And her oil and wheat were never gone!

Chorus:

These are the days of Elijah.
These are the days of Elijah.

There once was a prophet called Elijah,
And the widow's son
Fell ill and died,
And she blamed the prophet for his death.

'Have faith,' said the prophet called Elijah.
And he comforted the mother,
And he prayed for the son,
And the boy came back to life!

Chorus:

These are the days of Elijah.
These are the days of Elijah.

So God called a prophet named Elijah,
And he calls us, too,
To go out in the world
And to stand and speak for what's true.

Chorus:

These are the days of Elijah.
These are the days of Elijah.

Questions

1. Talk about a time when you wanted to run and hide like Elijah, because something God had asked you to do became 'too much' for you.

2. In that situation, God met Elijah's needs, both with the ravens and with the widow. Talk about a time when God met your needs, using someone else, in an unexpected way.

3. The widow gave what little she had and God returned a whole lot more to her. Talk about a time when you experienced something similar.

Elijah Number Two

(1 Kings 18)

Introduction

When I first did these readings, the church I pastored was working through the story of Elijah, so it just made sense to set up the sermon each week by doing the next part of the story in the same way. By the third week, folks were really looking forward to doing it again!

TELLING TIPS: Much the same as the previous reading. But, as you will see, the final verse is longer than the rest. You need to keep the beat going and make each line louder and more intense!

Chorus:

These are the days of Elijah.
These are the days of Elijah.

There once was a prophet called Elijah,
Who challenged the king
To a contest on Mount Carmel
To see whose god was really real.

'Here's the deal,' said the prophet called Elijah.
'You build an altar,
I'll build one, too,
And we'll see whose god provides the fire.'

Chorus:

These are the days of Elijah.
These are the days of Elijah.

'I'll call my prophets,' said the king to Elijah.
'Four hundred here,
Four-fifty there –
You're outnumbered. You won't stand a chance.'

'Bring it on!' said the prophet called Elijah.
'Nine hundred prophets of Baal
Against one prophet of the Lord.
I figure that's just about fair.'

Chorus:

These are the days of Elijah.
These are the days of Elijah.

'You go first,' said the prophet called Elijah.
So the prophets built their altar.
And they stacked up their wood.
And they waited for Baal to burn their bulls.

'Nothing's happened,' said the prophet called Elijah.
So the prophets danced.
And the prophets prayed.
From breakfast time to dinner time and more.

Chorus:

These are the days of Elijah.
These are the days of Elijah.

'What's the matter?' asked the prophet called Elijah.
'Is your god asleep?
Is he hard of hearing?
Or maybe he's just taking a break!

'Still nothing's happened,' said the prophet called Elijah.
So the prophets shouted
And threw themselves about.
From dinner time to tea-time and more.

Chorus:

These are the days of Elijah.
These are the days of Elijah.

'Now it's my turn,' said the prophet called Elijah.
And he built an altar,
And he stacked up the wood,
And then he added one final touch.

'Bring me water!' said the prophet called Elijah.
And he dumped it on the altar,
And he dumped it on the wood,
Until everything was soggy and wet.

Chorus:

These are the days of Elijah.
These are the days of Elijah.

'Help me, Lord!' prayed the prophet called Elijah.
'Send fire from heaven.
Show your power to the people
So they'll turn back and call you God again.'

So the Lord heard the prophet called Elijah.
And he burned up the bull,
And he burned up the wood,
And he burned up the stones,
And he burned up the soil,
And he boiled the water,
And sent it steaming to the sky,
And the people called him God again.
And the people called him God again.
And the people called him God again.

Chorus:

These are the days of Elijah.
These are the days of Elijah.

Questions

1. So how do you know which god is really real?

2. Elijah had to contend with the prophets of the false god Baal. And with the loyalties of his own people, who had chosen to follow that false god. Which false gods command the loyalty of the people who live around you? And what can you do to demonstrate to them that those gods aren't really real?

3. Can you think of any examples where people today might actually harm themselves to prove that their god is real?

Elijah Number Three

(1 Kings 19)

Introduction

And, yes, here's the third in the series!

> TELLING TIPS: Much the same as in the first two readings, but when you get to the 'still small voice', say it more and more quietly and encourage them to play along. You might even want to do the 'chorus' quietly following those lines. Then make the next verse big again.

Chorus:

These are the days of Elijah.
These are the days of Elijah.

There once was a prophet called Elijah.
The queen wanted to kill him
'Cause he'd beaten the Baals,
So God sent an angel to his side.

Now the angel made a cake for Elijah –
It was an angel sort of cake
From an angel sort of guy,
And it wasn't just pie in the sky!

Chorus:

These are the days of Elijah.
These are the days of Elijah.

'I'm all alone!' cried the prophet called Elijah
'I've done my best,
But I'm all that's left,
And I just want to run away and die.'

'Go to the mountain,' said God to Elijah,
'And wait for me to pass,
And wait for me to speak,
And I'll tell you everything you need to know.'

Chorus:

These are the days of Elijah.
These are the days of Elijah.

So to the mountain went the prophet called Elijah.
And the wind blew hard,
And the earth shook harder,
And a fire lit up the sky.

Then God spoke to the prophet called Elijah.
But he wasn't in the wind,
And he wasn't in the earthquake,
And he wasn't in the fire.
But he was there in the still small voice.
But he was there in the still small voice.
But he was there in the still small voice.
But he was there in the still small voice.

Chorus:

These are the days of Elijah.
These are the days of Elijah.

And God said to the prophet called Elijah,
'You're not alone,
You never were.
There are seven thousand just like you!'

'Seven thousand?' cried the prophet called Elijah.
'Then I'm not alone,
I'm not afraid.'
And he went off to do the work of the Lord.

Chorus:

These are the days of Elijah.
These are the days of Elijah.

Questions

1. Talk about a time when you did something you thought was good and someone else really disliked you for it.

2. Has there ever been a time in your life when, like Elijah, you just wanted to 'run away and die'?

3. All three of these stories have had to do with standing against what is wrong even when you feel as if you're the only one doing it. Can you think of any contemporary situations where someone has done that? Or maybe where someone needs to do that?

Songs in Search of a Tune: Shout Your Name

(Psalm 148)

Introduction

I like music. I like it a lot. And I've always wanted to write songs. So I sat down this past year and wrote some lyrics. The problem is that I'm not very good at the tune side of things. So we'll just call these pieces 'poems', which you can use as they stand, but which also might lend themselves to having music added by someone who knows something about such things!

TELLING TIPS: I wrote this one as a kind of modern 'All Creatures of Our God and King' where all creation is called to praise the Lord. There are two obvious differences, however. First of all, 'All Creatures of Our God and King' is much better. And secondly, I wanted to make my song personal, so the names in the song are all people in the church I pastor. I'm sure they wouldn't mind you using their names, too. And, who knows, you might have a Rex and a Marlene and an Alan and a Paul in your church, as well. But if your Stan and Margaret shouldn't really be holding hands, for example, that verse might be just a bit embarrassing and result in lots of unwanted pastoral issues. Therefore, I suggest that you might like to substitute the names of people that you know into the song. Be warned, however, that it's very difficult to find words that rhyme with Nigel.

Verse 1:

Novas and northern lights,
Sea lions, stalagmites,

84

Saturn and Mars and fish shaped like stars
Shout your name,
Shout your name.

Sunsets and snowstorms,
Single-celled life forms,
Photons and protons and goats on the hill
Shout your name,
Shout your name.

Bridge:

And Rex and Marlene,
And the girl dressed in green,
And the lad in between
Want to shout,
Want to shout your name, too.

And Wendy and Paul,
At the back of the hall,
And Allan who's tall
Want to shout,
Want to shout your name, too.

Chorus:

And they shout, 'Maker!'
And they shout, 'Earth Shaker!'
And they shout, 'Death Breaker!'
And they shout, 'God!'

Verse 2:

Peacocks and polar bears,
Sand dunes and solar flares,
Grass snakes and corncrakes and cold mountain lakes
Shout your name,
Shout your name.

Cherubs and chimpanzees,
Bull rushes, bumble-bees,
Antelopes, cantaloupes, pastors and popes
Shout your name,
Shout your name.

Bridge:

And Rex and Marlene,
And the girl dressed in green,
And the lad in between
Want to shout,
Want to shout your name, too.

And Margaret and Stan,
Who are still holding hands,
And the guys in the band
Want to shout,
Want to shout your name, too.

Chorus:

And they shout, 'Maker!'
And they shout, 'Earth Shaker!'
And they shout, 'Death Breaker!'
And they shout, 'God!'

Questions

1. I made my list of the things that might shout God's praise (and, yes, it would be interesting to see a cantaloupe pull that off!). What would you put on the list?

2. Apart from making the song that bit more personal, why do you think I put people from my church in the text as well?

3. If you could pick one aspect of the nature of God to shout about, what would it be?

Everything but You

(Ecclesiastes 3)

Introduction

This is another one of those pieces that I wrote in the middle of a conference. I really do love the thrill of writing from the moment – of trying to capture what's going on in a particular time and place. There's a power in it that comes from the immediacy, I think. I suppose it may make the reading less useful in another context, but I don't think that's true of this one. I like to think it's what might have happened if the preacher who wrote Ecclesiastes had met the preacher who was Paul.

TELLING TIPS: I read it on my own, with music playing in the background, as I recall, as a kind of meditative interlude between two worship songs. But it would work just as well with two or even three readers, alternating verses – and maybe working together as a chorus on the 'Everything keeps on changing. Everything but you' lines.

Yeah, everything keeps on changing
And everything has its place.
And everything keeps on changing,
Everything but you.

We greet our newborn children
And say goodbye to our dying parents;
We settle into the new neighbourhood
And move away from our old friends.

And everything keeps on changing
Everything but you.

We kill off our rivals and our passions and our dreams

And try to put a plaster on the pain.
We wreck the ones we care for
And erect a monument to our ambitions on the ruins.

And everything keeps on changing
Everything but you.

We weep like drunks for what love we have lost
And laugh like drunks for what love we have found.
We weep and we mourn,
We laugh and we dance.

And everything keeps on changing
Everything but you.

And we throw away what we later stoop to gather,
Embracing the sacred stones of wisdom that dropped from our hands in
    youth.

And everything keeps on changing
Everything but you.

And we look and we look and we look and we look
For purpose and value and meaning
Until we're too weary and worn out and wasted
To want to look any more.

And everything keeps on changing
Everything but you.

And we keep what's precious
And dispose of what's not,
Except for those of us
With big attics or garages or sheds,
Because surely we'll find a use for it someday,
Mending what's torn up and broken.

And everything keeps on changing
Everything but you.

And sometimes we just have to be silent
And stare
At the face of a lover
At the place of wonder
At the grave of the one who is gone.

And sometimes we just have to speak
And say
I love you
I praise you
I miss you.

And everything keeps on changing
Everything but you.

And we love and we hate
And we fight and make peace
With our friends
And our neighbours
And our husbands
And our wives
And our parents
And our children
And our churches.

Because everything has its time
And everything has its place,
And everything keeps on changing, Lord,
Everything but you.

Questions

1. What particular kind of hope do you find in God's constancy?

2. Is change good? Is it bad? Does it depend?

3. Which of the verses is most relevant to you at this moment?

The Passion

(Isaiah 53:5)

Introduction

A couple of years ago, there was a controversy among evangelicals in England over the nature of the atonement. Preachers and teachers and theologians weighed in with their opinions, and, on the whole, I found it helpful to hear and to read what they had to say. But, at the end of it all, I wondered if there might be a simpler way to talk about what God did through Jesus when he died on the cross. And this little piece was the result. As you will see, it doesn't explain any of the 'mechanics', mainly because I'm not entirely convinced that the 'mechanics' *can* be explained. Or even that there are 'mechanics'! I think the atonement is a lot more personal than that – and the result of God doing, in his way, what we see around us every day.

> **TELLING TIPS: This is one to read on your own. Or, if you like, you can have someone else read the italicised bits for emphasis.**

When I was six, I spilled my milk. And it poured over my plate, and onto my lap and down to the floor. So my mother soaked up the milk, and mopped up the floor, and stopped me from crying and popped me into a fresh set of clothes. And when she finally got back to the table, her dinner was cold.

When the milk gets spilled, somebody needs to clean it up.
And cleaning up means giving up something for someone else.

I turned on the evening news and there was a house on fire. No one knew how the fire started. Arson? Faulty wiring? A stray, smouldering cigarette? But everyone knew that there was an old woman trapped in that house. So a fireman went in and carried her out. And there he sat, sooty and sweaty and sucking down oxygen.

When the milk gets spilled, somebody needs to clean it up.
When the fire burns, somebody needs to put it out.
And putting it out means putting yourself at risk for someone else.

I watched *The Passion of the Christ* when it first came out. I sat through two hours of violence and pain. And I asked myself, 'Why? Why did Jesus have to die that way?'

Then I thought about my mother. And I thought about the fireman. And I thought about this world of ours, where people get knocked down and blood gets spilled and hatred burns. And I wondered, If it takes the sacrifice of a mum to mop up milk, and the sacrifice of a fireman to put out a fire, maybe, just maybe, nothing less than the sacrifice of God himself is adequate to clean up the whole of this mess of a world.

When the milk gets spilled, somebody needs to clean it up.
When the fire burns, somebody needs to put it out.
When the world goes wrong, somebody needs to fix it.
And fixing it up means God giving himself up for us.

Questions

1. How do you think Jesus' sacrifice took away our sins? How are we healed by his wounds?

2. Can you think of other, everyday, events where one person's sacrifice makes things better for another? Are those everyday sacrifices too small to compare with what God did through Jesus? Do they minimise what he did? Or are they perhaps a reflection of the love he showed when he died for us?

3. Other than Jesus, can you think of anyone who has given his or her life for you?

Some Things I Just Don't Understand

(Jeremiah 1:5)

Introduction

Quite honestly, I have never understood it. I really haven't. And I suppose I wrote this as a way of expressing that in as succinct a manner as possible. Either an unborn child is a baby, or she's not. And surely the worst scenario is that she should be a baby only if we decide she is. And a collection of cells – worthy of even less consideration than a fox in a hunt – if we decide she isn't. I guess what frightens me is that we have walked down this path before. Sixty years ago, in Germany, if you were tall and blonde, you were a human being. And if you were short and dark, you weren't. We fought a war to make it clear that every human life has inherent dignity and worth – above and beyond the whims of whatever powers-that-be. So why are we choosing again? Standing in that place of power and deciding who is human and who is not? I want you – you're my baby – you can live. I don't want you – you're only a foetus – you have to die. And that's what I don't understand. I just don't understand.

> **TELLING TIPS: You can do this one on your own. Or you might like to do it with someone else reading the scripture passage when it appears. Or you could even put the passage up on a screen and have the crowd read that as a kind of response to the rest of the text.**

Before I formed you in the womb I knew you,
before you were born I set you apart.

Here are some things I don't understand. I just don't understand.
  If, among other reasons, capital punishment is immoral because there is

the possibility that an innocent person might die, why is abortion acceptable? Are not all babies innocent? And even if there is just the possibility that what is growing in the womb is a person (just like the possibility that the convicted murderer is innocent), is not that possibility enough to keep us from ending the child's life?

> Before I formed you in the womb I knew you,
> before you were born I set you apart.

If a person thinks that abortion is acceptable, what do they do when someone they know has a miscarriage? If what is in the womb is not a person – if it is just a mass of cells – how can they honestly express any grief? Is it a person who has died, or isn't it? Surely the unborn child has to be one or the other. Or is it only a person if we want it to be?

> Before I formed you in the womb I knew you,
> before you were born I set you apart.

And why do we always say that a woman has a right to choose what she does with her body? How is the child growing inside her the same as her body? If you take a cell from the woman and a cell from the unborn child and compare the DNA, they will not be identical. The child may be 'in' the woman's body, but on the basis of the best scientific evidence, it's most definitely not the same.

> Before I formed you in the womb I knew you,
> before you were born I set you apart.

And why do we always say that abortion is about a woman's right to choose? Men often use the availability of abortion to force women to part with babies they would rather keep. When your boyfriend or your father or your husband says, 'Get rid of it or you're out!' that doesn't sound like much of a choice to me.

> Before I formed you in the womb I knew you,
> before you were born I set you apart.

And why do we spend thousands and thousands in one part of a hospital to preserve the lives of children born prematurely at twenty-three or twenty-four weeks, and then spend thousands in other parts of the same hospital bringing the lives of children of the same age to an end?

**Before I formed you in the womb I knew you,
before you were born I set you apart.**

And why does the phrase 'quality of life' always come up in this discussion? The world is full of people whose 'quality of life' is inferior to ours – people who suffer enormous hardship. But we don't advocate ending their lives for that reason. I have often wondered whether it is really the unborn child's 'quality of life' we are so concerned about – or our own.

**Before I formed you in the womb I knew you,
before you were born I set you apart.**

Maybe Jeremiah didn't really mean what he said. Maybe he didn't really think that God had plans for him, even while he was developing in his mother's womb. Maybe those words are just poetry.

Or maybe we're the ones who take the poetic licence.

'How's your baby?'

'When's the baby due?'

'Have you felt the baby kick yet?'

We know what we mean. Our language betrays us.

And that's why I don't understand. I just don't understand.

Questions

1. In what circumstances (if any) do you think that abortion is justified? And where do you find biblical justification for your answer?

2. 'Those in power decide who has worth and who does not.' 'Every human has inherent worth.' These are two very different approaches to human life. Where do you think these ideas come from? And what are their ramifications?

The Boys Who Liked to Say 'NO!'

(Daniel 1)

Introduction

This is one of my all-time favourite retellings! It started with the companion piece, 'The Men Who Liked to Say 'No!', which you will run across in a few pages and which originally appeared in one of my early books, *Angels, Angels All Around*. Having written about the men, it seemed only natural to consider the stubborn nature of these gentlemen at an earlier age. And because the book of Daniel is so full of detail and good storytelling anyway, it was easy.

> **TELLING TIPS:** 'NO' is the operative word in this story, so 'NO' is at the heart of the participation device as well. Tell your crowd that they are to say 'NO' every time it appears in the story. As in, for example, 'The boys who liked to say "NO" '. And also at those places in the text where one or more of the boys actually says 'NO'. Tell them to get louder and more determined each time. Tell them you'd like a full-blooded rebellion! And enjoy!
>
> The other way to do it is to divide the crowd into four groups (one for each boy) and teach them to say 'NO' in four different ways (a loud 'NO', a growly 'NO', a high-pitched 'NO', a silly 'NO', etc.). Then point to each group randomly when the 'NO' comes up in the text.

When the boys lived in Jerusalem, their Hebrew friends knew them as Daniel, Hananiah, Mishael and Azariah.

When Jerusalem was conquered, and they were taken as captives to the palace of King Nebuchadnezzar, they were given Babylonian names. And everyone knew them as Belteshazzar, Shadrach, Meshach and Abednego.

But anyone who knew them well, simply knew them as The Boys Who Liked to Say NO!

They were handsome, these boys. And clever and strong, to boot. Sons of Jerusalem's most important families. So Nebuchadnezzar decided to treat them well. He gave them soft beds to sleep on, rich food to eat and an education at his very best university – all in the hope that they would forget about Jerusalem and learn to call Babylon 'home'. And that the rest of their captured people would, too.

But Nebuchadnezzar hadn't reckoned on them being The Boys Who Liked to Say NO!

One of King Nebuchadnezzar's servants was an enormous man named Ashpenaz. He had a big belly and a bald head, and more than anything else in the world, he liked to eat! So he was put in charge of turning The Boys Who Liked to Say NO! into good Babylonians.

'For dinner tonight,' he announced, 'you will have the following choices from the king's own menu:

Pink pork sausages.

Plump pork chops.

Or my own personal favourite – Mrs Puffy's Perfect Pork Pies!'

Ashpenaz wiped the corners of his mouth with the back of his chubby hand. The thought of all those pork products made him quiver with joy. But The Boys Who Liked to Say NO! were calm. They knew exactly what to do.

The king's food looked good, and smelled even better, but they knew it was made from something their Law said they could not eat. The Law they had learned in Jerusalem. The Law their God had given them. The Law and the city and the God they were determined never to forget.

So they turned to Ashpenaz and together they said, 'NO!'

Ashpenaz could not believe it.

'No pink pork sausages?' he asked.

'NO!' said Shadrach. 'But I wouldn't mind a few carrots.'

'No plump pork chops?'

'NO!' said Meshach. 'I'll just have a green salad.'

'And not even one of Mrs Puffy's Perfect Pork Pies?'

'NO!' said Abednego. 'But a roast potato would be lovely.'

Ashpenaz wiped the sweat from his forehead.

'The king will be very angry,' he explained. 'If you do not eat this food, you will grow tired and ill. And then there is no telling what the king will do to me. He may throw me in prison, or torture me, or cut me up into tiny little pieces. Or worse still, take away my daily ration of bacon burgers. Please, won't you reconsider!'

'NO!' said Daniel. 'But we promise you that you will not get into trouble. For we will not grow tired and ill. Tell the king to put us to the test. For ten days, the four of us will have nothing but vegetables and water. The other boys in the palace can eat your food. At the end of that time, we shall see who looks more fit.'

Ashpenaz agreed, and so did the king, so for ten days, The Boys Who Liked to Say NO! said NO! to everything but vegetables and water – while the other boys ate their fill of pork sausages and pork chops and pork pies.

What happened? The God that Daniel, Shadrach, Meshach and Abednego would not forget did not forget them either! At the end of the test, The Boys Who Liked to Say NO! looked healthy and strong. And the other boys? Well, their bellies were bloated, their breath was bad, and I can't begin to tell you how they reacted when they discovered what was IN Mrs Puffy's Pork Pies!

So from then on, Daniel, Shadrach, Meshach and Abednego were allowed to eat whatever they liked. And even the king had to admit that they were both healthier and wiser than the rest. All because they were loyal to their God. And because they were The Boys Who Liked to Say NO!

Questions

1. When I did this story at a Christian conference, some people told me that they thought it was too negative – that it ought to be about saying 'yes' to God and not 'no' to the world. I could see what they meant, but what do you think?

2. What kinds of thing should we be saying 'No' to?

3. Daniel and his friends had to learn to live in a culture that was not sympathetic to their own. What can we learn from their example in this story when it comes to living as Christians in a Western secularised culture?

King Nebuchadnezzar's First Dream

(Daniel 2)

Introduction

This reading simply carries on with the story of Daniel. Once again, the detail found in the book itself makes for a really fun retelling.

TELLING TIPS: I think the statue is the best place to bring in audience participation, if you want to use it. Divide your crowd into six groups, one for each of the materials used in the statue.

Have the 'Gold' group look up in wonder and say 'Aaah!'
Have the 'Silver' group say 'Oooh!'
Have the 'Belly of Bronze' group pretend to tickle the person next to them and go 'Cootchie-cootchie-coo!'
Have the 'Iron' group stamp their feet.
And have the 'Iron and Clay' group make a squishy, squelchy sucking sound.
And have the 'Rock' group make a great big growly roar!

Then lead them in these sounds and actions at the appropriate places in the text.
Oh, and because the 'cutting up into tiny little pieces' shows up a lot as well, have everyone do a karate kick or move with you and shout 'Eee-Yaaa!' when you get to those points!

King Nebuchadnezzar had a dream.
A bad dream.
A troubling dream.

A dream that kept him up all night.

So he called together all his wise men – his magicians and enchanters, his sorcerers and astrologers.

'I have had a troubling dream,' he said. 'And I want you to tell me what it means.'

'No problem, your majesty,' grinned the wise men. 'Tell us your dream and we will tell you what it means.'

'Ah, but there is a problem,' said the king. 'If I told you my dream, you could make up any old rubbish to explain it. How would I know you were telling me the truth? So I have decided to set you a test. Pass, and you will receive a great reward. Fail, and I will chop you up into tiny little pieces.'

'And what kind of test would that be?' asked the wise men, not nearly so confident now.

'Tell me what my dream means,' said the king. 'But first, tell me what I dreamed!'

The wise men looked at each and trembled. No one had ever asked them to do this before.

'Seriously, your majesty,' they said at last, 'tell us your dream, and we'll tell you what it means.'

'I'm very serious,' said the king. 'And you're just stalling for time. You say you're wise. You say you're powerful. Then show me. Tell me what I dreamed, and then I will know for sure that you can tell me what it means.'

'But majesty,' stammered the wise men, every one of them trembling now. 'This is impossible. No one but the gods could do what you ask!'

King Nebuchadnezzar was furious, and declared that every wise man in Babylon should be chopped up into tiny little pieces. And so it was that the king's soldiers came looking for the wise man Daniel and his three wise friends – Shadrach, Meshach and Abednego.

Daniel did not tremble. No, he spoke to the soldier. He found out what the fuss was all about. He asked the king for just a little more time. And then he got together with his three friends – and had a prayer meeting!

They asked God to show them the king's dream. And when God did, Daniel went straight to Nebuchadnezzar.

'Do not chop the wise men into tiny little pieces,' he begged, 'for I can tell you what your dream means.'

'But can you tell me what I dreamed?' asked the king.

'I can't,' admitted Daniel. 'And neither can any other wise man or magician. But there is a God in heaven who can. He has shown me your dream, King Nebuchadnezzar. And now I will tell it to you.

'You saw a statue, your majesty – a giant statue!
   Its head was made of gold.
   Its chest and arms, of silver.
   Its belly and thighs were made of bronze.
   Its legs, of iron.
   And its feet were part iron and part clay.

'And then you saw a rock. A rock cut out of the hills, but not by human hands. The rock struck the statue on its feet of iron and clay and the statue broke into tiny little pieces that were swept away on the wind. But the rock? The rock grew into a mountain and filled the whole earth!'

Nebuchadnezzar was amazed. Daniel was right – down to the last detail. But before he could say anything, Daniel continued:
   'That was your dream, O King. And here is what it means.
   'Your kingdom is the head of gold. The kingdom to follow will not be quite as powerful as yours. That is the arms and chest of silver. The kingdom after that – the belly and thighs of bronze – will be less powerful still. But then will come another kingdom – the legs of iron – that will crush all before it. That kingdom will divide – the feet made of iron and clay – and in the days of that kingdom, the God of heaven will set up a kingdom of his own – the rock – that will never be destroyed.
   'God has shown you the future, your majesty – that is the meaning of your dream!'

King Nebuchadnezzar said nothing at first. He fell to the floor and bowed before Daniel. Then he exclaimed:

'Daniel, your God is the God of gods,
The Lord whose wisdom never ceases.
He showed me the meaning of my dream
And now no one shall be chopped up into tiny little pieces!'

Questions

1. If you had been one of the magicians or wise men, how would you have reacted to the king's request?

2. Have you ever been in a situation where God revealed something to you or to someone else that could not possibly have been known otherwise? Talk about that.

3. Again, what does this story have to teach us about being Christians in a culture that is not always sympathetic to our beliefs?

Songs in Search of a Tune: Praise to our God

(Daniel 2:20–23)

Introduction

This is another one of those 'Songs in Search of a Tune'. It's a rephrasing of the prayer that Daniel prayed when he asked God to show him King Nebuchadnezzar's dream.

TELLING TIPS: This is another one to tell on your own. And if you can come up with a tune, you could sing it instead!

Praise to our God for ever and ever,
Wisdom and power are his alone.
Praise to our God for ever and ever,
Wisdom and power are his alone.

He sets up the seasons – winter, spring, summer.
He knocks down the king – right off his throne.
He shines like a light into all that is hidden
And makes the deep, darkest mysteries known.

Praise to our God for ever and ever,
Wisdom and power are his alone.
Praise to our God for ever and ever,
Wisdom and power are his alone.

We praise you and thank you, O God of our fathers,
For all of the mercy that you have shown,

For sharing your wisdom and sharing your power
And making the secret things of kings known.

Praise to our God for ever and ever,
Wisdom and power are his alone.
Praise to our God for ever and ever,
Wisdom and power are his alone.

Questions

1. From what he says in this prayer, on what basis does Daniel have confidence that God can show him the king's dream?

2. How does God knock kings off their thrones? Can you think of both a biblical and a contemporary example?

3. If ultimate power and authority and wisdom belong to God, what does that say about the Christian's allegiance to nations, kingdoms and states?

The Men Who Liked to Say 'NO!'

(Daniel 3)

Introduction

As I said earlier, this is a companion piece to 'The Boys Who Liked to Say "No!"'. You could do one after the other in the same service, or use them both as an introduction to a sermon series on Daniel.

TELLING TIPS: Divide your crowd into three groups, as in 'The Boys...', and have them make three of the same 'NO' sounds. Then bring them in, as in the previous reading, every time you say 'Men who liked to say "NO!"' or when any of the men actually say 'NO' in the text. If you like, you could also have a fourth group to growl along with the king. Oh, and if you want to get your musicians involved, you could have them make some of the 'instrument' sounds. It's amazing what a keyboard with a sampler can do here! And as far as the 'made-up' instruments go, use your imagination!

One day, King Nebuchadnezzar's herald made an important announcement:

'All prefects and satraps,
All magistrates and judges,
All councillors and governors,
All big shots and hobnobs,
Must report immediately to the Plain of Dura.
King Nebuchadnezzar has a surprise for you!'

When the officials got there, they found a golden statue, three metres wide and thirty metres tall. It was the biggest statue they had ever seen. And gathered around the bottom of the statue was the biggest band they had ever heard.

The herald cleared his throat and took a deep breath:

'People of all nations and stations and languages,
People of all places and races and climes,
People of all landscapes and body shapes and backgrounds,
People of all time zones and hormones and kinds,
At the sound of
The trumpet, the trigon, the horn and the bagpipe,
The oboe, the zither, the harp and the lyre,
The wahoo, the farney, the honk and the oompah,
All of you must bow down and worship this golden statue.
And anyone who does not will be thrown into
A hot and humid, bright and blazing, flaming fiery furnace!'

While the herald caught his breath, King Nebuchadnezzar gave the signal and the band began to play. At once, everyone fell down and worshipped the statue.

Well, almost everyone.

For there were three officials, standing at the back, who did not bow down and who did not worship the statue. Shadrach, Meshach and Abednego. They were all grown up now – the *MEN* Who Liked to Say NO!

Now, most people knew King Nebuchadnezzar as the great and powerful ruler of Babylon. But anyone who knew him well, knew him simply as The King Who Liked to Say GRRR!

And when he saw the three men standing at the back, that is exactly what he did.

'GRRR!' he snarled. 'Who dares defy my order?'
'GRRR!' he growled. 'Who dares insult my god?'
'GRRR!' he roared. (For he was good at this!) 'Who dares? Who dares? Who dares?'

As it happened, there were several satraps and big shots and hobnobs nearby – native Babylonians, who didn't much like the idea of these foreigners from Jerusalem having such important jobs – who knew exactly who dared.

'Their names are Shadrach, Meshach and Abednego,' they told the king.

'GRRR!' snarled Nebuchadnezzar. 'Bring them to me at once!'

'Well,' snapped the king, when the men were brought before him, 'you heard the order and failed to obey. Will you worship the statue now?'

'NO!' said Shadrach. 'We will not worship your idol. Our God has told us that would be wrong.'

'NO!' said Meshach. 'And we will not forget our God, or his Law, or the land he gave us – the land from which we were taken.'

'NO!' said Abednego, 'And we believe that our God will not forget us!'

'Then off to the furnace!' roared the king.

Nebuchadnezzar GRRR-ed all the way to the furnace.

'Make it hot!' he growled. 'Seven times hotter than it's been before. And tie them up tight, so there is no chance for escape!'

And so, tightly bound, The Men Who Liked to Say NO! were thrown into the furnace. But the flames were so hot that the men who threw them in died immediately!

'Charred. Sizzled. Burned to a crisp,' noted the herald.

Things were different, however, for Shadrach, Meshach and Abednego. They weren't burning. They weren't boiling. They weren't even sweating. And they weren't alone.

They could just make him out, moving through the fire. A flash of orange hair. Flaming red fingers. And a pair of burning eyes. The angel flickered like the flames before them, now red and orange, now yellow, now white. Then, one by one, he touched a finger to the ropes that bound them, and they smoked and sizzled and burned right through. But there was not so much as a blister on the skin of Shadrach, Meshach and Abednego.

'God is with you,' the angel whispered. 'You have nothing to fear.' And a smile ignited on one cheek and burned like a fuse across his face. Then the angel took them by the hand and led them on a walking tour of the fiery furnace. They shuffled their feet through white, hot coals. They ran their hands along red, hot walls. They filled their lungs with black, hot air. And they blew out fat smoke rings!

Meanwhile, outside the furnace, Nebuchadnezzar's lips were no longer twisted in an angry snarl. No, they hung open and limp with amazement.

'I thought we threw three men into the furnace,' he said. 'But, look, there are four men in there now.'

The herald crept closer and looked. Then he turned to the king, his face red with the heat and dripping with sweat.

'It is an angel, your majesty. A creature from heaven. Perhaps even the god these men refused to forget. If so, he is a very powerful god indeed, for they are unharmed!'

Nebuchadnezzar leaped to his feet and ordered Shadrach, Meshach and Abednego to come out. They waded through the flames to the mouth of the furnace, kicking coals as they walked. But when they went to thank the angel, he just smiled and turned to smoke in their hands, leaving nothing but a whisper that curled around their heads, then disappeared.

'Don't forget. God is with you.'

Immediately, the officials gathered round them to have a closer look.

The satraps and the prefects inspected them carefully. 'Not a trace of smoke!' they noted.

The councillors and governors touched their hair. 'Not even singed!' they observed.

The big shots and hobnobs smelled their clothes. 'Fresh as a Babylonian spring!' they cried.

Finally, the king himself spoke up.

'Praise be to the God of Shadrach, Meshach and Abednego – the Supreme God! They did not forget him and he did not forget them – but sent his angel to save them. I therefore order that, from now on, anyone who says anything bad about this God shall be chopped up into tiny little pieces. And what is more, I shall promote Shadrach, Meshach and Abednego to even higher positions in my kingdom.

Then he looked squarely at the three friends.

'Surely,' he grinned. 'You can say yes to that?'

Shadrach looked at Meshach.
Meshach looked at Abednego.
Abednego looked at Shadrach.
Then, together, they looked at the king.

'NO... problem!' they said.

Questions

1. If you had been standing in the crowd at the foot of the statue and were asked to bow down, what would you have done? And why? Can you think of any contemporary examples where someone's life might actually be at risk because they refuse to worship a different god?

2. Are there any modern gods we bow to while claiming allegiance to the God of heaven? If so, what are they? Why do we do it? Should we stop? And, if so, how? Does any of this have something to do with wanting to be just like the people around us?

3. Again, what does this story have to teach us about being Christians in a secular culture?

Songs in Search of a Tune: There Was an Angel

(Daniel 3, John 5, Acts 12, Luke 24)

Introduction

I wanted to write a shorter piece about the angel who appeared to Shadrach, Meshach and Abednego in the fire, but got distracted in the middle and found myself thinking about stories in the Bible where angels appeared out of nowhere to bring God's help. Then it all got kind of personal. And this song/poem was the result.

TELLING TIPS: This is one to tell on your own.

Verse 1:

There was an angel in the fire,
There was an angel in the fire,
There was an angel in the fire,
Walking through the flame.

There was an angel in the fire,
There was an angel in the fire,
There was an angel in the fire,
And I heard him call my name.

And I heard him call my name.
And I heard him call my name.

There was an angel in the fire,
Walking through the flame.

There was an angel on the water,
There was an angel on the water,
There was an angel on the water,
And it rippled at his touch.

There was an angel on the water,
There was an angel on the water,
There was an angel on the water –
I want to feel that touch so much.

I want to feel that touch so much.
I want to feel that touch so much.

There was an angel on the water,
And it rippled at his touch.

Verse 3:

There was an angel in the prison,
There was an angel in the prison,
There was an angel in the prison,
And he opened every door.

There was an angel in the prison,
There was an angel in the prison,
There was an angel in the prison –
I'm not locked up any more.

I'm not locked up any more.
I'm not locked up any more.

There was an angel in the prison,
And he opened every door.

Verse 4:

There was an angel in the graveyard,
There was an angel in the graveyard,

There was an angel in the graveyard –
Said, 'There's nothing left to fear.'

There was an angel in the graveyard,
There was an angel in the graveyard,
There was an angel in the graveyard –
Said, 'You won't find the dead man here.'

'You won't find the dead man here.'
'You won't find the dead man here.'

There was an angel in the graveyard –
Said, 'There's nothing left to fear.'

And I heard him call my name.
And I heard him call my name.

There was an angel in the graveyard –
Said, 'You won't find the dead man here.'

Questions

1. This piece is based on four different angel appearances in the Bible. List some others that I might have used. And, hey, why not write verses to go along with those examples – along the lines of what I did in the reading?

2. Talk about a time when an angel visited you or someone you know.

3. Which verse (if any) means the most to you, in your life, right now?

King Nebuchadnezzar's Second Dream

(Daniel 4)

Introduction

This is probably the least well-known story in this Daniel series. But that doesn't make it the least important. Pride, arrogance and the sovereignty of God all make an appearance in this reading, and your group might find it the most interesting of them all.

> **TELLING TIPS:** I did this story originally with a really big crowd – like a few thousand! So I broke them up into three slightly less big groups and had each group make a sound. There was a bird group (I think they all clucked like chickens). There was an animal group (I think they all made monkey sounds). And there was a fruit group (they held out their hands as if they were holding a piece of fruit and said 'Pear'. Well, fruit doesn't make much noise – unless of course you want to use raspberries!) And, having said that (wish I'd thought of it earlier!), feel free to use whatever birds, beasts and fruit you think are funniest or more appropriate to your audience. I then brought each group in at the appropriate place in the text. I also had someone mime the king/stump role – and had a helper wet him with dew at the right moments (any super soaker will do!). As I recall, the 'king' grabbed the super soaker and got me on the last line. I'll leave that one up to you!

King Nebuchadnezzar had another dream.
  Another bad dream.
  Another troubling dream.
  Another dream that kept him up all night.

So again he called together all his wise men – his magicians and enchanters, his sorcerers and astrologers. But this time, the king must have been in a slightly brighter mood, for there was none of that nasty business about chopping up people into tiny little pieces.

Unfortunately, they still could not tell King Nebuchadnezzar what his dream meant. So the king did what he probably should have done in the first place. He sent for Daniel.

'Daniel,' he said, 'the spirit of the gods works in you and reveals the deepest mysteries. Explain to me what my dream means, please.'

And then King Nebuchadnezzar told Daniel his dream.

'There was a tree. An enormous tree. A beautiful tree. Its top touched the heavens and it could be seen from every place on earth! Every kind of bird nested in its branches. Every kind of beast sheltered beneath its boughs. And every creature in the world was nourished by its abundant fruit.'

'Sounds wonderful!' said Daniel.

But King Nebuchadnezzar just shook his head and sighed – for the dream did not end there.

'A messenger appeared before me – an angel sent from heaven. And he called out in a loud voice:

'Cut down the tree,

Strip bare its branches,

Tear off its boughs,

Scatter its fruit

And send the birds and the beasts away.

But leave the stump.

Bind it with iron and bronze

And for seven long years

Let it be drenched with dew

And dwell among the animals and plants.

For the Most High God wants you to know

That he and he alone sets up kingdoms

And knocks them down again, as well.'

Daniel trembled. Daniel shook.

He knew exactly what the king's dream meant.

And he knew just as well that the king would not like it.

'Oh, that this dream was about one of your enemies,' sighed Daniel. 'But sadly, your majesty, the dream is all about you.

'You are the tree, for your greatness stretches out across the earth. And like the tree, you will be cut down and driven out into the wild for seven years to be drenched by the dew and to dwell with the wild animals. But the stump will remain, so that your kingdom may be restored to you when you recognize that ultimate power belongs to God and God alone.

'Take my advice, your majesty. Tell God that you are sorry for the wrong things you have done. Stop taking advantage of the poor and the weak. And perhaps this dream will not become your nightmare.'

Did King Nebuchadnezzar take Daniel's advice? He did not! Twelve months later, as he was walking on the roof of his palace, he looked out across Bablyon and again was filled with pride.

'All that lies before me,' he boasted, 'This city and all its glory is down to my power and my majesty!'

And immediately, the dream came true! The king was overcome with madness, and for seven long years he was left to wander with the wild animals and be drenched by the morning dew. Until at last, sad and humiliated and alone, he lifted his eyes to heaven and asked God for help. And that's when the madness left him and eventually he was returned to his throne. And that's when he prayed this prayer:

'God and God alone is great,
Worthy of praise and honour, too.
His ways are right, his ways are just,
And those who are proud, he drenches with dew!'

Questions

1. What do you think is the point of the king's vision? What are we meant to learn from it?

2. How do you think Daniel felt about the king?

3. And, yet again, is there anything new to learn from this story about living as Christians in a 'foreign' culture?

Songs in Search of a Tune:
Daniel, Daniel

(Daniel 6)

Introduction

In my book *Angels, Angels All Around*, I did a retelling of the story of Daniel in the lions' den which suggested that the angel kept the lions from eating Daniel by distracting them with a variety of games. This is a sort of musical version of that story. There are lots of other body parts you might want to insert instead of the ones I have chosen. Just be careful (not that I have been – as you will see!) about which ones you choose.

> **TELLING TIPS: You might want to teach your crowd the chorus, and also have them repeat the 'sound effects' – 'Stinky, stinky', 'Oochy, ouchy' etc. – after you.**
>
> **It will also be helpful, when the lion speaks, to do that bit in a deep, growly lion voice.**

Daniel had some enemies.
They longed to see him dead.
And so they passed a brand new law
And this is what it said:

'You must not pray to any god,
Pray only to King Darius.'
But Daniel prayed. He disobeyed.
And things looked quite precarious.

They tossed him in the lions' den,
To make a lion's supper.

But God sent down an angel,
Those dinner plans to scupper.

Now you might think the angel
Simply grabbed the lion's muzzle,
But I think he found a nicer way
Of sorting out this puzzle.

Chorus:

Daniel, Daniel,
Sitting in the lions' den.
Daniel, Daniel,
It's dinner time again!

The lion said to Daniel,
'I want to eat your feet.'
The angel said to the lion,
'They don't smell very sweet!'

'Stinky, stinky, stinky, stink –
They don't smell very sweet!'

Chorus:

Daniel, Daniel,
Sitting in the lions' den.
Daniel, Daniel,
It's dinner time again!

The lion said to Daniel,
'I want to eat your arm.'
The angel said to the lion
'Don't do him any harm!'

'Oochy, ouchy, oochy, ouch –
Don't do him any harm!'

Chorus:

Daniel, Daniel,
Sitting in the lions' den.
Daniel, Daniel,
It's dinner time again!

The lion said to Daniel,
'I want to eat your nose.'
The angel said to the lion,
'The filling's kind of gross!'

'Ick, ack, ick, ack –
The filling's kind of gross!'

Chorus:

Daniel, Daniel,
Sitting in the lions' den.
Daniel, Daniel,
It's dinner time again!

The lion said to Daniel,
'I want to eat your thumb.'
The angel said to the Lion,
'Here, have some bubblegum!'

'Chew, chew, chew, chew –
Have some bubblegum!'

Chorus:

Daniel, Daniel,
Sitting in the lions' den.
Daniel, Daniel,
It's dinner time again!

The lion said to Daniel,
'I want to eat your belly.'

The angel said to the Lion,
'Why don't we have some jelly?'

'Yum, yum, yum, yum –
Why don't we have some jelly?'

Chorus:

Daniel, Daniel,
Sitting in the lions' den.
Daniel, Daniel,
It's dinner time again!

The lion said to Daniel,
'I want to eat your heart!'
The angel said to the Lion,
'Well, that'll just make you… start to have gastric disturbances that might
well result in unfortunate posterior emissions!'

'Raspberries, raspberries, raspberries, raspberries
Well that'll just make you…'
(Make 'raspberry' noises.)

Chorus:

Daniel, Daniel,
Sitting in the lions' den.
Daniel, Daniel,
It's dinner time again!

When morning came
King Darius saw that Daniel was alive.
He made his servants pull him out
And he gave him a high-five.

He then had Daniel's enemies
Tossed in the den instead.
The lion looked and licked his chops
It was time now to be fed!

Chorus:

Daniel's enemies,
Sitting in the lions' den.
Daniel's enemies,
It's dinner time. The end.

Questions

1. So how do you think the angel kept the lions from eating Daniel?

2. Talk about a time when you did something right and it caused you trouble.

3. Why not come up with a few body-part verses of your own. Try 'elbow': I dare you!

A Mouthful

(Daniel 6)

Introduction

This one is just a bit of fun, really. A light-hearted way of telling the Daniel and lions story. And, depending on the age of your crowd, you might want to start with a simple vocabulary lesson!

> **TELLING TIPS: This is one to tell on your own. If you want to get someone else involved, you could have a partner do the first two lines of each verse, and then turn to you for the rest. Or you could have the whole group repeat the 'Loyalty', 'Royalty' words, etc. after you at the beginning of each verse.**

Cupidity. Cupidity.
This is a tale of cupidity.
The king's advisers were jealous of Daniel.
They wanted that 'power' thing.
So they dreamed up a trick to put Daniel to death
And went to see the king.

Stupidity. Stupidity.
This is a tale of stupidity.
'You're like a god, King Darius!' they said.
You give us all we need!
So why should we pray to anyone but you?'
Flattered, the king agreed.

Royalty. Royalty.
This is a tale of royalty.
'Then what should we do?' asked the puzzled king.

120

'A new law!' his advisers grinned.
'If we catch someone praying to another god,
He'll be tossed in the lions' den!'

Loyalty. Loyalty.
This is a tale of loyalty.
Daniel was loyal to his friend King Darius.
But he was loyal to God even more.
So he knelt at the window and prayed his prayers.
In spite of the brand new law.

Ferocity. Ferocity.
This is a tale of ferocity.
The advisers cheered when they caught Daniel praying.
They roared with laughter and glee!
Then they tossed him into a den full of lions,
Who were waiting for their tea!

Velocity. Velocity.
This is a tale of velocity.
God sent an angel just as quick as he could
To shut the lions' jaws.
While Daniel slept soundly through the night
Safe from their teeth and claws.

Bonhomie. Bonhomie.
This is a tale of bonhomie.
King Darius was sorry he'd passed the law,
For Daniel was his friend.
So when he saw that Daniel was safe,
He had him pulled out of the den.

Gastronomy. Gastronomy.
This is a tale of gastronomy.
He arrested the men who'd made the law.
He tossed *them* into the den instead.
Then the lions snapped and snarled and roared
And had their breakfast in bed!

Cupidity – Stupidity.
Royalty – Loyalty.
Ferocity – Velocity.
Bonhomie – Gastronomy
(It's a mouthful, I know.)
But that is the story of Daniel!

Questions

1. Talk about a time when jealousy led you to do something you later regretted.

2. Daniel continued to do what he believed to be right, even though the consequences were painful. Talk about a time when you, or someone you know, faced a similar decision.

3. Daniel was delivered from the lions, but there are plenty of examples, throughout the history of the church, where Christians who also stood up for what was right got chewed up instead. What do you make of that?

The 'N' Word

(The book of Jonah)

Introduction

When I lead workshops on biblical storytelling, the story of Jonah inevitably shows up in the mix. And so I will usually ask, 'What do you think is the problem in the story of Jonah?' Just as inevitably, someone will say either, 'Getting out of the whale (or Big Fish, if they are a stickler!)' or 'Disobedience'. And my reply is always, 'Wrong!' Actually, to be fair, I concede that when we tell the story to small children, those two problems are probably fine. But neither of them is the real problem. No; Jonah's problem, the real problem from which his disobedience sprang, was that he hated the Ninevites – the very people God had sent him to rescue. Jonah's real problem was racism! And that's why I thought that a telling of the story that emphasised the 'N' word would be the most forceful way to make Jonah's problem clear and bring the point of the story home to us as well.

> **TELLING TIPS: It's important to say the word 'Ninevites' with as much disgust and hatred as you can muster. You need to get across the depth of Jonah's feelings, and that's probably why you need to do this as a solo reading. Having the crowd get involved might turn it into too much of a pantomime piece and work against the seriousness of the story.**

Jonah didn't mind using the 'n' word.
'Ninevites!' he grunted, the word like a curse on his lips.
'Why would God want to save Ninevites?
They're cruel. They're brutal. They're hardly human.
And I will not play a part in their rescue.'

Jonah didn't mind using the 'n' word.
'Ninevites!' he grumbled, as he boarded a boat for Tarshish.
'Conquerors. Oppressors. Monsters, not men.
I will not go. That's all there is to it.
They will not profit from this prophet's words!'

Jonah didn't mind using the 'n' word.
'Ninevites,' he whispered, as he eyed each sailor up and down.
'Dull, base and beast-like.
Some of these sailors have that look.
I'd better watch my back.'

Jonah didn't mind using the 'n' word.
'Ninevites!' he explained, as a storm swallowed up the ship.
'I won't take God's message to Ninevites.
That's why we're in this mess.
Throw me into the water and your troubles will be over.'

Jonah didn't mind using the 'n' word.
'Ninevites!' he cursed, as he sank like a stone in the sea.
'Uncaring, unfeeling,
Without an ounce of compassion.
I knew that they'd be the death of me.'

Jonah didn't mind using the 'n' word.
'Ninevites,' he sighed, as he sat in the belly of the fish.
'All right then. I'll go and talk to Ninevites.
I don't like them. I don't want to.
But I guess I've been saved for a reason.'

Jonah didn't mind using the 'n' word.
'Ninevites,' he muttered, as he walked around their city.
'They look funny. They smell funny. They talk funny.
But I'll do what I have to.
I'll do what I promised.'

Jonah didn't mind using the 'n' word.
'Ninevites!' he cried, forcing the word out as cheerfully as he could.
'You have forty days to change your ways.

124

Or God will destroy your city.'
And the Ninevites repented as one!

Jonah didn't mind using the 'n' word.
'Ninevites,' he sneered, as he climbed a hill outside the city.
'They're faking it. They haven't really changed.
And when they go back to their old ways,
I'll see them destroyed after all!'

Jonah didn't mind using the 'n' word.
'Ninevites!' he grinned, as he sat in the shade of a little tree.
'C'mon, Ninevites. I'm waiting to see you fall.
Waiting to see God's vengeance!'
But in the night, God sent a worm to kill the little tree.

Jonah didn't mind using the 'n' word.
'Ninevites!' he swore, as he looked at his little tree.
'They're responsible for this, I'm sure!
They're wicked and vile. They care for nothing!'
And that's when he heard God's voice.

God had a problem with the 'n' word.
But the 'j' word was driving him mad.
'Jonah,' God sighed. 'Jonah, don't be angry.
The people in that city are people just like you.
120,000 – men, women and children.
If the death of a tree is important
Should I not be concerned about their fate too?'

And that's where the story ends.
Not with an answer, but a question.
Will we love whomever God loves,
Whether we like them or not?

Jonah didn't mind using the 'n' word.
Do you?

Questions

1. So, if Jonah was a racist – how did he get to be a prophet? Why does God choose people who are much less than perfect to do his will? Why did he choose Jonah for this particular job?

2. Have a look at the end of Jonah – the bit after the Ninevites repent, which we often ignore. Why do you think that we never hear Jonah's response to God's final words?

3. We often think of racism in terms of one group that thinks it's superior looking down on a group it thinks is inferior. That might have been true of Jonah's attitude towards the Ninevites ('We are God's chosen people and you are not!'). But it is just as likely that his hatred stemmed from fear. Nineveh was the superpower of its day – a real and constant threat to Jonah's nation. Can racism work in that direction, too? Or would it be more accurate to call that something else?

Lights and Bells

(Matthew 1–2, Luke 1–2)

Introduction

Just a little Christmas poem that might fit nicely into a Christmas Eve or Christmas morning service.

> **TELLING TIPS: You might just want to read this one on your own – it's very short. Or you could get the group to do the 'Lights and Bells, Bells and Lights' parts with you.**

Lights and bells,
Bells and lights.
Cold pale mornings,
Long dark nights.
As winter's grey
Grabs hold and bites,
Christmas comes
With sounds and sights.
Lights and bells,
Bells and lights.

Lights and bells,
Bells and lights.
Angel songs,
Stars like kites.
Good News rings out
From Heaven's heights.
And Jesus comes
With sounds and sights.

Lights and bells,
Bells and lights.

Lights and bells.
Bells and lights.
Stable rafters
And starry brights
Paint shadow crosses
On wood uprights.
The baby turns…
Turns wrongs to rights.
Lights and bells,
Bells and lights.
For you and me
Turns wrongs to rights.
Lights and bells,
Bells and lights.

Questions

1. I put the bells and lights in because they are some of the things that remind me of Christmas and make me feel good when I think of them. When you think of Christmas, what physical things make you feel good about the season? And how might they connect with the coming of Jesus?

2. At the end of the poem I use the bells and lights to point us to the crucifixion. List some other elements in the Christmas story that do the same.

3. I have always lived in places where it's cold at Christmas time – and the poem reflects that. But how does the imagery work in a context where it's not cold and grey?

Follow Me

(Matthew 4:18–19, Matthew 9:9, John 1:43)

Introduction

Following Jesus and getting sucked into 'church culture': are they one and the same? That's the question this reading asks.

TELLING TIPS: Definitely one to read on your own, unless you'd like to have someone else read the 'scripture' parts at the start of each section.

As Jesus was walking beside the Sea of Galilee, he saw two brothers, Simon called Peter and his brother Andrew. They were casting a net into the lake, for they were fishermen.

'Come, follow me,' Jesus said. 'But first let me explain how this works.

'You'll have to be in church by 10.30 every Sunday morning. You can miss the odd service, but if you miss too many, the others may well begin to question your sincerity. They won't mention this directly, of course, but trust me, word will get around!

'Yes, I know that you may well already have something to do at that time. It's obvious that your work schedule involves some commitment in the early hours of the day, but we trust that you will find a way around that. This is, after all, the way that we have been doing it for years. It suits our schedule. It works for us. And we see no reason to change simply because the rest of society no longer sees Sunday as sacred! So leave the papers till Sunday afternoon, forget about the shopping, find someone else to coach the local boys' football team, and come and follow me.'

As Jesus went on from there, he saw a man named Matthew sitting at the tax collector's booth. 'Follow me,' he told him. 'But first let me explain how this works.

'You're obviously good with money, so I'm sure you'll understand. It's the roof, you see. And the walls and windows, as well. They're in constant need of repair, so there are a great many fund-raising events you will be expected to support: monthly flea markets; bake sales; the odd concert (We hope you like brass ensembles and children's choirs!); and of course, the Annual Christmas Fair. And with your contacts in the business world, we'll be counting on you to solicit the occasional donation – perhaps your winebibbing friends could cough up the odd bottle of booze for our raffle? So, what do you say? We need a new treasurer for our Building Fund. Why not come and follow me?'

The next day, Jesus decided to leave for Galilee. Finding Philip, he said to him, 'Follow me. But first let me explain how this works.

'The world, secular culture – call it what you will – is generally quite corrupting. So we expect you to leave that culture and join ours! You'll listen to Christian music, laugh at Christian comedians, spend your holidays at Christian conferences and even do Christian aerobics to Christian worship tunes! There will be Christian books for you to read, Christian films for you to watch, Christian fashion styles to which you must adhere, and we can even arrange for you to play football with your local Christian league. Corrupted by the world? You simply won't have the time! So leave your friends behind and come and follow me.'

'Follow me.' That's the invitation, pure and simple. But an invitation to what? To follow Jesus, or to join up with some specific church culture, to come and be a part of our Christian club? What are we asking and, more importantly, what are people hearing when we echo Jesus' invitation to 'Follow me'?

Questions

1. 'Church culture' of some sort or another is, of course, inevitable. When people get together to do anything as a group, they organise themselves in specific ways and engage in certain activities. And it's not long before those activities get formalised into a tradition. Just try doing one successful thing at your church, and see what happens the following year! But what happens if someone wants to follow Jesus but doesn't particularly buy into everything that's part of our church culture? What recourse do they have? What can we do?

2. What do you think of the Christian subculture – all those 'blessed' alternatives to 'worldly' activities?

3. Is it true that Christians often lose touch with their non-Christian friends when they get heavily involved in church culture? How does this affect evangelism? And what can the church do to minimise this effect? Do we just expect too much of people? Do we make ourselves too busy for our own good?

Foxes, Fish Food and Flying Things

(Matthew 8:19–27)

Introduction

OK, here's the deal. This reading was written, originally, for a church I pastored in England. And, over there, there is a long-established television character called Basil Brush. He's a fox puppet and his signature phrase (don't ask me why; I don't know!) is 'Boom! Boom!' So, for a British audience, a fox who goes 'Boom! Boom!' works nicely with a thundery storm that does the same. If you want to do this reading, you might explain that to your crowd (hey, a little insight into British TV culture won't hurt anyone. Then again…).

Or you could just tell them to go 'Boom! Boom!' at that point and hope they don't ask why.

> **TELLING TIPS: Divide your crowd into four groups and teach each group a different sound: 'Boom! Boom!', 'Zoom-Zoom!', 'No Room!', and (in a grave voice) 'Tomb-tomb'. Then bring each group in at the appropriate times, remembering to quieten them down to a whisper at the end.**

A teacher – a teacher of the Jewish law – came up to Jesus and said, 'I will follow you wherever you go.'

The man sounded serious. He sounded dedicated. He sounded keen. But Jesus wanted to make sure that the man knew exactly what he was getting himself into.

So he turned to him and said, 'Wherever I go? Really? Well let me tell you then. Foxes (*Boom-boom!*) have holes to hide in, and birds of the air (*Zoom-zoom!*) can always return to their nests. But I have nowhere (*No room!*) to lay down my weary head.'

Another man said to Jesus, 'I want to follow you, too. But my dad has just died and I need to go to his funeral.'

And I know this sounds harsh, but Jesus wanted the man to know just how important, how life-changing, how costly this decision was. So he turned to him and said, 'Then follow me. Follow me, now. And let the dead bury the dead.' (*Tomb-tomb!*)

It's not easy to follow. I think that's what Jesus was trying to say. Not a walk in the park. Not a piece of cake. Not a bowlful of cherries. Or any of the other 'happily-ever-after' clichés we sometimes build in to our appeals.

And to prove his point (could it be?), he boarded a boat with his followers and sailed right into a storm.

The thunder crashed. (*Boom-boom!*)

The waves rushed by. (*Zoom-zoom!*)

And his followers cried, 'Lord, save us! We're going to die. (*Tomb-tomb!*)

'There's no place (*No room!*) for fear, here,' said Jesus. 'Trust me, and you will see.'

So Jesus stood up, stood up in the boat in the middle of the storm.

And he silenced the thunder. (Whisper – *Boom-boom.*)

And he stilled the waves. (Whisper – *Zoom-zoom.*)

And nobody died. (Whisper – *Tomb-tomb.*)

For there was no place (Whisper – *No Room*) for anything but wonder and awe.

Questions

1. What has been most 'costly' for you when it comes to following Jesus?

2. Is there a sense in which Jesus' assertion that he had nowhere to lay his head is true for every Christian? Or was it just a specific feature of his ministry? What do you think, and why?

3. Do you think that Jesus' response to the man who had lost his father was harsh? Why do you think he said it?

A Table Story

(Matthew 9:9–13)

Introduction

Sometimes it's just a word that helps you find your way into a retelling. And in this case, as you will see, it's the word 'count'.

> **TELLING TIPS: This is definitely meant to be a solo piece. When I first did this reading, I sat behind a table on a stage and did it from there. I think it helped to give a sense of the story's setting. And because I hadn't memorised the story, it also gave me somewhere to put the text!**

Matthew looked around the table and counted.

Ten guests.

Six dishes.

Five stacks of thin, flat bread.

And eight – no, nine – bottles of his best wine.

Matthew couldn't help himself. Counting was on his mind. Counting was in his blood. Counting was his business.

Counting. And tables.

Matthew had sat behind the one and done the other for as long as he could remember. Because counting was what a tax collector's job demanded.

So much for the masters back in Rome.

So much for the men who watched his back.

And so much, of course, for Matthew!

Matthew grinned as he remembered.

Count well, and you could count on a pretty good living. And if the taxpayers should complain, or the accountants in Rome grow suspicious, then you could usually fob them off with just a little more creative counting!

'A few more denarii, please!'

'Another pile of coins, sir!'

'Yes, that's right, ma'am, I need both of your chickens. It's hardly my fault that they're the last you've got.'

'Not enough! Not enough! Not enough!' That was his mantra. And his bully boys were always there to back up those words with a broken arm or a twisted neck. Was it any wonder then that he was hated and despised and left to socialize with the rest of society's outcasts?

Matthew looked around the table and counted. The table was full of outcasts. But how many of his friends had imagined that they would ever be sitting here?

Not Adam, for a start, Galilee's best brothel keeper. Nor Daniel, drunk from the day he could carry a bottle. Nor Caleb the conman. Nor Benjamin the womanizer. Nor Jacob the thief.

But here they were, eating and drinking and joking around with a rabbi, of all people! A rabbi, for heaven's sake! A rabbi!

It didn't add up.

No matter which way Matthew counted.

He'd never had any time for religion.

Dos and Don'ts.

Rights and Wrongs.

Following the rules. Keeping the traditions.

It was just another kind of counting, as far as he could tell.

The scribes and the priests and the Pharisees sat behind their tables too. They called them altars, of course, but it was just the same. And they stacked up good deeds and bad deeds as if they were piles of coins.

'Too much drink.'

'Too many women.'

'Too much gambling.'

'Too many lies.'

And in the end, when the counting was done, their answer was always the same.

'Not good enough! Not good enough! Not good enough!'

So what was the point? If he couldn't be good enough for them, how could he ever be good enough for God? Surely, then, it made sense to stay away from their tables altogether.

Yet, here he was, at the table with a rabbi.

Matthew looked around the table and counted.

There was not one of his friends that anyone would even think of calling good. They were rogues, one and all. Rogues, himself included. And not even lovable rogues!

They were dishonest, perverted, selfish and mean. But this rabbi was still sitting there among them.

And that's what counted the most.

Matthew's friends had all asked him, 'Why?'

'Why did you leave your job?'

'Why did you give up your fortune?'

'Why did you leave it all to follow him?'

And the answer was here – at the table.

Rabbi Jesus was a good man. Matthew had no doubt of that. But unlike so many other religious people whom Matthew had met, Jesus did not make his goodness an excuse for judgment.

He could be holy, somehow, without being holier-than-thou. He could eat with good people and bad people alike, and treat them all with respect, treat them all the same. And if that's what lay at the heart of this new kingdom that Jesus was always going on about, then Matthew wanted to be a part of it.

Because, when it came down to it, Matthew was tired of counting. Wherever he had been, whatever he had done, somebody was always counting.

Counting the taxes to see who owed the most.

Counting the profits to see who was the richest.

Counting the bad deeds to see who was the worst.

Counting the good deeds to see who was the purest.

But at this table – the table where Jesus sat – nobody was counting. And when nobody was counting, then everybody counted!

Good or bad. Rich or poor. Sinner or saint. God loved them all and welcomed them all to his table. Surely that's what Jesus was trying to say.

And as for change – changing to be more like Jesus? Yes, who wouldn't want to be like him? Love life as he did. See through the hypocrisy. Cut to the heart of things. Surely that invitation – to come and follow and be changed – was part of the equation as well.

Matthew looked around the table again. Looked at all his friends. Would they stay with Jesus? Would they follow? Would they change?

Matthew couldn't tell. But one thing he did know – there was no chance of them following Jesus without some kind of welcome in the first place.

Without his acceptance.

Without his invitation.

Without this table.

Questions

1. What can Christians do to counter what is often the general impression that what we are most interested in is good behaviour – the counting of the rights and wrongs that Matthew found off-putting?

2. Talk about a time when you found it difficult to accept someone because of what you knew they had done. Or a time when you felt you weren't accepted because of your behaviour.

3. Who are the 'Matthews and his associates' in your community? Think hard about this. There are stereotypical answers that always come up in this discussion. But I have been to Christian conferences where, had I been a leader of industry, for example, I would have felt most unwelcome! Do we just have different 'Matthews', depending on our politics, or our backgrounds, or what we consider to be the most important aspects of Jesus' teaching? And how can we learn to live with the kind of grace that Jesus showed?

Peter Walks on Water

(Matthew 14:22–33)

Introduction

I sort of stumbled across this particular storytelling technique by accident. I wanted the crowd to really enjoy the participation, but discovered that they didn't always 'catch on' first time. So I thought I'd do it again. And once more for good measure! And if I was leading them in their bit three times, why not do the set-up lines in the same way? So what should really be a rather short story becomes a longer one – and the repetition and participation help the story to sink (sorry!) in.

TELLING TIPS: Before the story begins, teach the crowd the following words and actions:

'Boo!' (Make ghost motions and sounds.)
'Phew!' (Wipe forehead in a relieved motion.)
'Canoe' (Make a paddling motion.)
'You' (Point index finger.)
'Two' (Put up two fingers, like a peace sign, in the air.)
'Shoe' (Point at your foot.)
'Oh, poo!' (Say this sadly.)
'Woo-hoo!' (Say this joyfully.)
'It's true!' (Point finger in air.)

After I teach the actions, I sometimes ask the crowd if they can figure out the Bible story. I've had some great (but mostly wrong!) answers.
   Lead them in these motions during the course of the story – and don't worry if they don't catch on first time; they're probably just watching you to see what you do. As I said in the introduction, the repetition is there for them to really enjoy their part. And when you

Peter and his friends were sailing one night,
Peter and his friends were sailing one night,
Peter and his friends were sailing one night,
When they thought they spotted a ghost – Boo!
When they thought they spotted a ghost – Boo!
When they thought they spotted a ghost – Boo!

'That ghost looks like Jesus,' said Peter to his friends.
'That ghost looks like Jesus,' said Peter to his friends.
'That ghost looks like Jesus,' said Peter to his friends.
And all of his friends were relieved – Phew!
And all of his friends were relieved – Phew!
And all of his friends were relieved – Phew!

'But if it's Jesus,' said Peter, 'then he's walking on the water!'
'But if it's Jesus,' said Peter, 'then he's walking on the water!'
'But if it's Jesus,' said Peter, 'then he's walking on the water!'
'Without the aid of a canoe!
Without the aid of a canoe!
Without the aid of a canoe!'

'If you're really Jesus,' said Peter to the ghost-man,
'If you're really Jesus,' said Peter to the ghost-man,
'If you're really Jesus,' said Peter to the ghost-man,
'Then let me come walk with you.
Then let me come walk with you.
Then let me come walk with you.'

'Step out of the boat,' said Jesus to Peter.
'Step out of the boat,' said Jesus to Peter.
'Step out of the boat,' said Jesus to Peter.
'There's room out here for two!
There's room out here for two!
There's room out here for two!'

So Peter stepped out and walked to Jesus,
So Peter stepped out and walked to Jesus,
So Peter stepped out and walked to Jesus,
With nothing but sea under his shoe.
With nothing but sea under his shoe.
With nothing but sea under his shoe.

Then Peter got scared and stopped trusting Jesus.
Then Peter got scared and stopped trusting Jesus.
Then Peter got scared and stopped trusting Jesus.
And he started to sink – Oh, poo!
And he started to sink – Oh, poo!
And he started to sink – Oh, poo!

So Jesus helped Peter back into the boat.
So Jesus helped Peter back into the boat.
So Jesus helped Peter back into the boat.
And all of his friends cheered, 'Woo-hoo!'
And all of his friends cheered, 'Woo-hoo!'
And all of his friends cheered, 'Woo-hoo!'

'You're somebody special!' they said to Jesus.
'You're somebody special!' they said to Jesus.
'You're somebody special!' they said to Jesus.
'The Son of God – it's true!
The Son of God – it's true!
The Son of God – it's true!'

Questions

1. How would you respond if you spotted one of your friends walking on water?

2. What was the point of this miracle?

3. Talk about a time when you were short on faith, like Peter, and it made you lose sight of Jesus. What happened? How did you find your way back into the boat?

Two Answers

(Matthew 16:25)

Introduction

My tenth-grade social studies teacher was a guy named Dave Shrecengost. We called him Shrec for short, but he was no ogre. On the contrary, he was one of those teachers whom you could feel close to and yet still respect. And, better still, he was the kind of educator who understood that his job was not simply to pass on facts and figures, but to teach you how to process and think about them. He's the one who asked the question. And the fact that one of his students is still working on the answer some thirty-five years later shows just how good a teacher he was!

> **TELLING TIPS: You could either do this one by yourself, or tell it with someone else – with one doing the verse and the other the text in between. You could also put the Bible verse up on a screen and have the group read it at the appropriate times. (This is better than having them do it from their Bibles, simply because they will, more likely than not, have different translations, and then it just sounds like church in the Tower of Babel! It will work, though, if everyone is reading from pew Bibles.)**

Jesus said, 'Whoever wants to save his life will lose it,
but whoever loses his life for me will find it.'

When I was at school, when I was only fifteen, one of my teachers asked the class a question: 'What do you want to do with your life?'

Jesus said, 'Whoever wants to save his life will lose it,
but whoever loses his life for me will find it.'

The answers broke down into roughly two groups.

Half of the class simply wanted to be happy.

And the other half wanted to do something that would make the world a better place.

Jesus said, 'Whoever wants to save his life will lose it, but whoever loses his life for me will find it.'

Thirty years have passed.

Thirty years and more.

And I've watched my classmates.

And my friends.

And my family.

And my workmates.

And I've finally figured it out.

Only just figured it out.

Those weren't two answers.

Not two answers at all.

No, those answers were one and the same!

Jesus said, 'Whoever wants to save his life will lose it, but whoever loses his life for me will find it.'

Questions

1. How would you have answered my teacher's question when you were fifteen? How would you answer it now?

2. Talk about a time when the two answers came together for you.

3. As you can tell from the introduction, I am firmly in the middle of the baby-boomer generation. How do you think that generation has done with regard to the 'two answers'?

One Out of a Hundred

(Matthew 18:12–14)

Introduction

This is a really short reading, but it's the brevity, I think, that makes it powerful. It's one of those readings that can be dropped into a service, like a little surprise, to make a really big point.

TELLING TIPS: One to do on your own, but as with others of this kind, you could have another reader do the scripture verse.

One out of a hundred.
A penny on the ground.
You'd hardly bother if you dropped it,
Or bend down to pick it up.

But God would.

One out of a hundred.
Statistically insignificant.
Well within the margin of error.
Hardly worth counting.

But God would.

One out of a hundred.
A face in a crowd.
A voice in a chorus.
You'd hardly notice if they were missing.

But God would.

What do you think? If a man owns a hundred sheep, and one of them wanders away, will he not leave the ninety-nine on the hills and go to look for the one that wandered off? And if he finds it, I tell you the truth, he is happier about that one sheep than about the ninety-nine that did not wander off. In the same way your Father in heaven is not willing that any of these little ones should be lost.

Not even one.
One out of a hundred.

Questions

1. Can you think of a time when you let someone slip by, almost without notice, because something else had your attention?

2. There can be a lot of pressure associated with keeping one's eye on every sheep in the flock, especially for church leaders. Is that expecting too much? How can they deal with that pressure? What might the rest of the church do to help (apart from saying, in an accusatory tone, 'Why haven't you visited Mrs So-and-so recently?')?

3. How is this story related to the prodigal son?

Hey, That's OK!

(Matthew 18:21–35)

Introduction

As you will see, the participation device in this story is very simple and almost silly. But when I did this reading the first time, there were people in the crowd who really had fallen out with each other. And, in the midst of the 'silliness', some very serious things started to happen.

> **TELLING TIPS: Divide the crowd into two groups and have them face each other. Standing might make this easier – but don't have them keep getting up and down. That will just distract them from the story. Just ask them to stand the whole way through. Or, if you want them to sit, have them swivel a bit. In either case, the 'facing each other' part is the key to the story. Lead one group in saying 'I'm really sorry' at the appropriate points in the story. And lead the other group in responding 'Hey, that's OK!' Teach them their lines before you start the story and make it clear that you really want them to say it like they mean it!**

Peter asked Jesus a question. 'If somebody hurts me,' he said, 'and then says, "I'm really sorry," how many times should I forgive them and say, "Hey, that's OK"?'

Before Jesus could answer, however, Peter offered an answer of his own. He thought it would sound good. He thought it would sound big-hearted. He thought it would be the kind of thing Jesus would like to hear.

'Should I forgive them... seven times?' said Peter.

It seemed like a lot of times to Peter, but Jesus was not impressed. Not at all.

'No,' answered Jesus. 'Not seven times. But *seventy times seven*!'

Peter did some quick maths. (Count on fingers) And somewhere on the way to 490, he ran out of fingers. That was a lot of times. Far more times than Peter had ever forgiven anybody.

So Jesus told him a story.

'Once upon a time there was a king,' said Jesus, 'and one of his servants owed him money.

'Not a little money. Not some money. Not even lots of money. But loads and loads and loads of money – millions and millions and more!

'The servant was brought before the king. And because the servant could not pay what he owed, the king commanded that the man, his wife and even his children be sold as slaves.

'The servant fell to his knees.

'"I'm really sorry!" he cried. "Be patient with me, please. Just give me another chance. And I promise I will pay back everything I owe."

'The king looked at his servant. He felt sorry for him. And then, much to the servant's surprise, the king smiled and said, "Hey, that's OK."

'Then he cancelled the debt, and set him free!

'The servant left the palace celebrating. And that's when he ran into another servant – a servant who owed HIM money.

'Not loads of money. Not a lot of money either. Just a little money, actually. A bit of spare change – that's all.

'Did the first servant remember what the king had done for him? Not for a minute.

'He grabbed the second servant by the throat and demanded to be paid.

'So the second servant fell to his knees.

'"I'm really sorry!" he cried. "Be patient with me, please. Give me another chance and I will pay back everything I owe."

'But instead of saying, "Hey, that's OK," the first servant had the second servant thrown into jail.

'When the other servants heard about this, they told the king. And he was so angry that he had the first servant dragged before him again.

'"When you came to me and said, 'I'm really sorry,' I cancelled your debt and said, 'Hey, that's OK.'"

'"Why couldn't you do the same for someone else?"

'And with that, the king had the servant thrown into jail until he could repay the debt.

'Peter,' said Jesus. 'God is like that king.

'We say to him, "I'm really sorry" – more times than we can count. And even more times than that, he tells us, "Hey, that's OK." And all he really wants is for us to tell that to each other too.

146

'I'm really sorry,' said Peter. 'I didn't understand.'
And Jesus just smiled and said, 'Hey, that's OK.'

Questions

1. Talk about a time when you were like the first servant – or someone behaved like the first servant towards you.

2. Talk about a time when you behaved like the king (in the beginning of the story!). Or someone acted like that towards you.

3. We're all different, and, for most of us, forgiveness is not only a problem of quantity (How many times?) but also quality (I find that sort of behaviour really offensive!). What kinds of thing do you find particularly hard to forgive?

Feed the Poor!

(Matthew 25:34–36)

Introduction

I have this theory. I think that a lot of us like talking about helping the poor of the world because it brings us comfort and lets us believe that we have actually done something for them. And I suppose that, in a limited sort of way, talking or singing or preaching or writing about the problem does keep our attention focused on it. But it doesn't solve it – not by a long way! Particularly when we conclude our talk/song/sermon/article by demanding that 'someone out there' do something about it! (Usually someone whom we perceive to be richer or more powerful or better connected than we are.)

Of course, there are some problems facing the developing world that can only be solved politically or economically. But there is a whole lot more that could be done if we stopped pointing our fingers and used our hands to reach into our own pockets instead. Not just during the annual celebrity-driven fund-raising bash, but regularly, in a consistent and (dare I say it) sacrificial way. That would, of course, make us less comfortable. Real sacrifice always does. But it would bring real comfort to those who need it most. That's what this reading is about.

> **TELLING TIPS: This is another one of those solo readings. You'll need to do it from the book – just to make the point at the end. And it might be nice to have another voice – or set of voices – to do the 'feed the poor' bits at the start of each section. Maybe even folks dressed up a bit to look like the characters they are giving voice to.**

'Feed the poor!' cried the vicar.

And the Lord said, 'Hey, I've got an idea! Why don't you sell the churches? The market's strong. Prices are high. The places are well-positioned. And besides, they're costing you an arm and a leg to maintain!

'So why not sell them and give the money to the poor? You can move into houses or schools or community centres. And if people suggest that you're abandoning your legacy, just tell them that your legacy has to do with restoring people, not twelfth-century buildings!

'Go on. You can do it! Why ask someone else to pay the price? Sell the churches and feed the poor. Because preaching about sacrifice is not the same as making one.'

'Feed the poor!' cried the politician.

And the Lord said, 'Hey, I've got an idea! Why don't you raise the taxes? I know it will make you unpopular and put your position at risk. But isn't it time to be honest for a change? The only way to feed the poor (and improve the hospitals and educate the children and fix the infrastructure, now that I think of it) is to find the money. And the only place to find it is from the people.

'This is about more than your image, more than the polls, more than New Labour or Compassionate Conservatism. So stop acting as if you care about the poor and do something to help them.

'Go on. You can do it. Why ask someone else to pay the price? Risk your position and raise the taxes. Because campaigning about sacrifice is not the same as making one.'

'Feed the poor!' cried the celebrity.

And the Lord said, 'Hey, I've got an idea! Why don't you put your hand into your own pocket? The poor know it's not Christmas time. There's nothing comical about the relief they need. And they still haven't found what they're looking for.

'And that's because, in spite of your good intentions, you still live like kings while much of the world starves. So instead of begging the guy who stocks the shelves at Tesco's to give another fiver, why not forego that next Ferrari, or that third country house, or that million-pound wedding? And meet the needs of the poor yourself.

'Go on. You can do it. Why ask someone else to pay the price? You could cancel the debts of some developing nations with a stroke of your own pen. Because singing about sacrifice is not the same as making one.

'Feed the poor!' cried the people.

And the Lord said, 'Hey, I've got an idea! Why don't you re-mortgage your house? It's worth – what? – five, ten, twenty times what you paid for it? That's money you didn't earn. It's just come your way. So why not take out a second mortgage, and instead of adding that conservatory or taking that "holiday of a lifetime", why not give the money away? Go on. You can do it. Why leave it to someone else? Because hoping for sacrifice isn't the same as making one.'

'Feed the poor,' wrote the author.

And the Lord said, 'Hey, I've got an idea! You know those royalties you're getting for this book...?'

And that's when the author put down his pen.

Questions

1. OK, so I'm speaking for the Lord here. And quite possibly speaking out of turn. What do you think of the specific suggestions that the Lord makes to each character? Are they practical, possible and realistic, or aimed in the wrong direction entirely?

2. What specifically could you do, on a regular basis, that you are not doing now, to help the poor of the world? What would it cost you? How much are you willing to give? What might happen if, say for a year, Christians in the West would tithe to the poor of the world as they tithe to their churches? What if churches would do the same?

3. What do you think are the obstacles to helping the poor of the world? Is there anything we can do about them? And, even though those obstacles sometimes make us cynical, should they stop us from helping at all?

The Tree of Life *or*
A Tale of Three More Trees

(Genesis 3, Matthew 27)

Introduction

Just a bit of speculation here. If the Tree of Life stood in the heart of Eden, then perhaps it also stands at the heart of our return. I think I wrote this about the same time I was writing *Angels, Angels All Around*.

TELLING TIPS: This is very much one for you to tell on your own. It would be fitting at Easter, but I think you could probably use it at any time. It's a more dramatic reading than many of the others in this collection, so it needs practising and careful pacing.

And the angel who guarded the gates of Eden took one last look at Adam. He burned those features for ever in his mind – sad eyes, sorry brow, the face of loneliness and rejection – then raised his fiery sword into the sky. And there he remained, blocking the entrance to the Garden and the path to the Tree of Life.

Age after age, he stood at his post, the beauty of the Garden all about him. He knew its smell and its taste and its sounds, but he had no time to enjoy it. For all he could do was watch, in case the face of Adam should return.

And perhaps that is why, one day, the impossible finally happened.

It wasn't a sound that caught his attention. It was more like a feeling. A sense, deep inside the angel, that something was wrong. And that is why he lowered his sword, turned and ran through the Garden. And that is how he discovered that the Tree of Life was gone!

Only a ragged hole remained, as if the tree had been torn out by its roots. The angel drove his sword into the ground, its flaming orange dimmed to a flickering blue. Then he knelt beside it and buried his face in his hands.

What was he going to do? Guarding the tree had been his responsibility. But somehow he had failed. And there was only one course of action he could take: he must find the Tree of Life and watch over it once again.

So like Adam before him, he walked sadly out of the Garden of Eden. But he did not wander over the unplowed wilderness of the world. No, he opened his wings and flung himself through the fabric of time and space – in search of the Tree of Life.

There was a smell to Paradise – a purity, a freshness – that he was certain he could recognize. And so he sniffed his way through aeons and epochs until, finally, he picked up the scent. Then he raised his sword and sliced his way into one particular time and place.

The air was cold, the clouds icy with the promise of winter. Below the clouds there were hills, mile after mile of them, portioned off by rivers and valleys. And trees? There were more trees than the angel had ever seen. But they were stripped bare of leaves. All but one, that is, whose pointed branches burned bright from the window of a single house. That was the one he headed for, until his senses picked up something else – chimney smoke and the sound of human voices.

'Adam!' the angel cursed, as he flew, invisible, into the house and hovered next to a small plastic replica of himself.

Adams were everywhere below, their hands full of bright and shiny things. The angel looked long and hard, but he could find no one who resembled the sad Adam he had chased from the Garden.

Instead, these Adams were laughing – big ones and little ones, brown ones and pale ones – all together. Then finally, they settled themselves on the furniture and on the floor, and one of the Adams spoke.

'Let us give thanks to God!' he said. 'For the gift of his Son, for the gifts we hold in our hands, and for the gifts we are to each other.'

That is when a voice whispered to the angel from among the bright branches. 'I am not the tree you seek,' it said. 'I am the Tree of Laughter. Where sadness turns to joy, where tears give way to smiles, where all that oppresses or frightens is conquered by hope and peace, that is where you will find me. But you must look elsewhere if you would find the Tree of Life.'

And so the angel left the Tree of Laughter, and the merrymakers gathered in its shade, and burst the curtain of time once more – in search of the Tree of Life.

It was not long before he caught the scent again. So he pulled out his sword and slashed a path into another place.

The sun was red against the horizon – red as the angel's sword – and it burned the land brown and bare. Except for one tree, that is, whose leaves hung cool and green over the banks of a sleepy river.

There were noises beneath this tree as well. Strange, muffled sounds – human sounds that made the angel cautious.

'Adam!' he whispered, and invisible once more, he hovered closer to have a look.

They were Adams, certainly – a male and a female, skin black as the river's edge. And they were holding one another and caressing one another and pressing their lips together. And then they just sat there and stared at each other and said nothing for hours and hours. Nothing at all.

'I am not the tree you seek,' the branches quivered at last. 'I am the Tree of Love. Watch and you will see.'

And in a moment, the sun rose and fell, thousands upon thousands of times! The two Adams became four, then ten, then a hundred. Their hair bleached white, their bodies bent and stooped, and they held children and grandchildren and great-grandchildren in their ever-more-feeble arms. But they never grew tired of staring into each other's eyes and saying nothing for hours. Nothing at all.

'Where there is tenderness,' the tree continued. 'Where there is commitment and kindness and passion, that is where you will find me. But you must look elsewhere if you would find the Tree of Life.'

And so the angel resumed his search, determined that he would not be foiled again. This time, however, the scent was nowhere to be found. He had almost given up hope, in fact, when he smelled it – the faintest odour of Paradise. Skeptical, he stopped and sniffed, and the longer he waited, the stronger the scent became. The Tree of Life was near. He was sure of it. So he drew his sword and ripped, one more time, through the fabric of heaven and earth.

And immediately, he was sorry that he had.

The sky shuddered dark around him. Thunder clapped. A fierce wind blew. And below all was lifeless and grey. Surely he had made another mistake.

But the scent was stronger than ever. So he plunged, invisible, towards the earth. And all at once, he knew. He was in the right place after all. For there, on a hill, stood Adam!

Sad eyes. Sorry brow. The face of loneliness and rejection. He would recognize those features anywhere!

'Adam!' he bellowed. 'Adam!' he cursed. 'What have you done with the Tree of Life?'

But Adam would not answer. His head lolled heavily to one side. His lips were blistered and bruised.

'He cannot hear you,' whispered a voice. 'He hears no one. He is dead.'

'Dead?' the angel wondered. 'Adam? Dead?'

'Not Adam,' the voice replied. 'But Adam's son. And the Son of God as well. Sent by the Maker himself to undo Adam's damage and repair the path to Paradise.'

'And who… who are you?' the angel asked. But there was no need to wait for an answer. All he had to do was look – beyond the face, beyond the hands, beyond the outstretched arms of the man before him. And, sure enough, there was wood. Wood cut and shaped. Wood hammered and pierced. Wood stripped bare of all beauty and blossom and life.

'No!' the angel cried, falling to his knees. 'This is not possible. Who could have done this to you?'

'The Maker of all things,' the voice said softly. 'It was he who plucked me from the Garden. He who brought me here. He who planted me in this place. For where evil is overwhelmed by goodness, where failure is comforted by grace, where sins are forgiven and debts are repaid and darkness is blinded by light, that is where you will find me. For I am what the Maker always intended me to be. I am the Tree of Life.'

'And what about me?' the angel pleaded. 'What am I to do now? What am I to be?'

'What the Maker made you for,' answered the fading voice.

And so the angel climbed slowly to his feet and, with his sword raised like lightning to the sky, stood guard on the hill of death and watched over the Tree of Life.

Questions

1. I made a Christmas tree the Tree of Laughter, but when I first wrote the story it was an oak tree, I think, at the first Thanksgiving. What tree would you make the Tree of Laughter?

2. What tree would you make the Tree of Love?

3. The angel in this story is pretty aggressive – not your stereotypical white glowy being in a bathrobe. What do you see when you think about angels?

The Apostle Paul and Sir Isaac Newton

(Matthew 28, Luke 24, John 20, 1 Corinthians 15)

Introduction

The idea for this very short reading came from a song by Julie Miller called 'Speed of Light', on her *Broken Things* CD. I just love the way she links together the spiritual and the physical, the emotional and the scientific, and thought that a similar approach might work in this situation too.

TELLING TIPS: It's short, really short – and that's its strength. So do it on your own. Play with the repetition. And then slow down and take your time over the end. I think this works very well either to start an Easter service or to finish it.

The tomb was sealed.
But the tomb couldn't hold him.

The guards were armed.
But the guards couldn't hold him.

Three days had passed.
But time couldn't hold him.

The man was dead.
But death couldn't hold him.

Mary Magdalene tried.
But she couldn't hold him.

The door was shut.
But the room couldn't hold him.

And when he walked to the top of the hill
And bid his friends goodbye, gravity,
Even gravity could not hold him.

So how come we can hold him
Closer than a brother?
How come we can hold him
Where two or three are gathered?

Death has been swallowed up in victory.
That's how.
And even gravity is no match for love.

Questions

1. In this reading, I focus on our continuing relationship with the risen Christ as one of the benefits of his resurrection. What aspect of the resurrection means the most to you? Or does that change, depending on times and circumstances?

2. Is there anything else that couldn't hold him? And what does the resurrection prevent from taking hold of us?

Jesus' Media Consultant

(Mark 1:21–39)

Introduction

There are several readings like this in the book, and I probably enjoyed writing them most of all. The key is to make the commentary flow naturally along with the biblical text, and also to highlight or provide a contrast to some aspect of that text – in this case, the modern preoccupation with spin and PR and media (in the church as well as the world), versus Jesus' commitment to be led by prayer and his relationship with the Father.

TELLING TIPS: The most important thing is that the biblical text and the inserted text should work together smoothly as a whole. So it will take two readers and a little practice. The nice thing about this one is that the person reading the scripture can do it from a Bible, and the 'media consultant' can read from a laptop or a clipboard. So no one has to worry about memorising anything!

They went to Capernaum, and when the Sabbath came...

Jesus' media consultant said, 'We've got an 11 o'clock at the synagogue, Rabbi. There's time for a little teaching, a little healing – but you'll have to make it quick. We've got a full schedule today.'

Jesus went into the synagogue and began to teach. The people were amazed at his teaching, because he taught them as one who had authority, not as the teachers of the Law.

Just then a man in their synagogue who was possessed by an evil spirit cried out, 'What do you want with us, Jesus of Nazareth? Have you come to destroy us? I know who you are – the Holy One of God!'

And Jesus' media consultant said, 'A heckler! That's the last thing we need. Do something, quick!'

'Be quiet!' said Jesus sternly. 'Come out of him!'
The evil spirit shook the man violently and came out of him with
a shriek.
The people were all so amazed that they asked each other, 'What
is this? A new teaching – and with authority! He even gives orders
to evil spirits and they obey him.'

'That was quick thinking,' said Jesus' media consultant. 'It could have been a disaster, but now I think we can use it to our advantage. I've got some friends in the local press. I'll make a few calls.'

News about him spread quickly over the whole region of
Galilee.
As soon as they left the synagogue...

Jesus' media consultant said, 'We have a light lunch scheduled next. At the home of a local businessman called Simon. I think he has something to do with the fishing industry.'

They went with James and John to the home of Simon and Andrew.
Simon's mother-in-law was in bed with a fever and they told Jesus
about her.

'Not good,' said Jesus' media consultant. 'This is going to put us way behind schedule. I say we get out as quick as we can and grab something on the way. Burgers. A kebab. What do you think?'

So Jesus went to her, took her hand and helped her up. The fever
left her and she began to wait on them.

'I've got to hand it to you,' said Jesus' media consultant. 'You know how to get yourself out of a difficult situation. I would never have thought of that. But we're gonna have to hurry. I've got several more appearances scheduled for today. There's a five o'clock, a six o'clock, and an eight o'clock if we can squeeze it in.'

That evening after sunset the people brought to Jesus all the sick and demon-possessed. The whole town gathered at the door...

'Male, female. Gen X, Gen Y!' said Jesus' media consultant. 'I like the demographics!'

And Jesus healed many who had various diseases. He also drove out many demons, but he would not let the demons speak because they knew who he was.

'I'm not so sure about that,' said Jesus' media consultant. 'You know what they say; "any press is good press". And then I want you to get a good night's sleep, it looks as if we've got a long day ahead of us tomorrow. We can't let this momentum slip. These people are just itching for more!'

Very early in the morning, while it was still dark, Jesus got up, left the house and went off to a solitary place, where he prayed.

'So where'd he go?' shouted Jesus' media consultant. 'Talk to me, people! We've got briefings and meetings scheduled here. We're on the edge of something big. This is not a good time for the rabbi to disappear on us!'

Simon and his companions went to look for him, and when they found him, they exclaimed: 'Everyone is looking for you!'

Jesus' media consultant exclaimed too. 'Praying? What do you mean, you've been praying? We've got make-up in ten minutes. And a list of appearances as long as my arm. This is important stuff, Rabbi. Another day in this town and I think this messiah thing of yours will go right through the roof.'

Jesus replied, 'Let us go somewhere else – to the nearby villages – so that I can preach there also. That is why I have come.'

'Somewhere else?' cried Jesus' media consultant. 'When this place is ripe for the picking? What about the schedule? What about the appointments? We've got a slot on Oprah, for goodness' sake! What am I supposed to tell her – that you can't come on because you PRAYED?'

So Jesus travelled throughout Galilee, preaching in their synagogues and driving out demons.

And Jesus' media consultant? He packed up his laptop and went home.

Questions

1. So, is there any place for media consultants, PR and spin in the life of the church today? Why or why not?

2. Talk about a time when prayer led you to do something that didn't seem to make much 'sense' but that was the right thing anyway.

3. How do you think Jesus defined 'success'? Compare and contrast that with the way you think the church defines success today.

So Sow!

(Mark 4)

Introduction

I wrote this originally for an event that celebrated the work of Sunday-school teachers and children's leaders. The parable of the sower set the theme for the day and I wanted to do a retelling that reflected both the realism and the hope of that story.

TELLING TIPS: Teach your crowd three actions:

'So go!' (Have them stretch out their right arms and point their finger as if to say 'Go!')
'So Sow!' (Have them stretch out their left arms in a 'sowing-seeds' motion.)
'And know' (Have them point a finger to their temple.)

You can have the crowd say the lines with you, and you can also break the crowd into three groups and have each group do an action. Whatever works best for you!

So Go!
So Sow!
And Know
The seeds you throw
Are seeds not sown in vain.

Yeah, some of them will fall along the path
Miss the soil altogether
And have no chance to hear
As Satan's sneaky sparrows steal them all away.
But others will land on the good earth

And seeds will sprout and buds will blossom
And fruit will weigh down branches
Thirty and sixty and a hundred times more!

So Go!
So Sow!
And Know
The seeds you throw
Are seeds not sown in vain.

And, yeah, some will fall on the rocky ground
Sink down and take root right away.
Till trouble comes like a scorching sun
And the soil is not deep enough
To save them from the withering day.
But others will land on the good earth
And vines will grow and wine will flow
And grapes will weigh down branches
Thirty and sixty and a hundred times more.

So Go!
So Sow!
And Know
The seeds you throw
Are seeds not sown in vain.

And, yeah, some will fall on the thorny ground
And the weeds of worry
And the weeds of wealth
Will strangle and shut out the light.
But others will land on the good earth
And rising right up to an elephant's eye
(or so the song says anyway)
The corn will reach to the sky
Thirty and sixty and a hundred times high.

So Go!
So Sow!
And Know

The seeds you throw
Are seeds not sown in vain.

Questions

1. Talk about the 'seeds' you know that were stolen away, or withered in the shallow soil, or were strangled by the weeds. Is there anything we can do to make a difference there? Or are we ultimately only responsible for the sowing?

2. Why do you think Jesus told this story? What was he hoping to accomplish with it?

3. What is the 'fruit' that the growing plant produces?

A Little Shining, a Little Sowing

(Mark 4:21–32)

Introduction

Just a little reading, this one – tying together three of Jesus' sayings about the kingdom. Probably more of an all-age service piece.

TELLING TIPS: Teach everyone the chorus first – you might want to put it up on a screen so they will remember. You might also want to teach them a few actions to go along with the words.

'A little shining' – hands open beside face in a glowing motion.
'A little sowing' – pretend to toss seeds in a sowing motion. (It wouldn't hurt to explain this. You can't take it for granted that everyone will know what 'sowing' is, and because knowing that is pretty much essential to understanding the reading – and what Jesus has to say – it's important that the whole group is clued in to this from the start.)
'The kingdom of God keeps growing and growing' – reach out arms, wider and wider, or reach above head, taller and taller.

A little shining, a little sowing,
the kingdom of God keeps growing and growing.

'If you have a lamp,' said Jesus, 'you've got to let it glow. Under a bowl. Under the bed. It's no use there at all! But put it on a lampstand – for everyone to see – and all that once was hidden is revealed!
'If you have a lamp,' said Jesus, 'you've got to let it glow.'

A little shining, a little sowing,
the kingdom of God keeps growing and growing.

'If you have a seed,' said Jesus, 'you've got to let it go. Drop it into the ground. That's your part, and God will do the rest. Seed to stem. Stem to stalk. Stalk to bushy head. You couldn't make it happen if you tried.

'If you have a seed,' said Jesus, 'you've got to let it go.'

A little shining, a little sowing,
the kingdom of God keeps growing and growing.

'So plant your seed,' said Jesus, 'then stand back and watch it grow! A mustard seed is small. The smallest seed of all. But it grows into a great big bushy... bush! With great big bushy branches for birds to roost and rest. So plant your seed,' said Jesus, 'then stand back and watch it grow!'

A little shining, a little sowing,
the kingdom of God keeps growing and growing.

Questions

1. What 'lamp' is Jesus talking about here? And, practically speaking, how are we to let it glow?

2. What is the 'seed' we're supposed to drop into the ground?

3. Talk about the difference between our part and God's part in the growing of seeds.

The Dazzler

(Mark 9:2–13)

Introduction

There is just something about Peter, isn't there? Up one minute and down the next. Getting it so right and then getting it so wrong. Maybe that's why we're drawn to him, because we see our own struggles reflected so clearly in his. This is one of several readings I've done that looks at some aspect of Jesus' life from Peter's perspective.

> **TELLING TIPS:** Because the reading aims to put us in Peter's shoes (sandals, whatever!), the participation focuses on Peter's reactions – on all the 'p' words. So teach the actions before you begin. Have the crowd 'huff and puff' with you when Peter does. And make it bigger the second time. As in – 'Peter was huffing' (little huff) 'Huffing and puffing' (bigger huff and puff). Have them shriek on 'petrified' and shriek even louder on 'Really petrified'. Have them go 'Ahhh' on 'peaceful'. And a bigger 'Ahhhhh' on 'Peaceful at last'. Then have them go 'Huh?' on 'puzzled'. And an even bigger 'Huh?' on 'Really puzzled'.

Peter was puffing! Huffing and puffing! He and Jesus and James and John had just walked up a mountain. But before he could catch his breath, something strange happened. Something he'd never expected. Jesus started to shine. That's right – shine! And his clothes were like an advertisement for some brand new laundry powder – brighter than any bleach could make them!

And that's not all. Moses was standing there with him! Moses, who had led God's people out of slavery!

And Elijah – the prophet who stood up to King Ahab and faced down the prophets of Baal – was there too! Even though he and Moses had been dead for hundreds of years!

Now Peter was petrified! Really petrified! What could he say? What could he do? So he just blurted out the first thing that popped into his head.

'Jesus!' he stammered. 'Why don't we put up three shelters, three tents, three tabernacles? One for you and one for Moses and one for Elijah, to savour this special moment.'

And that's when the cloud appeared. A cloud that surrounded them all. And out of the cloud came a voice. And Peter was more petrified than ever.

'This is my Son!' said the voice. And there was no mistaking whose voice it was. 'This is my Son whom I love. Listen to him!'

And then as suddenly as everything had happened, it was over. Jesus was standing alone.

So Peter was peaceful. Peaceful at last. And then Jesus led them back down the mountain. 'I don't want you to mention this to anyone,' he said. 'Keep it to yourselves until after I have come back from the dead.'

Now Peter was puzzled. Really puzzled. 'Back from the dead?' he wondered. 'What does Jesus mean by that?' And James and John wondered too. But the question troubled them so much that they decided to ask a different question instead.

'Why do the teachers of the Law say that Elijah must come before the Messiah?'

'Elijah has come,' said Jesus. 'Just as the scriptures said he would. Just as they also said that the Messiah must suffer and be rejected.'

And even though they were now more puzzled than ever, Peter and James and John dared ask no more. And they walked down the mountain in silence.

Questions

1. Is there anything that Jesus said or did during his ministry that puzzles you? That you just don't understand?

2. Why do you think Jesus let Peter, James and John join him in this experience?

3. What is the significance of Moses and Elijah appearing alongside Jesus? And the significance of what God says?

Drinking and Dunking

(Mark 10:35–45)

Introduction

It's that 'way in' thing again – finding a word that ties the text together and helps to make it that bit more clear and memorable. Except it's three words this time – drinking and dunking. And dying.

> **TELLING TIPS: You can either do this one on your own, or find a couple of helpers to play James and John. You'll want to practise it with them ahead of time – there's too much for an on-the-spot volunteer to do. But you could get the crowd involved if you taught them the lines of the rest of the disciples and had them shout those lines out at the appropriate time.**

James walked up to Jesus and stood on his right side.

John walked up to Jesus and stood on his left.

Then the brothers each put an arm around Jesus' shoulders and whispered so that no one else could hear.

'Jesus, we'd like to ask a favour. When you finally set up your kingdom, and sit down upon your throne…'

'Could I have the throne on your right side?' asked James.

'And could I,' asked John, 'have the throne on your left?'

Jesus didn't know whether to laugh or cry. These two were his closest disciples. Yet their question showed that they understood so little of what he'd tried to teach them.

'You don't realize what you're asking for,' he said at last. And then, like any good teacher, he followed their question with a question of his own.

'Can you drink the cup I drink?' he asked. 'Can you join me in my baptism?'

James and John glanced at each other. They were strange questions. But drinking and dunking seemed a small price to pay for the chance to reign in Jesus' kingdom.

'Of course we can,' they whispered back.

And Jesus just sighed. For he knew the cup was a poisoned chalice, and his baptism was a drowning pool. Death was the only way to the kingdom. A cross, the path to the throne. And despite their innocence and lack of understanding, Jesus knew that his friends would walk that path too.

'You will drink my cup,' he sighed again. 'You will join me in my baptism too. But as for thrones – that's not my decision to make.'

James and John wanted to know more. But before they could ask, their secret meeting was interrupted by the other ten disciples.

Someone had been listening in. Or maybe James and John were just lousy whisperers. But a chorus of 'Hey!' and 'What's going on here?' and 'I wanted that throne!' was finally brought to an end by Jesus.

'Listen. Listen. Listen!' he said. And he wasn't whispering now. 'You lot seem awfully interested in thrones. Fear, power, position and authority: that's how those who sit on them get their way. That's how they show their greatness. And I'm here to tell you that it must not work that way among you!

'In my kingdom, the slave will be master and the servant will sit on the throne. And greatness will be measured by how well you give yourselves to one another. For even I did not come to be pampered and preened and catered for, but to live as a servant and die as one too – to give myself up as a ransom for the world.'

'Drinking and dunking,' James whispered to John.

'Drinking and dunking and dying,' John whispered back.

And there were no further questions about thrones.

Questions

1. What do you think prompted James and John's request?

2. Can you think of examples where the church has taken Jesus' teaching on power and authority to heart?

3. Can you think of examples where the church has missed Jesus' point altogether?

A Christmas Eve Service for Those Who Don't Feel Like Celebrating

(Luke 2)

Introduction

My dad died in the autumn of 2002, following a long and painful illness, and by the time that Christmas rolled around, I really didn't feel like celebrating very much. Maybe it was selfish, but I wrote this piece for our annual Christmas Eve service that year and, from the response I got, even people who did feel like celebrating found it helpful.

TELLING TIPS: The individual sections are best read by you, or a variety of readers, taking the sections in turn. During the gaps in the text, I inserted carols and prayers that reflected the themes in the section I had just read. I think we lit candles, as well, as the reading suggests.

Every now and then, I read a familiar passage from the Bible, and something strikes me for the very first time. A line I've never really heard before – or never really thought about. There's a line like that at the end of the passage that we're going to focus on now. I'd like you to listen for it as I read Luke 2:8–18. (*Read Luke 2:8–18 NIV.*)

The shepherds spread the word. They went and told people what they had seen and heard. Friends. Relations. Citizens of Bethlehem. And when those people heard the story, they were amazed. Well, who wouldn't be?

But were they moved? Convinced? Or changed? That's a different thing altogether, isn't it? And it's true for us as well.

Because sometimes, even though it's Christmas – maybe even the first

Christmas – we're just not in a Christmas-y mood. We just don't feel like celebrating.

The shepherds' first port of call is the local pub. 'Bethlehem's Best' – that's the brew they serve. And while the punters sit and sip, the shepherds tell their story.

There's a lot of ooh-ing and aah-ing and 'Never!' But when the shepherds repeat the angels' message – 'good news of great joy!' – a man in the corner grunts and gulps down what's left of his pint. He's a merchant, travelling up and down the land of Palestine and beyond. And he knows, because he's seen it, that good news is in very short supply.

Famine to the east. Rebellion to the west. Higher taxes and even higher crime. Hospital queues. Inadequate transport. Falling pensions. Failing schools.

And, just like us, he wonders: How do you do it? How do you celebrate good news – how do you even believe in the possibility – when all the news you hear is bad?

So let's light a candle. And let's pray. For everyone who wonders with him. For everyone this Christmas who struggles to believe that the news – any news – can be good.

'Good news of great joy!' the shepherds repeat. And they're standing on the tables now and flapping pretend wings!

Some punters laugh. Some punters cheer. But the barmaid turns round and wipes her eyes with a dirty towel. Her husband is out of work. One of her children is seriously ill. And just last week, her grandmother died. Everything seems to be falling apart. Everywhere she looks is dark. She wants to share the shepherds' excitement – or at least she feels she should. But she can't. Not now. Because everything is still too painful, too close, too hopeless, too sad.

And just like us – because we've been there, or one day will be – just like us she wonders: How do you sing 'Joy to the World' when all you feel is sadness?

So let's light a candle. And let's pray a prayer. For everyone who wonders with her. For everyone this Christmas who's sad.

The shepherds are in full swing now. And even though they can't begin to sound like angels, the message is the same. 'Glory to God in the highest. And peace to people on earth.'

One punter has had enough. It's not just their singing he can't stand. Nor the disruption of a quiet night's drink. It's that line that galls.

'Peace on earth,' he mutters. And he slams the door on his way out. 'Peace on earth? While the Romans rule over us? While they crush us and control us and lay claim to God's own land? Peace on earth? Impossible!'

And surely we wonder with him.

Afghanistan and Iraq. Korea and Africa. India and Pakistan.

And Israel. Still Israel. Always Israel.

How can we possibly sing about peace on earth, when the world is on the brink of war?

So let's light a candle. And let's pray a prayer. In the hope that, one Christmas, the angels' song might come true.

The shepherds' tale is almost done. But the punters are losing interest. Angels are one thing – strange, exotic, amazing! But a baby? Everyone's seen a baby. And so the end of the story is a bit of a dud.

But it's also the beginning of an answer. The answer to all we have felt and worried over and wondered about. You see, Christmas promises are one thing. Sometimes, by God's grace, they come true. And sometimes, foiled by man's stubbornness and sin, they fall short. Their complete fulfilment lies ahead – in the kingdom to come.

Christmas promises are one thing. But a Christmas present is something else. For God's gift to us is God himself. God in a very specific way:

God in a manger.

God in a stable.

God vulnerable and fragile and small.

God like us, in fact.

God with us in the bad news.

God with us in the sadness.

God with us when we cry for peace.

God with us when the promises come true.

And God with us when they don't.

God in a cradle. And God on a cross.

God puts himself in our hands. To suckle and to nurture. To receive or to reject.

God's gift is God himself.

So let's light a candle. And let's pray a prayer for everyone who wants God's gift this Christmas. For everyone who longs for God himself.

Questions

1. Have you ever been in a worship service in which everyone else seemed to be celebrating, and that was the last thing you wanted to do? How did you react? And how can we order worship in such a way that there is room for a variety of feelings to be expressed?

2. Which of the Christmas promises means the most to you? Which have you seen fulfilled? Which are you still waiting for?

3. In the conclusion to the piece, I suggest that the promises are less important than the present that is God's presence among us. Is that a cop-out or an answer? And why?

The Birthday of a King

(Luke 2)

Introduction

Here's another one of those 'What was it like?' stories. Although I suppose this is more of a 'What would you do?' In any case, it helps the listener to crawl into the Christmas story and also to consider what kind of king Jesus was born to be.

> **TELLING TIPS:** As with the other stories in this series, you need to start by teaching your crowd the actions and sounds that go along with the key word in each section.
>
> 'You have a parade.' (March in place like a marching band. Or hum '76 Trombones' from *The Music Man*.)
> 'You find a special place.' (I suppose you could continue the show-tunes theme by having everyone sing 'OOOOO-klahoma'! Or simply saying 'There's no place like home' from *The Wizard of Oz*. Or maybe you could shout out the name of a place that is special to your crowd.)
> 'You shoot off fireworks.' (Have everyone shout 'Ka-Boom!')
> 'You send out invitations.' (Have everyone say 'RSVP, please!')
> 'You bring presents.' (Have everyone say 'For me?')
> 'You throw a party.' (Have everyone cheer or sing 'Happy Birthday to You!')

What do you do for the birthday of a king?
    You have a parade.
    With fancy floats, and marching bands and giant bouncing balloons.
    Jesus was a king.
    And there was a parade for his birthday, too.

A long walk from Nazareth, way down south to Bethlehem.

A caravan of people, off to pay their taxes.

Rich and poor.

Old and young.

Men and women.

And one couple in particular – a man named Joseph, and Mary, his very pregnant wife.

What do you do for the birthday of a king?

You have a parade.

What do you do for the birthday of a king?

You find a special place.

A ballroom, maybe – with marble floors and painted ceilings and gold chandeliers.

Jesus was a king.

And his parents found a special place for his birthday, too.

There were no ballrooms. And the hotel rooms were all full. But there was room in an empty stable.

With a dirt floor.

And a wooden roof.

And a dangling cobweb or two.

What do you do for the birthday of a king?

You find a special place.

What do you do for the birthday of a king?

You shoot off fireworks!

You fill the sky with pinwheels and daisies and a rumbling rocket racket.

Jesus was a king.

And there were fireworks at his birthday, too.

Shooting stars,

Heavenly hosts,

And a great big angel band!

What do you do for the birthday of a king?

You shoot off fireworks!

What do you do for the birthday of a king?

You send out invitations.

To dukes and knights and lords and ladies.

Very important guests.

Jesus was a king.
And there were invitations to his birthday, too.
'You are invited,' said the angel to the shepherds,
'To a stable in the town of Bethlehem.'
'You are invited,' said the angel to the shepherds and their sheep.
'There will be plenty of straw for all!'
What do you do for the birthday of a king?
You send out invitations.

What do you do for the birthday of a king?
　　You bring presents.
　　Bright and shiny things.
　　Fun and fancy things.
　　No boring things, like pants or socks.
　　Jesus was a king.
　　And he got presents, too.
　　His father's care.
　　His mother's love.
　　And a very nice set of swaddling clothes (whatever they are!).
　　What do you do for the birthday of a king?
　　You bring presents.

What do you do for the birthday of a king?
　　You throw a party.
　　You eat treats and sing songs and give gifts.
　　And every member of the royal family is there.
　　Jesus is a king.
　　And every year, we throw a party for him.
　　A party that goes right round the world!
　　We eat treats and sing songs and give gifts.
　　And every member of the royal family is there –
　　His brothers and sisters, you and me!
　　What do we do for the birthday of a king?
　　We throw a party.
　　And we call it Christmas.

Questions

1. What would you do for the birthday of a king?

2. What does this story have to say about the nature of Jesus' kingship?

3. Talk about some special, out-of-the-ordinary thing that you or your family or someone you know did for Jesus at Christmas time, as a way of celebrating his birth.

Every Baby Wants

(Luke 2)

Introduction

I came up with this reading just after Christmas a couple of years ago, while listening to a CD called *Befriended* by The Innocence Mission. There weren't any Christmas songs on the CD, but the music just set me thinking about women from all over the world – women of different races and backgrounds and situations – all holding their babies in their arms. And Mary holding her baby, too. And what it is that holds them all together.

> **TELLING TIPS: You could just read this one, but it's very short, so, if you have access to the technology, it might be nice to show a picture of a mother and her baby to go along with each line in the first section. (Mothers from different cultures, as I suggest in the introduction.) And then, in the second section, you could show pictures or traditional paintings of Mary and the baby Jesus.**

Every baby wants
To be held safe and warm,
To hear her first lullaby,
To drink from his mother's breast,
To snuggle up against a soft blanket,
To sleep and dream a dream of peace.

So maybe that is why
When God came to visit,
He came to us as a baby.

To be held safe and warm,
To hear his first lullaby,

To drink from his mother's breast,
To snuggle up against a soft blanket,
And to dream with us a dream of peace.

Questions

1. Is there anything I've missed? Anything else that every baby wants?

2. What comes to mind, what do you think of, when you consider the God of all creation as a baby in a mother's arms?

3. What does the incarnation have to say about motherhood?

Midnight – A Meditation for Christmas or Good Friday

(Luke 2:1–20, John 3:1–21, Luke 22)

Introduction

This is one of the oldest readings in the book. I wrote it for a Christmas Eve service twenty years ago or so, but, as the title suggests, I think it would also work nicely on Good Friday. It needs that lights-down, candles-burning, crowd-huddled-in-the-dark atmosphere to really work.

> **TELLING TIPS: You could have a different reader for each of the three sections, if you didn't want to read it all yourself. And it works really well to insert songs and prayers and scripture readings between the sections – perhaps even introducing each section with the Bible passage to which it refers. In that case, you probably will want someone else to read the scripture, just for a bit of variety.**

Midnight One

It's midnight, and the stillness is ripped by the first wailing breath of a newborn baby. A traveller, asleep in the inn, stirs and turns over and pulls his blanket up around his shoulders. A dog sits up and barks. A child, sickly and half awake, calls for a drink of water.

It's midnight, and on a hillside outside the town only the sheepdogs have heard the cry. Their masters are stretched out around the campfire, talking and laughing and sharing a drink – keeping the night at bay, along with the wolves and bears. But they're tired and so, gradually, their talk winds down to a murmur. The hillside is still now. Still, like the town. It's midnight. And things happen at midnight.

As if to echo the baby's cry, or maybe even to answer it, the silence is torn again – but, this time, by a very different kind of voice.

'Don't be afraid,' the voice says. And if the shepherds weren't so terrified, they might just burst out laughing. Don't be afraid? Don't be ridiculous! The blanket of night has been yanked off their backs and replaced by a vision of heaven-only-knows-what! And it tells them not to be afraid.

'Listen,' the voice goes on. 'I have good news for you, and for everyone else, as well. Today is the Messiah's birthday. And Bethlehem is his birthplace!'

What can the shepherds say? What can they do? They know how to deal with thieves and bears, but night visitors like this are well beyond their expertise.

'Here is how you will know what I say is true,' the angel continues. 'Look for a cowshed. Look for a manger. And that's where you'll find the baby!'

And the shepherds are even more confused – for it's not the place that any of them would have thought of finding a baby, much less a Messiah. But then, there's not much time to think, because the next few moments are like a multiplication table of the first – more angels, more light, more sound and a song this world won't hear the likes of again until eternity.

When it's all over, the shepherds hurry off, flock and all, as fast as feet and hooves will carry them. Innkeepers are awakened and late-night revellers stopped until the shepherds finally find directions to the stable they've been looking for.

The angel was right, of course – right down to the swaddling cloth! And there he is – the baby, the sign, the Messiah!

What follows is a lot of handshaking and backslapping, and baa-ing and barking to boot. And then, not waiting around for the wise men (as some tableaux suggest!), the shepherds rush off to share their good news with the rest of the town.

They didn't understand fully what they had just experienced. And they wouldn't for another thirty years or so. But they were sure of one thing. It was midnight. And at midnight, things happen. God breaks the back of night and calls forth a brand new day.

Midnight Two

It's midnight, and there's a baby crying again. Two men, deep in thought and discussion, lift their heads and listen. One of them thinks, 'Why doesn't somebody shut that kid up?' The other one just smiles. It's midnight. And he knows – at midnight, things happen.

'Nicodemus,' he says, 'If you're ever going to see the kingdom of God, you're going to have to be born all over again. Like a newborn baby, you're going to have to start fresh – seeing God and this world and yourself in a completely new and different way.'

Nicodemus can't quite get his head round that. The baby's still crying – there's a light on now – and what began as a secret midnight rendezvous between a radical rabbi and a highly respected member of the religious establishment is in danger of being seriously compromised. Born again? Born again? What do nappies and baby wipes have to do with God?

Jesus tries again.

'The world is in darkness,' he says. 'Dark as midnight. People go their own way and do their own thing without regard for the needs of others or the will of God.'

Nicodemus has read the papers. He watched *Newsnight* before he came out. The darkness he understands.

'Thirty years ago, Nicodemus, God sent a light into this dark world, a light to chase away the darkness and lead us to a brand new day. I am that light, Nicodemus, but I've got to tell you that we have all developed such good night vision that some of us are still going to prefer the darkness. That's why I say that you must be born again. Because anything short of a brand new start – any compromise with the darkness – is a return to midnight.'

Scurrying home, darting from pillar to pillar, Nicodemus still doesn't quite understand what he has just heard. But he's sure of one thing. It's midnight. And at midnight things happen. God is up to something here. And he wants to be part of it – to leave the darkness behind and find that brand new day.

Midnight Three

'Tis midnight, and on Olive's brow,
The star is dimmed that lately shown:
'Tis midnight in the garden now,
The suff'ring saviour prays alone.

It's midnight, and at midnight things happen. Thirty-three years on, and the baby whose first breath disturbed Bethlehem's sleep is less than twenty-four hours from his last. One of his closest friends has betrayed him. There is a crowd coming to arrest him. And the followers who have sworn to defend him are asleep. There are no shepherds on the way, no guiding star above. For all practical purposes, he is alone.

What the angels sang about so joyfully all those years ago must now come to pass. He must be the Messiah, redeemer and saviour, but in a way that not even the angels could have imagined. He smiles at the irony of it. To be the Prince of Peace has little to do with living a peaceful life. There has been plenty of bother and misunderstanding and controversy – and now, finally, this.

There is a part of him that wants to run off – off into the darkness. But he is confident, because he has prayed, that nothing but his death will bring that darkness to an end.

He can see torches now, slicing through the night in his direction. He is a torch, as well, about to be consumed for his father's sake, and for the sake of the world.

As the arresting soldiers obey their orders, they have no idea what they are doing – and understand even less what God is doing. For it's midnight, and he is up to something again. He sent the baby to Bethlehem, the rabbi to the religious leader, and now he sends his own Son to a cross, that those soldiers and a world just like them might have their darkness turned to light.

Because it's midnight. And at midnight, things happen.

One day ends. And a brand new day is born.

Questions

1. This reading attempts to trace the life of Jesus through three midnight events. Are there any other times or places (mornings, mountains, seas?) that you could use to do the same? What would they be, and which events in his life would they touch?

2. The reading suggests that 'at midnight, things happen'. Has anything significant ever happened at midnight for you?

3. Talk about an experience in your life in which you moved from a kind of 'midnight' to a 'brand new day'.

When Heaven Breaks In

Introduction

I wrote this originally for a Christmas Eve service, I think. You could use it as I did, with prayers and carols between each section, or you could just read it all in one go.

> **TELLING TIPS: When my brother used it at his church, he had different people read each section, and that worked nicely. Otherwise, just read it yourself.**

1. When heaven breaks in
   When heaven breaks in
   When heaven breaks in
   You just know!

   Angels appear
   You're filled with fear
   And you don't need a pastor or a priest to tell you
   That there's something divine going on here.

   And there were shepherds living out in the fields nearby, keeping watch over their flocks at night. And an angel of the Lord appeared to them, and the glory of the Lord shone around them, and they were terrified.

   That's what happens
   That's what happens
   That's what happens
   When heaven breaks in.

2. When heaven breaks in
   When heaven breaks in
   When heaven breaks in
   It shows!

   There's a sign
   You can find
   And you can see with your own eyes
   That God is at work in this place and this time.

   But the angel said to them, 'Don't be afraid, I bring you good news
   of great joy that will be for all people. Today in the town of David, a
   saviour has been born to you. He is Christ the Lord. This will be a
   sign to you. You will find the baby wrapped in cloths and lying in a
   manger…' Suddenly a great company of the heavenly host
   appeared, praising God and saying, 'Glory to God in the highest.
   And, on earth, peace to men on whom his favour rests.'

   That's what happens
   That's what happens
   That's what happens
   When heaven breaks in.

3. When heaven breaks in
   When heaven breaks in
   When heaven breaks in
   You just go!

   You run from the stable
   To each house, home and table
   You say what you saw
   And you don't need
   A Workshop
   A Seminar
   A DVD presentation
   Or an inspirational talk
   To make you willing and able.

When the angels had left them and gone into heaven, the shepherds said to one another, 'Let's go to Bethlehem and see this thing that has happened, which the Lord told us about.' So they hurried off and found Mary and Joseph and the baby, who was lying in a manger. When they had seen him, they spread the word concerning what they had been told about the child, and all who heard it were amazed at what the shepherds said to them.

That's what happens
That's what happens
That's what happens
When heaven breaks in.

4. When heaven breaks in
   When heaven breaks in
   When heaven breaks in
   You bow down low.

You praise God all through the night
You give your sheep another fright
And you don't need a video or an overhead projector
To get the words just right.

The shepherds returned, glorifying and praising God for all the things that they had heard and seen, which were just as they had been told.

That's what happens
That's what happens
That's what happens
When heaven breaks in.

Questions

1. Talk about some experience you have had during which you felt that 'heaven broke in'.

2. Is it true that we find we know how to react when God does something amazing in our lives – that it doesn't require seminars and workbooks and lessons?

3. There is something quite wonderful, in this story, about the way God appeared to people at work! It's not the place we usually expect to find him, is it? Why do you think that is so? And if you don't agree, talk about a time when you ran into God at your workplace.

Mary Went Looking for Jesus

(Luke 2:41–50, John 19:25)

Introduction

Sometimes writers get a 'gift' – and this piece is one of them. I was at an Eastertime conference in 2002, and the scripture for one of the evenings was the passage from Luke 2 about the young Jesus in the temple. I was talking with some of the leaders in the afternoon, and they asked me if I had a reading that would fit. I didn't, but said I'd be happy to put something together. So I went back to my room and prayed, and the Luke 2 story and the passion story just sort of came together. As I said, a gift.

> **TELLING TIPS: This is definitely one to do on your own. You need to read the Bible passage at the start really well, and 'sell' the idea that the Luke 2 story is what you're doing. I always pick up the pace and the sense of desperation as Mary looks for Jesus, and then slow it right down with 'And finally she found him. But it wasn't like that other time', because you need to give your group the time to make the transition to the other story with you. You also need to make sure you leave time for some reflection or response at the end. I've found that it just needs working through – some quiet time or a quiet song works best.**

Every year his parents went to Jerusalem for the Feast of the Passover. When Jesus was twelve years old, they went up to the Feast, according to the custom. After the Feast was over, while his parents were returning home, the boy Jesus stayed behind in Jerusalem, but they were unaware of it. Thinking he was in their company, they travelled on for a day. Then they began looking for him among their relatives and friends. When they did not find him, they went back to Jerusalem to look for him.

Mary went looking for Jesus. Her heart was pounding, her hands sweating. She hadn't seen him for days.

Mary went looking for Jesus. 'Have you seen my son?' she asked. 'Have you seen my son? My boy?'

Mary went looking for Jesus. The hot wind biting her face, chasing the tears from the corners of her eyes.

Mary went looking for Jesus. Up and down, and in and out, the crowded streets of Jerusalem.

Mary went looking for Jesus. And suddenly she remembered. The same search. The same crowded streets. But, oh, so long ago.

Mary went looking for Jesus. And finally she found him. But it wasn't like that other time. Not at all.

Then, she had looked down at his twelve-year-old face. Now, she was forced to look up.

Then, the temple teachers had praised him, amazed! Now, they shouted and swore.

Then, his face was adolescent fresh. Now, it was covered in blood.

Mary went looking for Jesus. 'Why are you looking for me?' he'd asked. And he'd fixed her with a look both innocent and wise. A look that said: 'I'm sorry you're worried. I know what I'm doing. Everything will be all right.

'Didn't you know that I'd be here in my Father's house, doing my Father's will?'

Mary went looking for Jesus. He was looking at her now as well. And it was the same look. The very same look. The bright boy. The dying man. 'I'm sorry you're worried. I know what I'm doing. Everything will be all right.'

They say you never stop being your mother's son.

Or your father's either, I guess.

Mary went looking for Jesus. And she found him in a temple. And she found him on a cross. Where she always knew he'd be – doing his Father's will.

Questions

1. The story ties together two times when a desperate mother went looking for her son. Have you ever 'lost' one of your children – in a shop or a park – for even a short time? What did it feel like as you went looking for them?

2. What would have been the similarities between Mary's two 'searches'? What would have been the differences?

3. 'You never stop being your mother's son. Or your father's either, I guess.' In what sense was that true of Jesus?

Bzz-y

(Luke 10:38–42)

Introduction

This is a quick reading – and all the more appropriate for it! It would make a lovely introduction to a sermon about Mary and Martha, and works really well right across the age range.

> **TELLING TIPS:** Teach the chorus to your crowd, first of all, and make sure they can do it quickly (and that you repeat it each time). Do it ever more quickly as the reading progresses, to give a sense of Martha's increasing busyness and frustration. And then slow it right down when Jesus speaks. Let them join you on the first two lines of the last chorus (which you can do a little more slowly), and then cut them off and do the last two lines yourself.

Busy, busy, busy,
Busy as a bee.
Martha was so busy,
She could hardly even breathe!
(x2)

Wash the dishes, cook the meals,
Put the kettle on.
Clean the windows, sweep the floor,
Work is never done!

Busy, busy, busy,
Busy as a bee.
Martha was so busy,

She could hardly even breathe!
(x2)

Jesus came to visit once,
She put on such a spread!
Home-made bread and fancy cakes
And pickled chicken heads.

Busy, busy, busy,
Busy as a bee.
Martha was so busy,
She could hardly even breathe!
(x2)

'I do all the work,' she moaned,
'It all comes down to me!
While sister Mary chats with Jesus
Idle and carefree.'

Busy, busy, busy,
Busy as a bee.
Martha was so busy,
She could hardly even breathe!
(x2)

'Slow down, Martha,' Jesus smiled.
'Take it easy, please.
Hospitality is good,
But you still need time to breathe.
Time to think and time to pray,
Time to spend with me.
So join your sister Mary,
And then we'll sort out tea.'

Busy, busy, busy,
Busy as a bee.
So Martha sat and listened
And at last found time to breathe!

Questions

1. I know lots of people (busy people mostly!) who, in spite of Jesus' words, still feel really sorry for Martha. How do you feel?

2. Does the weekly programme of the average church encourage us to be more like Mary or Martha? Give some examples. And what might Jesus say to the church today in this regard?

3. Hey, I like doughnuts and coffee, or cakes and cups of tea after a service as much as the next person! And somebody has to get all that ready – and do all the other 'busy' stuff that Christians do in the context of a worship service – not to mention during all the other activities. Again – what would Jesus say to us?

Untie the Ox

(Luke 13:10–17)

Introduction

This is another one of those 'spur-of-the-moment' readings that showed up in the middle of a conference! But it works as a really effective set-up for a sermon on this passage.

TELLING TIPS: Before the story begins, divide your crowd into two groups. Get one group to say 'Untie the ox!' in a deliberate sort of way. And get the other group to say 'And set the woman free!', again in a deliberate manner. Oh, and be prepared for the odd 'Boo'. For, at this point, some members of the audience may assume that you are moving into mildly misogynistic territory! Assure them that all will be well, once they see the point of the reading. And then do it – quick! Oh, and it helps if you pick up the pace and the energy as the reading progresses, so that by the end it becomes quite a rant!

Jesus was teaching in the synagogue.
Untie the ox and set the woman free!

When he spotted a woman, her back bent double.
Untie the ox and set the woman free!

He called her forward. He laid his hands on her.
Untie the ox and set the woman free!

She stood up straight and gave thanks to God!
Untie the ox and set the woman free!

But the ruler of the synagogue was angry and indignant.
Untie the ox and set the woman free!

'You've healed on the Sabbath! You've broken our laws!'
Untie the ox and set the woman free!

'There are six days for healing. Do it in your own time!'
Untie the ox and set the woman free!

But Jesus just sighed and shook his head.
Untie the ox and set the woman free!

'You hypocrites,' he muttered. 'You hypocrites!' he cried.
Untie the ox and set the woman free!

'You'd loose an ox and lead it to the water.'
Untie the ox and set the woman free!

'You'd do it on the sabbath and think nothing of it!'
Untie the ox and set the woman free!

'So why not the same for this daughter of Abraham?'
Untie the ox and set the woman free!

'Why not the same for this daughter of Abraham?'
Untie the ox and set the woman free!

'So why not show mercy to this daughter of Abraham?'
Untie the ox and set the woman free!

Bound by ropes and bound by illness.
Untie the ox and set the woman free!

Bound by rules and regulations.
Untie the ox and set the woman free!

Bound by tradition, bound by theology.
Untie the ox and set the woman free!

Bound by institutions, bound by bureaucracy.
Untie the ox and set the woman free!

Bound by everything but mercy.
Untie the ox and set the woman free!

So let's follow the one who died on the cross.
Untie the ox and set the woman free!

And set us free by his pain and loss.
Untie the ox and set the woman free!

Let's untie the ox and set the woman free!
Let's untie the ox and set the woman free!
Let's untie the ox and set the woman free!

Because that's what it means to live in Jesus' community.

Questions

1. In what way is the church today bound by rules and regulations?

2. In what way is it bound by traditions or theology?

3. In what way is it bound by institutions and bureaucracy? Talk about a time, in your experience, when any of these stood in the way of showing mercy.

Untie the Ox (Again)

(Luke 13:10–17)

Introduction

Sometimes I get two ideas for a reading and just can't decide which I like better. This piece is very different from the previous one, and yet (after an admittedly much longer journey!) it finishes up in pretty much the same place. Which one you choose will probably have a lot to do with the time you have and the style of reading you prefer.

TELLING TIPS: Unlike the previous reading, there is no participation here. This one will require your best reading and performing skills, because you have to convince the group that you really are the officious bureaucrat who penned this 'letter'. I have found that taking my time with this reading and really enjoying the Matathias character makes it work best. And it might help to have someone read the Bible passage first.

My Dear Eli,

As a fellow Pharisee, you have asked for my reaction to the incident at the synagogue this past sabbath, and I ask, in turn, for your patience and understanding, because my answer may not be exactly what you wanted to hear.

The facts are clear enough. I was, as you know, present myself and witnessed all that was said and done.

The rabbi, Jesus, was teaching. The nature of his discourse is not relevant to the issue at hand. Suffice it to say that he is, as many have already noted, a clear and intelligent communicator, who appeals to the educated and the uninformed alike.

He was in the middle of his message when he noticed the old woman. As far as I could tell, she made no effort to attract his attention (and is therefore, in my opinion, innocent of any wrongdoing with regard to the subsequent violation of the sabbath Law). No, I think it is fair to say that HE spotted HER – bent over nearly double with some affliction or other.

I have, by the way, attempted to ascertain the exact nature of her infirmity. While there are many opinions on the matter – ranging from some birth defect, on the one hand, to the influence of demonic powers, on the other – there is no question that the woman was genuinely ill, and not, as some of our more cynical colleagues have suggested, a 'plant'.

So, Jesus spotted this woman. And interrupting his own discourse, he invited her to come forward. To be honest, I would have thought that this was the time for the ruler of the synagogue to act. It was a highly irregular and uncomfortable moment, not in keeping with the usual order and decorum of the service. Had I been in his position, I would have sent the woman back straight away, and all would have ended happily. As it was, he failed to exercise his responsibility at this juncture, and the woman responded to Jesus' invitation.

'Woman,' he said – so that everyone could hear, 'Woman, you are set free from your infirmity.' Then he laid his hands on her, and immediately she stood up straight and gave thanks to God for her healing.

It was at this point that the ruler of the synagogue finally decided to act. And his timing could not have been worse. The crowd was understandably impressed, indeed, excited by what had happened, and were in sympathy with the woman and her plight. Yes, the Law had been violated. There is no question of that. And, yes, something needed to be done. But this was not exactly what you might call 'a teachable moment'.

Playing right into Jesus' hands (more on this later), he rose with great indignation and tactlessly suggested that the sick should seek healing not on the sabbath but on the other six days when it was allowed. This produced an angry murmur from the crowd – rightly, I think, because it placed the blame on the sick woman and not on Jesus, who, as I have already said, was clearly at fault for instigating this situation in the first place.

Perhaps the ruler of the synagogue aimed his comments at the woman because he was afraid to attack Jesus directly. We are all aware, by now, of his combative reputation where matters of the Law are concerned. But the ploy failed miserably, and Jesus launched into yet another of his famous invectives against hypocrisy and the keeping of the Law.

We have heard it all before: 'Whitewashed tombs, dirty bowls, murderers of the prophets, etcetera and so forth, blah, blah, blah...' But I must say that on this particular occasion, he argued his point rather well.

198

Jesus compared the loosing of the woman from her illness to the loosing of an ox or an ass from its stall.

'If an animal needs to drink,' he suggested, 'the sabbath law permits us to do what little work is necessary to untie it and lead it to water. And therefore,' he argued, 'Why should we not also be permitted to do what work is necessary to loose a woman from her infirmity?'

You and I, of course, can see the flaws in this argument immediately. Scholars have debated for centuries over the nature of the knots, the effort involved in the untying, and the distance to the water. The situation is nowhere near as clear-cut as Jesus suggested.

But my point is that, to the untrained mind – and I mean no disrespect here, but that would include the bulk of the congregation in the synagogue that day – Jesus' argument would seem quite plausible.

It certainly convinced THAT crowd, and the upshot was their overwhelming approval for what Jesus had done and abuse and scorn for those of us who see things in a more scripturally exact light.

So what is to be done? That was your question. And here, as promised, is my answer.

Nothing.

I told you, you wouldn't like it. But I am totally convinced that it is the right course. I know what many of our colleagues have said. I have heard plans to challenge him, debate him, even trump up charges against him. But these are either useless or unethical or both.

The very incident that we are considering is a perfect illustration of my point. Confrontation is counterproductive. The best thing is to do nothing – and wait!

Follow me for just a moment here. Have we not dealt with movements and splits and sects in the past? Everything from serious ascetics like the Essenes to that ridiculous Braying Brotherhood of Balaam's Ass? Do you remember? Palm-frond ears tied to their heads. Rope tails hanging from behind. All in the hope that an hour's hee-hawing would result in some word of prophecy!

It still makes me shudder to think about it. But what did we do? We waited – that's what – and let the weight of time and institution and regulation and rule bring these groups back to their senses. And so now the Essenes are quietly at work in the desert, and, the last I heard, the few remaining Braying Brothers had composed a thoughtful commentary on the care and feeding of donkeys – all thoughts of prophecy and hee-hawing banished for ever.

We waited. It worked. And that is why I say we do the same with Jesus.

His group is small now. He can move freely among them, tailoring his teaching to their daily needs and changing situations. They don't need rules. He is there, beside them, to answer any question, to advise on any problem.

But the success of his movement will create a whole new dynamic!

'Success?' I hear you say. 'Success is the last thing we want!'

But hear me out. Success means growth. Not one band of disciples travelling from place to place, but lots of little bands who will have to settle eventually into communities of some kind or other. Communities dotted, here and there, all over our land.

Will Jesus be able to advise them daily in that situation? Of course not. There will need to be rules to govern their behaviour, regulations to order their communities, structures to provide leadership. And inevitably, there will be discussions and debates over the nature of all of these. And, in the midst of that, they are sure to forget all about their 'radical agenda', their newfound 'freedom', and, best of all, their criticism of us!

Inside information that I am privy to suggests that there have already been questions.

Jesus says that we must love our neighbour.

'Who exactly is my neighbour?' someone asks.

Jesus says that we must forgive.

'How many times?' That's what one of his followers wants to know.

You can already imagine the commentaries, the scholarly debate and the regulations that will arise from just these two issues.

Don't you see, Eli? It's inevitable. There is no other way.

Rules. Regulations.

Committees. Commentaries.

Bureaucracy. Hypocrisy!

And quicker than you can say, 'The Braying Brotherhood of Balaam's Ass', the followers of Jesus will be sitting where we're sitting now!

I ask you, what is the alternative? Unless Jesus can find some way to spirit himself from group to group, here and there and everywhere, he will no longer be able to advise his followers personally on how they should follow his teaching. And what happens when he dies? What choice will they have then but to enshrine his words in some kind of fixed rule? And then who will help them apply and interpret? Jesus is not likely to live for ever, is he?

So let's wait. Time and human nature and the grinding process of institutionalization are on our side. And it won't be long until someone stands up in the midst of Jesus' followers, cries, 'Hypocrite!' and asks why they put their own rules and traditions above some basic human need.

Thank you for patiently wading through this lengthy epistle. I hope that you can see my point, or, at the very least, would be happy to engage in further discussion on this matter – perhaps at the next meeting of the Kid Boiled in its Mother's Milk Exclusionary Subcommittee.

But in the meantime, let us wait. Just wait. For I am confident that this approach will do more to slow the progress of Jesus' movement than anything else we could imagine.

All the best, then.

Your brother and friend,

The Pharisee, Matathias

Questions

1. So, in what ways, if any, has the Pharisee's prediction come true?

2. There is, of course, a lot of irony in the Pharisee's analysis of what Jesus will and won't be able to do, with regard to leading his followers in the long term. Where did the Pharisee get it wrong?

3. You might want to consider the questions from the previous reading as well.

The Parable of the Great Feast

(Luke 14:15–24)

Introduction

As you will see, there is a lot of 'local detail' in this story. Well, local to me, at least! If you are telling stories to the same group all the time, it can be really helpful to weave those kinds of detail into your stories, because it really does help everybody feel 'at home' and more a part of what you're doing. So, in this case, there are references to several of the people who belonged to the church I pastored when I wrote the piece. Alan Ridout keeps bees; Julie Harris makes a great apple cake; Joan Hunt bakes the best ginger cake you will ever eat. And lots of people at that church frequent a local cafe called Berkeley's. You will obviously not want to use those references when you do the reading! But I'm sure there are equivalent places and individuals at your church. And if you're doing this reading at a conference or a camp and you don't know the crowd all that well, you can leave that section out entirely.

TELLING TIPS: Speakers are always telling audiences to turn off their mobile phones. What's fun about this story is that you get to ask the crowd to turn them ON! This will work only in a setting where people know each other reasonably well. Ask for three volunteers who have the phone numbers in their 'memory' of three other volunteers in the room (who also have their phones with them and switched on!). Then ask them, in turn, to ring those people at the three 'phone' moments in the story. It will work really nicely if the person who is 'calling' is sitting some distance away from the person who is 'answering'.

If people don't know each other well, then just divide the crowd into three groups and have them make three different 'ring-tone' sounds. Again, you can ask someone in each group to switch their phone on and mimic that particular ring tone.

Once upon a time, there lived a king who decided to host a great banquet.
He sent out invitations to some very important guests. Then he
commanded his servants to fetch the finest food from the four corners of
his kingdom.

Honey cakes from the Rivers of Ridout.

Ginger cakes from the House of Hunt.

Apple cakes from the Hamlet of Harris.

And blueberry cheesecakes from the kitchens of Berkeley Castle.

When all was ready, he sent his servants out again to tell his guests that the
time had come.

The servants came to the first guest. But as soon as they'd opened their
mouths, the man's phone began to ring (*mobile phone sound*).

'I'm very sorry,' he said. 'That was my estate agent. I've just bought a field
(The prices are coming down – don't you know!), and I must go and see it. Tell
your master that I cannot come to his banquet.'

The servants came to the next guest. But as soon as they'd opened their
mouths, her phone began to ring, too (*mobile phone sound*).

'I'm very sorry,' she said. 'That was my stockbroker. I've just bought
shares in the cattle market and we need to take care of some paperwork.
Tell your master that I cannot come to his banquet.'

So the servants went to the next guest. And it was just the same. As soon as
they'd opened their mouths to speak, his phone rang, as well (*mobile phone
sound*).

'I'm very sorry,' he said. 'That was my wife. We've just got married you
see, and we need to spend some quality time together – at IKEA. Tell your
master that I cannot come to his banquet.'

When the king heard all these excuses, he was furious! His banquet was ready, the hall was a picture, and the cakes looked amazing. And so he came up with another idea.

'Go into the streets and the alleys,' he said to his servants, 'and invite the poor, the blind and the lame to my feast!'

So that's what the servants did. They went into the alleys and the streets. And when the poor received their invitations, they cheered. When the blind heard the news, they cheered even louder. And when the servants spoke to the lame, they cheered loudest of all!

They followed the servants to the banquet hall, but when they had all sat down, there were still more empty seats.

'Go out to the country!' ordered the king. 'To the roads and to the lanes. And invite the country folk, as well.'

So the servants went to the country. And when the country folk received their invitations, they all said 'Yee-ha!'

And the poor and the blind and the lame and the country folk gobbled down the delicious cakes (*gobble sounds*). And apart from the guests who had made their excuses, they all lived happily ever after.

Questions

1. What point was Jesus originally trying to make with this story? What might it mean for us, today?

2. What do you think of the excuses the people in the story made? Do they seem reasonable to you?

3. What excuses have you made for not turning up at 'The King's Feast'?

Count the Cost

(Luke 14:25–35)

Introduction

I first did this reading at the end of a conference, just before everyone went home – thus the travelling imagery. But I think it works well in other contexts too – even at the end of a Sunday service, when we wander off into the next week.

> TELLING TIPS: Teach the chorus to the group before you start the story. Counting on fingers is more fun, but you can have them count in their heads instead. You also might want to shorten the chorus. Some people prefer to use just the first and last lines. Whatever you like best.

1, 2, 3, 4, 5, 6, 7.
Count the cost. Count the cost.
Count the cost in the kingdom of heaven.

Once there was a large group of people following Jesus.

A large group at church on Sunday. A large group at a conference. A large group on retreat perhaps. Who knows?

But a large group of people who'd just had an important and significant time and were feeling really close to Jesus.

1, 2, 3, 4, 5, 6, 7.
Count the cost. Count the cost.
Count the cost in the kingdom of heaven.

So Jesus turned to them and shared a few hard truths about the journey home.

Not the congestion. Not the road works. Not the food at the service stations. But the journey after that – the following days and weeks and months.

1, 2, 3, 4, 5, 6, 7.
Count the cost. Count the cost.
Count the cost in the kingdom of heaven.

'If you want to follow me,' said Jesus, 'you will have to hate your father, your mother; your husband, your wife; your brother, your sister; your child, your own life.'

Now, the people had been on trips with their families before, and they figured that this was likely to happen at some point on the way home, in any case.

So Jesus continued.

1, 2, 3, 4, 5, 6, 7.
Count the cost. Count the cost.
Count the cost in the kingdom of heaven.

'And if you want to be my disciple,' he said, 'you will have to pick up your cross and follow me.'

This was getting more serious!

'You wouldn't build a house,' he said, 'or a garage, or anything, without first working out the price. What if you could only afford the concrete slab floor and then had to stop? Imagine how the neighbours would laugh!

'Or what if you were a king, about to fight a battle. You had ten thousand soldiers and your enemy had twice that number. You'd think long and hard about it, wouldn't you? And try to find a peaceful solution if you didn't think you could see it through.'

1, 2, 3, 4, 5, 6, 7.
Count the cost. Count the cost.
Count the cost in the kingdom of heaven.

'Let me make this as simple as possible – if you're not willing to leave behind what's most important to you, then you cannot be my disciple.

'You are salt. And salt is good. But if it loses its saltiness – the thing that makes it special and distinct – then it's no good for anything and just gets chucked in the bin.'

1, 2, 3, 4, 5, 6, 7.
Count the cost. Count the cost.
Count the cost in the kingdom of heaven.

What does it cost to follow Jesus?
It costs nothing at all – but it costs everything we've got.
How can that be?
Because nothing good happens in this world without sacrifice.
I'll say it again. Nothing good happens in this world without sacrifice. Nothing good happens without one person giving up something for someone else.
That's what Jesus did for us when he died on the cross.
And if we're going to follow him – live as he lived and see it through to the end – then we are going to find ourselves giving up things too. Even the most precious things we've got.

1, 2, 3, 4, 5, 6, 7.
Count the cost. Count the cost.
Count the cost in the kingdom of heaven.

That's the truth. That's the bottom line. That's what the journey is all about.
He who has ears, let him hear.

Questions

1. Talk about a time when you had to 'count the cost' with regard to your faith and something or someone else that was important to you.

2. I know I made light of the 'hating your family' quote, but what do you suppose Jesus meant by that?

3. Is it true that nothing good in this world ever happens without sacrifice? Offer examples to support your opinion.

A Maths Problem

(Luke 15:1–2, 8–10)

Introduction

There's an awful lot of arithmetic in the Bible. Two by two. Seventy times seven. Ninety-nine sheep out of a hundred. In fact, one of these days I'm going to write a whole book of Bible maths stories, so that kids can learn about Deuteronomy and long division all in one go! In the meantime, here's a story in which the numbers really matter.

> **TELLING TIPS: Before the story begins, teach your group the little counting rhythm. Let them use their fingers if they have to – it's more fun, anyway! Then bring them in at the appropriate times.**

Jesus was talking with the tax collectors and their friends. But the Pharisees and their friends (who always seemed to be eavesdropping) were listening as well.

'Look at that!' they muttered. 'He says he's a religious man, but he spends all his time with sinners!'

So Jesus turned to the Pharisees and said, 'I've got a maths problem for you. Add, subtract, multiply, divide. Use your fingers, use your toes if you like. Here's the problem: "What number makes an angel smile?"'

The Pharisees groaned. They hated maths – and those word problems in particular. So while they were undoing their sandals, Jesus told them a story.

Once there was a woman who had ten coins. And each coin was worth a day's wage. One afternoon, she went to count her coins. And suddenly, she had a maths problem too!

One, two, three.
Four, five, six.
Seven, eight, nine and ten.

That's how many there were supposed to be. But somehow, someone had done some subtracting. And now there were only nine!

Desperate for a solution, the woman tackled the problem at once. She lit a lamp. She swept the floor. She lost track of how much time it took. Inch by inch. Metre by metre. Cubit by cubit. The woman looked carefully into every crack and crevice. And finally, she found it!

Her deficit diminished. Her budget balanced. The woman counted her coins again.

One, two, three.
Four, five, six.
Seven, eight, nine and TEN!

And then she smiled. For that one last coin had made all the difference.

What number makes an angel smile? The answer is the same.

One.

Just one.

Each one.

Every one.

One missing soul swept out of the darkness and into the light. One lost sinner found. Do the maths. Add, subtract, multiply, divide. Use your fingers, use your toes if you like. You'll see that it all adds up.

Questions

1. The woman in the story was desperate to find her lost coin. But, as Jesus points out at the end, the story is really about 'lost' people. Are we as desperate for them as the woman was for her coin? Why? Why not?

2. How much time do you intentionally spend with people who are not Christians? Do you think you are more like Jesus or more like the Pharisees in this regard?

3. What do you think are the most effective ways to find the 'lost' – to sweep them out of the darkness and into the light?

The Prodigal

(Luke 15:11–32)

Introduction

A couple of years ago, I was asked to do a retelling of the story of the prodigal son at an outdoor festival sponsored by one of the local churches. Outdoor festivals can be some of the most difficult places to do storytelling, because crowds are more widely dispersed, there are lots of distractions, and even the best sound systems struggle to make your vocals clear. Lots of words just don't work in that situation, so it seemed the perfect place for one of those repetitive, rhyming, participation stories you will run across several times in this book!

TELLING TIPS: Teach your group these sounds and actions ahead of time.

'Foo!' (Put hands on hips, show a disgusted look on face.)
'Two.' (Put two (as in peace sign!) fingers in the air.)
'Ooh!' (Say this in a high–pitched lady's voice, with hands on hips.)
'Blue!' (Put lower lip out, use sad voice.)
'Eeugh!' (Pinch nose with fingers.)
'Crew.' (Salute while saying 'Crew.')
'Do!' (Swing arm, with fist clenched, in a determined fashion in front of the body while saying 'Do!')
'Flew!' (Flap bent arms as wings, with fingertips stuck in armpits.)
    (Option: 'Rue?' (Put finger to chin, in thinking style.)
'Phew!' (Wipe hand across forehead in a relieved manner.)
'Moo!' (Put fingers as cow horns at both sides of head.)
'Woo-hoo!' (Say joyfully.)

As in other stories of this kind, the lines get repeated three times to help the story stick and also to give the crowd a chance to catch on to and enjoy the actions.

There once was a man who had two sons.
There once was a man who had two sons.
There once was a man who had two sons.
But the younger son was fed up. *(Foo!)*
But the younger son was fed up. *(Foo!)*
But the younger son was fed up. *(Foo!)*

'I want half of your money,' the younger son said.
'I want half of your money,' the younger son said.
'I want half of your money,' the younger son said.
So the father divided it in two. *(Two.)*
So the father divided it in two. *(Two.)*
So the father divided it in two. *(Two.)*

The son took the money and went far away.
The son took the money and went far away.
The son took the money and went far away.
And wasted it on wine and women. *(Ooh!)*
And wasted it on wine and women. *(Ooh!)*
And wasted it on wine and women. *(Ooh!)*

Then the money ran out and a famine came.
Then the money ran out and a famine came.
Then the money ran out and a famine came.
And the son turned kind of blue. *(Blue!)*
And the son turned kind of blue. *(Blue!)*
And the son turned kind of blue. *(Blue!)*

The son went to work for a local farmer.
The son went to work for a local farmer.
The son went to work for a local farmer.
And had to clear up piggy poo. *(Eeugh!)*
And had to clear up piggy poo. *(Eeugh!)*
And had to clear up piggy poo. *(Eeugh!)*

'I've really messed up,' said the son to himself.
'I've really messed up,' said the son to himself.
'I've really messed up,' said the son to himself.
'I'm worse off than my father's crew.' *(Crew.)*

'I'm worse off than my father's crew.' *(Crew.)*
'I'm worse off than my father's crew.' *(Crew.)*

'I'll go back and beg to be one of his servants.'
'I'll go back and beg to be one of his servants.'
'I'll go back and beg to be one of his servants.'
'That's exactly what I'll do.' *(Do!)*
'That's exactly what I'll do.' *(Do!)*
'That's exactly what I'll do.' *(Do!)*

So the son headed back to his father's house.
So the son headed back to his father's house.
So the son headed back to his father's house.
He ran, he raced, he flew! *(Flew!)*
He ran, he raced, he flew! *(Flew!)*
He ran, he raced, he flew! *(Flew!)*
(Option:Was this a decision he would rue?)

The father was waiting and saw his son coming.
The father was waiting and saw his son coming.
The father was waiting and saw his son coming.
And welcomed him with open arms. *(Phew!)*
And welcomed him with open arms. *(Phew!)*
And welcomed him with open arms. *(Phew!)*

Then the father gave him a ring and a robe.
Then the father gave him a ring and a robe.
Then the father gave him a ring and a robe.
And a roast beef dinner, too! *(Moo!)*
And a roast beef dinner, too! *(Moo!)*
And a roast beef dinner, too! *(Moo!)*

'It's like you were dead,' the father said.
'It's like you were dead,' the father said.
'It's like you were dead,' the father said.
'But you're alive again!' *(Woo-hoo!)*
'But you're alive again!' *(Woo-hoo!)*
'But you're alive again!' *(Woo-hoo!)*

Questions

1. What do you think Jesus was trying to teach when he told this story?

2. Talk about a time when you ran away from the 'Father'. What brought you back?

3. Quite often, we go running after 'prodigals', in the hope of bringing them back or of protecting them from the bad things that might happen to them while they are 'away'. What do you think is the significance of the fact that the father in the story watched and waited for his son to return, but did not pursue him?

Songs in Search of a Tune: I Just Want to Drive

(Luke 15:11–32)

Introduction

This reading/song was inspired by Nick Page, who wrote a book called *Now Let's Move into a Time of Nonsense: Why Worship Songs are Failing the Church*. Among other suggestions for improving the lyrics in contemporary worship songs, Page recommends using modern and urban imagery as opposed to ancient and pastoral. I'm not sure that this piece is what Nick had in mind (particularly since it ended up sounding like a country-and-western song. OK, maybe alt-country!), but it was my attempt to recast the prodigal story in twenty-first-century terms.

TELLING TIPS: One to do on your own (with a steel guitar!).

Verse 1:

It's a struggle to admit it,
But I've taken the wrong road.
Gone to places I've regretted,
Where I never thought I'd go.
Now I'm leaving that far country,
Doing what I have to do.
And I just want to drive.
I just want to drive
Back home to you.

Verse 2:

I hate to have to say this
But I can't stand the shape I'm in.
Thought that things would turn out different,
That I was only made to win.
But I've lost – there's no way round it,
Lost the plot and road map, too.
And now I just want to drive.
I just want to drive
Back home to you.

Chorus:

And they say that you've been waiting,
Waiting since the day I went –
Pacing up and down the pavement,
Wearing holes in the cement.
So I guess that means you love me,
Love me like I never knew.
And now I just want to drive.
I just want to drive
Back home to you.

Verse 3:

It's not easy to confess this,
But I've acted like a swine.
Turned my back on those who loved me,
Thought of me, myself and mine.
But I want things to be different,
No matter what I have to do.
So I just want to drive.
I just want to drive
Back home to you.

Chorus:

And they say that you've been waiting,
Waiting since the day I went –
Pacing up and down the pavement,

Wearing holes in the cement.
So I guess that means you love me,
Love me like I never knew.
And now I just want to drive.
I just want to drive
Back home to you.

Questions

1. So, does the imagery work? Or have I missed the point? Or, worse still, trivialised the story?

2. Why not try taking a psalm and finding contemporary and urban images to replace the ancient and pastoral ones? Is it hard? Is it easy? Is it even appropriate? And what do we gain (and lose?) from such an exercise?

3. Does it matter, do you think, where the images come from? Do some biblical images make it more difficult for twenty-first-century people to understand what the Bible is saying? Is that really a roadblock to faith? Or do Christians worry too much about it? Is there an argument (other than stubborn-minded traditionalism) for keeping and cherishing and employing images that non-believers might initially struggle to understand?

The Other Prodigal

(Luke 15:25–32)

Introduction

At the very first church I pastored, an elderly woman in the congregation asked me to visit her following a sermon I had preached on the prodigal son. She had a bone to pick with me. When she was young, she had been left to support her ageing mother, while her younger siblings left home, and married, and got on with their lives. As a result, she felt a great deal of sympathy for the 'older brother' in the story, and couldn't understand why he always came off as the 'bad guy'. What was wrong, she wondered, with doing one's duty – and resenting those who had shirked theirs? It's a good question. And, even though Peggy passed away a long time ago, I'm sure that she's not the only one who has asked it. So, twenty years later, here's my shot at some kind of an answer.

> **TELLING TIPS: This is one to tell on your own, although you might have someone else read the father's part. The important thing is to reflect the feelings of the older brother accurately. When I read it, I just try to remember what Peggy looked like! But I'm sure that, even if you haven't found yourself in an 'older brother' situation, you know someone who has.**

The older brother became angry and refused to go in. So his father went out and pleaded with him. But he answered his father...

I can't go in. I just can't go in. I know you love him. I can see that you've forgiven him. But I can't forget the look on your face the day he left.

You were gutted. Devastated. Destroyed. You couldn't eat or sleep for weeks. Surely you remember.

And it wasn't easy for me either. There were jobs that needed to be done.

Responsibilities he'd accepted that had to fall to someone else – me! To be honest, I felt abandoned too.

And yes, I can see that you're happy now. Just happy to see him again. To talk with him. I understand that. I really do. But how long will it last? That's what I want to know. Surely, you've asked yourself the same question?

He went away once. He took what he wanted. He left you for dead. So how long before he does it again? How many times will you let your heart be broken? That's what I want to know.

I mean, you can't really imagine that he's back for good. Things got hard for him out there – that's all. And he figured that things would be easier here. Oh, I know he said he'd gladly work as one of your servants. But he knows how well the servants are treated here. This is just the easy way out for him again. It's always the easy way out. So he swallows a little pride and comes back. Worst case scenario, you put him to work and he still gets three square meals a day and a warm place to sleep. Best case? Well, I think he's looking at the best case. Robes and rings and a feast the likes of which I've never seen.

I know. I know. I shouldn't bring it up. They're your robes and rings and caterers. Yours to do with as you please. It's just that… it's just that… if someone has to break your heart to get your attention, then your heart's going to be broken a lot.

'My son,' the father said, 'you are always with me, and everything I have is yours.'

I'm not saying I'm perfect. I'm not saying that for a minute. But I do try to do what's right. I really do. And I can't see what's wrong with that.

Loyalty. Commitment. Duty. OK, maybe those qualities aren't exciting. Maybe they're not compelling or sexy. But they are the qualities that hold things together. And they're qualities that I've learned from living with you!

I mean, what kind of state would the world be in if everyone acted like him? That's what I want to know. Taking what you want when you want it. Shirking your responsibilities. Running off at a moment's notice. Living for yourself, regardless of how your actions affect anyone else. That's what his life has been like. His and the millions of others who are just like him.

The problem is that it's the rest of us – the loyal, committed, duty-bound ones – who have to pick up the pieces, clear up the mess and pay the price when they're done.

And then, when they finally come running back home because the mess is too big, when they finally want some kind of help and support, we're not even allowed to criticize or complain. Oh no, because then WE would be in the wrong – uncaring, unsympathetic, unforgiving.

Well, who makes the effort to sympathize with us? That's what I want to know. Those of us who play by the rules and at least try to do what's right. Who takes the time to see things our way? To walk in our shoes?

No one. That's who. We just get called names. Legalists. Moralists. Conformists. Prudes.

'My son,' the father said, 'you are always with me, and everything I have is yours.'

I mean, what's so wrong with trying to do what's right and suggesting that if a few more people tried a bit harder, there might be less mess to clean up in the first place? What's so bad about encouraging people to take a little more responsibility for themselves?

I know. I know. I know. No one's perfect. Life's not like that. And I'm not always responsible either. Of course, we all need to be forgiven at one time or other. But some people – people like him – just seem to go out of their way to make a habit of it! As if the failing and the forgiving provides some kind of assurance – again and again and again – that they will be loved no matter what they do.

Maybe you don't mind. But I find it tiring. And frustrating. Living always with that uncertainty.

It reminds me of church camp. That's what it does. There were these boys – popular boys. The ones who were good at sports and getting the girls. Well, year after year, these boys would mess up. They'd break the rules and get into all kinds of trouble. But then, the last night, around the campfire, they'd come forward in a flood of tears and say how sorry they were and how they were going to change and how things would be different. And they would cry and the camp counsellors would cry and the girls would cry.

But I didn't. I couldn't. And I could never figure out why no one seemed to remember that the same thing had happened the year before. And the year before that.

Were they just a bunch of dumb suckers, falling for the same old trick, year after year? Or was I the sucker? Because the other thing I could never figure out was why the same camp counsellors who got all choked up about those kids never had more than two words for the likes of us who kept the rules and didn't cause any trouble and memorized our verses without complaint. There were no tears for us. Not much attention of any kind, as I recall.

And so I have to ask. Have to ask again. What does it take – what does it take to get their attention? What does it take to get yours? Are you like the girl who ignores the guy who's kind to her because she finds the prospect of reforming the bad boy more appealing? Is that what this is all about? Because if it is, I feel duty-bound to remind you that she often ends up hurt and abused and pregnant.

And the nice guy? The nice guy just gets ignored.

The problem is that there's a world full of us. We're married to alcoholics and related to druggies. Our brothers-in-law are adulterers, our uncles are gamblers. Our mothers pop pills and our sisters abandon their kids.

So we mop up the puke and change the extra nappies and visit the hospitals and pay for the rehab and cancel the debts and put up with so much crap.

And what do we get in return? We get taken for granted most of the time. Or condemned – if we should so much as suggest that they should get their act together.

But do you know what we really want? All we really want is for someone to pay us a little bit of attention too.

'My son,' the father said, 'you are always with me, and everything I have is yours.'

He'd said that before. A couple of times, I think. And at first, it sounded like condemnation.

'Stop your moaning. Don't complain. You have everything you need.'

But maybe it sounded that way because that's what I was expecting to hear.

Because when he said it the third time, it didn't sound as if he was criticizing me at all. It sounded more like a welcome. It sounded more like – I don't know – an invitation?

All right, it wasn't a feast he was offering. But then, I didn't need a feast. I hadn't been sharing scraps with sows, had I? I'd been eating well all along. And as for rings and robes, I had them too.

What I needed was... well, what I needed was him, I guess. Or at least the assurance that he understood.

But then I realized that's what he'd been giving me.

'You are always with me,' he'd said. 'I do pay attention to you. I do recognize and regard you. You're not alone. Not alone in your obedience, your faithfulness, or even in your frustration with a world that is not as it was meant to be. Not alone when you try to fix what's wrong, or hang in there with someone. Not alone when you hold things together.

'Everything I have is yours,' he'd said. 'My goodness is so that you can be good. My faithfulness so you can be faithful. My patience so you can be patient. My strength so you can endure. You can't do any of that without me.'

And then there was that last thing. The thing that annoyed me when I first heard it, but that finally made sense in the end.

'We had to celebrate and be glad, because this brother of yours was dead and is alive again; he was lost and is found.'

It was the word 'dead' that did it. That finally changed my mind. How had my brother become a prodigal? By treating my dad as if he was dead. So if I did the same thing to my brother, if I left him in the grave when I could welcome him back to life, would that not make me a kind of prodigal too?

'All right,' I said. 'I'll do it.' And with the noise of the feast ringing in my ears, I swallowed my pride, like my brother had swallowed his. And I went in and sat down at my father's table.

Questions

1. Talk about a time when you felt like the older brother. Is the response of the older brother in the story an accurate reflection of how you felt?

2. Does the world really fall into two categories – 'younger brothers' and 'older brothers'? Or is it more complicated than that? And if so, how?

3. Does the resolution in the story 'work'? Or is it forcing too much into what the father says? What do you think the father meant when he answered the older brother? How would you have answered Peggy?

Kids, Camels and the
Kingdom of God

(Luke 18)

Introduction

Here are two stories from Luke 18 that are linked together by the disciples' very different response to the people who came to see Jesus. The alternative ending makes the reading a bit more specific, and may not work in every situation, but I have included it in case it works for you.

> **TELLING TIPS: There are two motions at the heart of this reading – 'welcoming' (arms open wide, ready to receive) and 'pushing away' (hands out in front, pushing). Teach these to your group and then lead them in doing the motions at the appropriate points in the text.**

When the women came to Jesus with their children, the disciples pushed them away. But Jesus opened wide his arms and said, 'Don't keep the kids away from me. The kingdom of heaven belongs to them. They're little and powerless, dependent and small. And you need to be like them to find your way in!'

But when the ruler came to Jesus, with his goodness and his goods, the disciples welcomed him with open arms. 'If this man can't be saved,' they said, 'then who can?'

Jesus welcomed the man as well. But this is what he said: 'The only goodness there is, is God's. And as for your goods – give them to the poor!'

So the man walked sadly away.

Jesus was sad as well. So he turned to his friends and said, 'The rich own many things. But not the kingdom of God. It does not belong to them. They are big and powerful, strong and independent. And, like a camel shoved through the eye of a needle, they find it hard to let go of enough hump and hoof to squeeze in!

God's values are different from ours. That's all Jesus was trying to say. He welcomes those we push away. And those we welcome, he welcomes too. (They just can't push their way in!)

It sounds difficult. It sounds complicated. But it's simple really.

It's all about kids and camels and the kingdom of God.

(Alternative ending – pick up after '… hump and hoof to squeeze in!')

So when the rich man came to our church, we welcomed him with open arms. We gave him a cup of coffee and a comfy seat in a state-of-the-art sanctuary.

And when the children came, we welcomed them as well. We let them stay in the sanctuary (for the first thirty minutes). Then we sent them to the corner of the fellowship hall (which, admittedly, could use a coat of paint), with Mrs Robertson, who has served the Sunday School faithfully for ages (on a fifty-pound-per-year budget).

And that's when Jesus came to our church too. 'This is not hard,' he said. 'I'll go through it slowly if you like, because so much depends on you getting this.' And he told us again about kids and camels and the kingdom of God.

Questions

1. Are there certain kinds of people we welcome or push away in the church today? If so, how do we do that?

2. Do we still kowtow to the rich? Why or why not?

3. Statistics suggest that something like 80% of Christians made their initial commitment to Christ before the age of eighteen. And yet church budgets often reflect a far greater percentage of resources going to 'adult' programmes and ministries than to programmes that are focused on kids. What would a church look like if it took those statistics seriously and focused its energies wholly on passing the gospel to the next generation?

Another Maths Problem

(Luke 18:18–27)

Introduction

Here's another take on Jesus' encounter with the rich young ruler. And, once again, from a mathematical point of view.

TELLING TIPS: This is one to tell on your own.

A disciple is a learner, a pupil, a student – someone who goes to school. So when the rich man asked his question – 'Good teacher, what must I do to inherit eternal life?' – Jesus' disciples thought it was time for Sunday School.

Jesus knew different however. He was the teacher after all. And he could see, quite clearly, that the rich man's question was all about Maths.

'You know the commandments,' said Jesus.

'Don't murder;

'Don't commit adultery;

'Don't steal;

'Don't lie;

'Don't cheat;

'Honour your father and your mother.'

And like a man punching numbers into a calculator, or stacking up coins, or counting on his fingers, the rich man nodded, one by one.

'I have kept them all,' he said, 'ever since I was a boy!'

And that's when Jesus changed the subject – or at least the subject matter. 'You think the kingdom of God is all about addition,' he said. 'The problem is that no one can be as good as God – or add up enough good deeds to deserve eternal life.

'No, the kingdom is not about addition. It's about subtraction – taking away anything that stands between you and God and keeps you from devoting yourself to him. So if you want treasure in heaven, then you'll need to take away your earthly treasure and give it to the poor.'

The rich man was good at addition – in financial terms and in moral terms as well. But his calculator didn't even have a minus key, so he walked away sadly.

The disciples, meanwhile – the learners, the students – were trying to take all this in. Jesus could see the shocked looks on their faces. He could smell the smoke as their brains buzzed round at a million miles a minute!

Riches are a blessing from God... That's what they were thinking. So a rich man should be closer to God than anyone!

'No,' said Jesus. 'You've got it all wrong. Riches make it harder for a man to get into the kingdom. His wealth becomes his god – it's what he depends on, treasures and serves. And it blocks his view of the true God in heaven.'

And that's when Jesus changed the subject again – to Zoology, and a bit of Home Economics.

'I tell you, it's easier for a camel to squeeze through the eye of a needle than for a rich man to get into God's kingdom.'

'Then how can anybody be saved?' cried the disciples.

'It's down to God,' said Jesus at last. 'It's always down to him – we must trust him to do what only he can do. None of us can save ourselves – no matter how many riches or good deeds we add up. But with God, anything and everything is possible!'

Questions

1. Is the kingdom of God about addition or subtraction or maybe even some other kind of calculation?

2. How do riches make it hard for us to get into the kingdom? Is there anything else that works the same way?

3. Do you think Jesus is too hard on rich people? Does he want every rich person to give all they have to the poor? Why or why not? And, given the place in the world that most Westerners occupy (rich beyond the wildest dreams of most of the people on this planet), that makes 'camels' of the vast majority of the people reading or using this book! That's right, in the eyes of the world, we're all 'rich rulers'. How do you respond to that?

The Anatomy of Faith

(Luke 18:35–43)

Introduction

This is just a quick and punchy way of telling the story of the blind beggar Jesus healed. And because it's so physical, it helps us to understand both the man's infirmity and his strengths. And maybe to see him as a whole person – and not just a blind beggar.

> **TELLING TIPS: You might just want to point to your ears, mouth, head and heart as you work your way through the reading. And then do it again, at the end, finishing off with your eyes.**

He couldn't see. But there was nothing wrong with his ears.

'Who's there?' asked the blind beggar. 'What's going on? There's a crowd on its way, isn't there?'

'Jesus is coming,' said a beggar nearby. 'The crowd's with him.'

He couldn't see. But there was nothing wrong with his mouth.

'Jesus!' he shouted. 'Jesus, son of David, have mercy on me!'

And when there was no answer, he shouted even louder. 'Jesus!'

'Quiet!' said the people in the crowd. 'Stop your shouting, beggar!'

He couldn't see. But there was nothing wrong with his head.

He knew all about squeaky wheels. And grease.

So he shouted louder still, 'Jesus, son of David, have mercy on me!'

So Jesus stopped.

'What would you like me to do for you?' he asked.

He couldn't see. But there was nothing wrong with his heart.

'I don't want to be a blind beggar,' he said. 'I want to see.'
And Jesus said, 'So be it then. Your faith has made you whole.'

And now there was nothing wrong.
    Not with his ears.
    Not with his mouth.
    Not with his head.
    Not with his heart.
    And not with his eyes either.
    Not any more!

Questions

1. Why does Jesus ask the beggar what he wants him to do?

2. Talk about the problems inherent in identifying a person solely by one particular infirmity. Or even by one characteristic or talent or experience.

The Ballad of a Little Man

(Luke 19:1–10)

Introduction

Apparently, in Middle Eastern societies, one is honoured not so much by being invited to the home of someone important as by having that someone accept an invitation to your house. This retelling of the story of Zacchaeus is built upon that premise, with the 'great and the good' of Jericho lined up to invite Jesus into their homes. I think it makes his decision to eat his supper with the diminutive tax collector even more outrageous and even more profound.

> **TELLING TIPS: I generally just read this on my own. But you might want to get some helpers to play Abraham and Nathaniel, and even someone small for Zacchaeus. They could just mime their parts (it will take a bit of practice). And as for the sycamore tree, well, you could always use a chair or a pew or a very tall deacon! Just check your insurance cover first!**

Abraham was the town butcher.
He stood tall. He was honest and kind.
He sold chicken and cow.
The folks loved it – and how!
(And he never touched fried bacon rind!)

But Zacchaeus was a wee little man,
And a wee little man was he.
He was hated and feared.
No one wanted him near.
He was Jericho's taxman, you see!

Nathaniel was the town baker.
A big man, with five strapping sons.
All Jericho slobbered
And globbered and drooled
At the smell of his freshly baked buns.

But Zacchaeus was a wee little man,
And a wee little man was he.
For a few pennies more
He'd cheat you for sure
He'd do anything to increase his fee.

Now the word went around
Old Jericho Town
That Jesus was coming for tea.
'Twas an honour, a treat
For this teacher to eat
At one's house – so they lined up to see.

'Come eat with me!'
Tall Abraham said.
'We'll have drumsticks and lamb chops and beef!'
But Jesus just smiled
And passed on through the crowd,
Leaving Abraham stricken with grief.

'To my house he'll come,'
Nathaniel explained
To those standing 'round, with a boast.
But when he was asked
Jesus wandered right past.
Nate's mood turned as black as burnt toast.

Many others came next.
I suppose that you've guessed –
Jesus said 'no' to each of them too.
In fact, he said 'nay'
To all good folk that day,
And shaded his eyes for a view.

Zacchaeus, meanwhile,
With a chimpanzee's style,
Had climbed up a sycamore tree.
He was just curious
But the crowd might get furious
If they saw him. So he hid there safely!

Jesus looked down,
Quite close to the ground,
And failed there to find his prey.
A rustle. A cry.
So Jesus looked high.
The branches were starting to sway.

'So that's where you're hiding,
You wee little man.
I'm hungry, and that's why I say:
Put your feet on the ground.
ZACCHAEUS, COME DOWN!
I'm eating at your house today.'

Zacchaeus was shocked.
And you could have knocked
The crowd over with a feather. And so,
Honoured and humbled,
He climbed down then stumbled
Homeward, with Jesus in tow.

The crowd muttered and moaned.
'A sinner!' they groaned.
'A scoundrel, a swindler, a swine!
It's a scandal, a curse.
It couldn't be worse!
Jesus sharing his bread and his wine.'

They talked all through tea.
What they said, no one knows.
No keyhole to hear or peep through.
But when they came out,

Jesus said, with a shout,
'Zacchaeus has now changed his view!'

'He's different, he's sorry.
He's forgiven. He's saved.
He's brand-spanking, fresh-smelling new.
He's still rather small.
But his heart's ten feet tall.
And now he will prove it to you.'

'To those that I've cheated,'
Said Zac with a smile,
'I'll pay back times two – no, times four!
And I've emptied my coffers.
I've got some great offers
For anyone out there who's poor.'

The people applauded.
They couldn't believe it.
'He's gentle and kind as a dove!'
Jesus said, with a grin.
'See, there's no one whose sin
Takes him out of the reach of my love.'

Questions

1. Why do you think Zacchaeus climbed the sycamore tree to get a glimpse of Jesus?

2. After Zacchaeus talks with Jesus, he gives away loads of his money. Did you do anything like that when you became a Christian? Not giving away money, necessarily, but doing something really obvious that showed the change that had taken place in your life. If not you, then perhaps you know someone else who did.

3. This isn't the only story in which Jesus shows a preference for associating with sinners over 'good' or 'religious' people. The Pharisees criticised him for this on several occasions. Do you think that Jesus had a problem with 'good' and 'religious' people? Do you think he does now? Why or why not?

Onward, Christian Soldiers

(Luke 23:33–34)

Introduction

There is a lot of ox-goring in this reading, and your own personal bovine might feel just a little bit beaten up as you read it. So feel free to add or delete according to your own preferences, prejudices and pet peeves.

TELLING TIPS: Again, one to do on your own – unless you'd like someone else to read the Bible passage at the start.

> When they came to the place called the Skull, there they crucified him, along with the criminals – one on his right, the other on his left... And they divided up his clothes by casting lots.

Each of the soldiers had a hand on the garment. And with the other hand, they rolled the dice.

'When I win the garment,' said the first soldier, 'I will build a great church. And the church will reach out to the young, to the poor, to the vulnerable and we will tell them exactly how to live. And if they do what their shepherds say – and I mean *exactly* what they say – then they will be allowed to wear the garment. And if they do not, the garment will be taken from them.'

'The garment is filthy,' said the second soldier. 'But God wants only the best for his people. The nicest suits, the flashiest cars, the best jobs, the biggest houses. So I will take the garment and wash it and tailor it and cover it with jewels. And only those who have the faith to name the garment will be able to claim it.'

'The garment is so old-fashioned,' said a third. 'But I have heard from God himself. And he told me that I must lead a part of my local fellowship away from the old garment and that we must put on new clothes.'

And now there were more hands and more voices and the rattling of many more dice.

'Only socialists can wear the garment,' cried the soldiers on the left.

'He who does not work, should not eat,' countered the soldiers on the right.

'Only those who sing choruses should wear the garment,' sang one group, accompanied by a five-piece band.

'Only those who sing hymns,' sang another in four-part harmony.

'Only those who manifest the gifts!'

'Only those who believe in the rapture!'

'Only Protestants.'

'Only Catholics.'

'Only Orthodox.'

'Only those who come to my house group at half-past seven on a Tuesday night.'

'Only those who will allow homosexuals to become bishops.'

'Only those who will not."

Only those who will eat my bread and drink my purple Kool-aid.'

So Jesus looked down at the soldiers. The Onward Christian Soldiers. His body was torn, his clothes divided.

And he said, 'Forgive them, Father, for they do not know what they are doing.'

Questions

1. What do you think are the disadvantages of division in the body of Christ? Are there any advantages? If so, what?

2. Is it realistic to expect every Christian to believe exactly the same thing? If not, then how do we live in unity (remember Jesus' prayer in John 17) in the midst of diversity?

3. Talk about a time when you came into contact with a Christian who, in spite of your own convictions, did not believe you were a Christian at all because of your differing beliefs. How did you deal with that?

A Death Rewound

(Luke 24:1–12, Matthew 28:8–10, John 20:14–18)

Introduction

I really like that scene in the first *Superman* movie where the Man of Steel sends the earth spinning backwards so he can bring the woman he loves back to life. It's something we've all wished for, I suppose – at one time or another. To rewind time and undo what we've done, or what's been done to someone we love. I know that, strictly speaking, resurrection is much more than that. It has a future, remaking, reshaping dimension that is so much more amazing than the hands ticking backwards on a clock. But when you compare the details of Jesus' crucifixion to his resurrection, that might be how it would appear to someone who was there – and who just wanted to see him again.

> **TELLING TIPS: Again, this is very much a solo reading. It would fit nicely at the start of an Easter service, or as a prelude to an Easter sermon.**

Mary Magdalene remembered.

How could she ever forget? The drawn face. The sunken eyes. The final breath. The moment he died. Then the thunder and the lightning and the shaking of the ground. The shaking of her shoulders and his mother's shoulders too as their tears mixed with the rain.

There was no rain now. But there were tears. Tears and dew and early morning mist, as she made her way slowly to the tomb. Suddenly, the ground began to shake, and she feared for a moment that it was happening all over again. And in a way – in a backwards kind of way – it was!

There was thunder and there was lightning, and the soldiers were terrified as they had been three days before. Then the tomb split open – wide open like the curtain in the temple – and all in a great rush, an angel told Mary and her friends that Jesus was alive. His face was shining bright and he had so much more to say. And perhaps the other women listened, but Mary Magdalene just looked. For there was only one face she wanted to see. And when at last she did see it, that other picture was erased for ever. This face was not drawn; it sported a wide and knowing smile. These eyes were not sunken; they burned bright with life and promise. And the breath he took to speak finished not with a goodbye, but with a warm and glad hello.

Jesus was alive! And even though he went away again, Mary remembered. Mary Magdalene remembered. How could she ever forget?

Questions

1. How do you think that 'resurrection' differs from a simple rewinding of the clock?

2. Talk about a time when you wished you could rewind some event in your life.

3. Have you ever watched someone die? Talk about how that felt and how it would feel to see that person alive again.

Three Men and a Fig Tree

(John 1:43–51)

Introduction

Sometimes it's the characters who help you find your way into a retelling. Sometimes it's the setting. In this case, it was both! The differences between the characters of Jesus, Nathanael and Philip are the key to understanding this passage. But the fig tree is pretty important, too! So I thought I'd wrap them up together in a kind of chorus to make that clear. This piece was originally written for a family service at the church across the street, so it works well across a wide age range.

TELLING TIPS: Divide your crowd into four groups: one for Jesus, one for Nathanael, one for Philip and one for the fig tree! Teach them the following actions before the story begins:

Jesus – arms wide open, in a welcoming gesture.
Nathanael – arms crossed in a defensive posture, suspicious look on his face.
Philip – waving, as if to say 'Come with me'.
Fig tree – arms as branches – either waving or fixed in a 'branchy', contorted manner.

Then, as you read the story, have each group do its motion in turn, during the 'Jesus, Nathanael, Philip and the fig tree' chorus lines.
    The other option, which is more chaotic (but also more fun!), is to teach everyone every motion and then point to a group when you say each name in the 'chorus', but do it randomly – so they never know what's coming! The only downside is that this might distract their attention from the rest of the reading. Probably not a good thing if you want them to actually remember the story! A milder version of this is to teach each group the fig tree motion,

only, and move that around, from group to group, during the 'chorus'.

Jesus said to Philip, 'Follow me!'
Jesus, Nathanael, Philip and the fig tree.
So Philip found his friend, sitting under a tree.

'We've found him, Nathanael! The one we've been waiting for!'
Jesus, Nathanael, Philip and the fig tree.
'The Messiah, promised by Moses and the prophets!'

'His name is Jesus – Jesus of Nazareth.'
Jesus, Nathanael, Philip and the fig tree.
Nathanael scoffed. He was a bit of a snob.

'Nothing good has ever come from Nazareth!'
Jesus, Nathanael, Philip and the fig tree.
'You'll see!' said Philip. 'Just come and see!'

So they left the fig tree and went to find Jesus.
Jesus, Nathanael, Philip and the fig tree.
And when Jesus saw them coming, he opened his arms.

'Nathanael!' he said. 'Nathanael, I know you!'
Jesus, Nathanael, Philip and the fig tree.
'You speak your mind. You mean what you say.'

'And when you see the truth, you want to embrace it.'
Jesus, Nathanael, Philip and the fig tree.
'A true Israelite – with nothing false about you.'

Nathanael was puzzled. 'But how do you know me?'
Jesus, Nathanael, Philip and the fig tree.
'We've never met. Not that I can recall.'

'I saw you,' said Jesus. 'Underneath the fig tree.'
Jesus, Nathanael, Philip and the fig tree.
'I saw you while Philip was on his way.'

Nathanael was amazed – amazed and astounded.
Jesus, Nathanael, Philip and the fig tree.
'Then you must be the Messiah – the Son of God!'

'Surprised?' said Jesus. 'We've only just started.'
Jesus, Nathanael, Philip and the fig tree.
'You'll see angels in heaven by the time we're done.'

So Nathanael followed Jesus, just like Philip.
Jesus, Nathanael, Philip and the fig tree.
And off they went. What adventures they had!
Jesus, Nathanael, Philip and the fig tree.

Questions

1. Nathanael didn't have a lot of respect for people who came from Nazareth. Is there a group of people you don't have a lot of respect for – or maybe whom you didn't respect once upon a time?

2. How do you feel about people like Nathanael – who speak their minds and mean what they say?

3. Philip needed to tell his friend Nathanael that he had met the Messiah. Talk about someone you know who needs to meet the Messiah too. Particularly someone who might be sceptical, as Nathanael was. What would convince that person that Jesus is who he says he is?

Water into Wine

(John 2:1–11)

Introduction

Just a bit of fun, this one. But it would make an entertaining introduction to a sermon or a lesson on Jesus' first miracle. If you like the tone of this piece, I'd also recommend 'Have a Jar on Me!', a Celtic rendition of the water-into-wine story by the Scottish band The Electrics. You can find it on their CD *Livin' It Up When I Die*.

TELLING TIPS: Divide your audience into four groups. Get one group to hum the first two lines of 'Here Comes the Bride'. Get the next group to sing the first line of 'Red, Red Wine' (either the Neil Diamond or UB40 version will do). Get the third group to sing 'Yes, We Have No Chardonnay' to the tune of 'Yes, We Have No Bananas' (You'll have to mangle 'Chardonnay' to get there – emphasis on the second syllable, please). And the last group can do a Jar-Jar Binks impersonation with their line, saying 'Me-sa Jar-Jar'.

Tell each group its cue:

1) 'wedding'
2) 'wine'
3) 'servants' and
4) 'jars'

You'll want to lead them the first few times, so cues have been provided within the text below for your benefit.

Jesus, his mother, Mary, and his disciples were invited to a wedding (*'Here Comes the Bride'*) in Cana of Galilee.

Everyone was having a wonderful time. And then they ran out of wine (*'Red, Red Wine'*).

So Jesus' mother took Jesus to one side.

'They've run out of wine *('Red, Red Wine')*' she said. 'Is there anything you can do?'

'Mother!' said Jesus. 'Why are you getting me involved? It's not time for me to do this kind of thing yet.'

But Mary took no notice and went to speak to the servants *('Yes, We Have No Chardonnay!')* 'See that fellow standing over there?' she said. 'That's my boy! Do whatever he tells you.'

Nearby, there were six large stone jars *('Me-sa Jar-Jar')*. They were used for ceremonial washing and held between twenty and thirty gallons of water each.

So Jesus said to the servants *('Yes, We Have No Chardonnay')*, 'Take those jars *('Me-sa Jar-Jar')* and fill them up with water.'

The servants *('Yes, We Have No Chardonnay')* did as they were told. And they filled the jars *('Me-sa Jar-Jar')* to the brim.

'Now draw some out,' said Jesus, 'and take it to the man in charge of the wedding *('Here Comes the Bride')*'.

So that's what they did. And when the man tasted it, the water had turned into wine *('Red, Red Wine')*!

Immediately, the man in charge of the wedding *('Here Comes the Bride')* went to the bridegroom.

'This is amazing,' he said. 'Most people serve the cheap stuff at the end of the feast, when everyone is too drunk to notice. But you have saved the best for last!'

And that is how Jesus performed his first miracle and showed his glory to his disciples.

He turned water into wine *('Red, Red Wine')*.

At a wedding *('Here Comes the Bride')*.

With the help of a few servants *('Yes, We Have No Chardonnay')*.

And six huge stone jars *('Me-sa Jar-Jar')*.

Questions

1. If it wasn't yet time for Jesus to reveal himself and do his miracles, why do you suppose he did it anyway?

2. Put yourself in Mary's place. What do you imagine was going on in her mind – what was she thinking and feeling – when she volunteered Jesus' 'services' at this wedding?

3. You might disagree with me here, and I might be skating on thin theological ice, but turning water into wine doesn't quite match up to making blind people see, stilling storms and raising the dead on the 'importance' scale – unless of course it's your family's wedding that looks like being ruined! And, even if it was your own wedding, you'd probably still rather have your mother's arthritis cured or your uncle's deafness healed, if you see what I mean. So what was the 'point' of this miracle? And why do you think it was included in the gospels?

The Woman at the Well

(John 4:1–26)

Introduction

I think it was John Ortberg who suggested that Jesus' sympathy with 'fallen' women might have had something to do with the suspicious nature of his own conception. This reading simply tries to bring that out. If the language is too rough for your particular group, feel free to soften it with other terms.

TELLING TIPS: It's important that you carry on quite naturally from this into the scripture passage, and that the passage is also read with a lot of feeling and understanding. At the conference where I first performed this, I read the first part and then had someone else do the Bible reading. You could just as easily do the whole thing on your own, but it might be helpful to pick up a Bible at the point where you start to read it, to make it clear that the first part is just an interpretation and not part of the text itself.

In Samaria, Jesus came to a town called Sychar. Jacob's well was there, and Jesus, tired out by his journey, sat down by the well.

It was about noon. And a Samaritan woman came to draw water. A Samaritan woman with a reputation. A Samaritan woman with five ex-husbands and one current live-in. A Samaritan woman who had to come looking for water in the hottest part of the day so she could be sure she was on her own.

Jesus looked into her eyes, and suddenly, he could see it all:

The gossiping neighbours.

The hostile stares.

The eyes at the windows.

And the whispering chorus of voices in the market.

'Slut! Slapper! Slag! Who does she think she is, parading herself round here?'

'Oh, I've heard some stories in my time, but this one takes the biscuit!'

'We know what she's been up to. We know what's been going on. She can't fool us.'

'It could be anybody's husband next.'

'Go on, get out of here! Get out, d'ya hear? And take that little bastard with you.'

'You heard us, Mary!

You heard us, Mary!

You heard us, Mary!

Get out!'

Jesus looked into her eyes, and he remembered it all. So he turned to the woman, and as tenderly as he knew how, he spoke.

Read John 4:7b–26.

Questions

1. So what do you think of the idea behind the reading – that Jesus understood, first hand, what it meant to be linked to someone with a questionable reputation?

2. List the social and religious conventions that Jesus violated when he spoke to the woman at the well.

3. Is there anyone you might be reluctant to speak to? Can you think of any contemporary situations that might pose a risk to you or to your reputation?

Another Woman at the Well

(John 4:1–30)

Introduction

This is another one of those story/song combos, but, in this case, I've already supplied a bluesy little tune for the chorus. It was the 'Well, well, well' that set me off in this direction in the first place, and I think it makes for a completely different way of telling a Bible story.

> **TELLING TIPS: Start by teaching your crowd the chorus. You can snap your fingers while you read the verses, or maybe even have a drummer do something light on a snare. Don't have the crowd do it, though – you'll never keep the beat throughout the whole of the reading! And hey, if you want to come up with a tune for the verses as well, you can just sing the whole thing.**

Well, well, well

Chorus:

Well, well, well.
Well, well, well.
Well, well, well.
Jesus met a woman at a well.

Jesus had to travel up north to Galilee;
Had to travel over hill and over dell.
He stopped for a rest in a place called Samaria
And there he met a woman at a well.

'I'm tired,' said Jesus. 'Could you give me a drink?
I've got a thirst that I really need to quell.'
'But your folk and my folk don't get along.
We shouldn't speak,' said the woman at the well.

Chorus:

Well, well, well.
Well, well, well.
Well, well, well.
Jesus met a woman at a well.

'If you knew who I was,' said Jesus with a grin,
'If you could even begin to tell,
You'd ask ME for water, for living water.'
'I'm confused,' said the woman at the well.

'Your water,' said Jesus, 'will quench my thirst.
Yet I'll be thirsty in an hour, as well.
But the water I give will quench your thirst for ever.'
'Gimme some!' said the woman at the well.

Chorus:

Well, well, well.
Well, well, well.
Well, well, well.
Jesus met a woman at a well.

'Go call your husband,' said Jesus to the woman.
Said the woman, 'I've no husband to tell.'
'That's right,' said Jesus. 'You've had five husbands
And you're living with a man, now, as well.'

The woman changed the subject. 'I believe that you're a prophet –
It's a fact that anyone could see or smell.
So tell me, should we worship at a temple or a mountain?
Tell me please,' said the woman at the well.

Chorus:

Well, well, well...

'A mountain or a temple, it doesn't really matter.
The time is coming when neither will excel.
But worship in truth and worship in spirit.
That's the Father's wish, O woman at the well.'

'The Messiah will set us all straight when he comes,'
Said the woman. 'Everything will be swell!'
'I'll let you in on a secret, you're looking at him, Sister!'
Said Jesus to the woman at the well.

Chorus:

Well, well, well...

So the woman went to town and announced to all her neighbours,
Her voice ringing clear as a bell.
'I just met the Messiah, he told me all I ever did.
And he was only sitting by the well!
And he was only sitting by the well!
And he was only sitting by the well!'

Chorus:

Well, well, well...

Questions

1. What do you suppose Jesus meant when he told the woman he could give her 'living water'? Why was she confused?

2. Why was the woman concerned about whether it was appropriate to worship on a mountain or in a temple?

3. What do you think it means to worship God in spirit and in truth?

A Word about Worship

(John 4:21–24)

Introduction

Yeah, I was in a bad mood when I wrote this one. I'd just finished a conversation with someone who had gone on and on about 'real worship', which really meant the worship tradition they were accustomed to as opposed to the worship traditions of other groups. I do get tired of that conversation and of explaining again and again that every tradition has those moments in its worship where God seems most present and most real. And that we simply need to respect that, even if it doesn't do the same for us. So I thought I'd write this piece and just pass it round the next time the subject comes up!

TELLING TIPS: This is one to tell on your own. But, depending on your group, and your background, you might want to change some of the references.

He hardly said a word about worship.
But we talk about it all the time.
'Oh, so you're not doing that song, yet?' (said in a faux compassionate, slightly condescending, mildly amused tone)
Or how about this one?
'So you're still using an overhead projector, are you?'

He hardly said a word about worship.
But we can't let it rest.
'Is your church "moving on"?'
'Is your worship Spirit led?'
'Are you doing things decently and in order?'
'Are you going deeper with the Lord?'

He hardly said a word about worship.
But we use it as a measuring rod. A whipping post.
Wesley, Sankey, Kendrick, Redman.
We do them all a disservice when we use them as the means by which we judge each other.

He hardly said a word about worship.
So does he care, does he really care if we're
Chanting with the Gregorians,
Harmonizing with the Victorians,
Or chuckling with the Canadians?

He hardly said a word about worship.
So how do we know which of the following statements are true?
Real worship is when the bell rings and the bread and wine become flesh and blood.
Real worship is when the guitar strikes 'that' chord and the hands go up in the air.
Real worship is when we reach the third verse of 'Just as I Am' and the crowds stream down to the altar.
Real worship is when we're singing in tongues.
Real worship is when the pastor raises his voice and wipes his forehead with his hankie and the congregation shouts 'amen' and 'hallelujah'.
Real worship is when we pray the 'Our Father'.
Real worship is when we sit and just wait for the Spirit to move.
Real worship is when we reach that point in the creed where it says ' … world without end'.

He hardly said a word about worship.
Except for this.

> A time is coming when you will worship the Father neither on a mountain in Samaria nor in Jerusalem. A time is coming and has now come when the true worshippers will worship the Father in spirit and truth, for they are the kind of worshippers the Father seeks.

Samaria or Jerusalem?
Prayer meetings or high mass?

Mountains or temples?
Choruses or hymns?
Like the Jews and the Samaritans, we're still stuck on style.
When all he cares about is substance.

He hardly said a word about worship.
'A time is coming,' he said, 'and has now come.'
But I've had a good look around, and much as I hate to disagree,
I don't think the time has come yet.

(Alternative ending)

He hardly said a word about worship.
So maybe the time has come
To keep quiet about our differences
And be content with what he said.

Questions

1. A colleague of mine observed quite wryly, one time, that God seemed to make his presence known at our services only after we had sung two fast songs and two slow ones! I know exactly what he meant, and I figure you do, too. In your tradition, when is God 'supposed' to show up? When does 'real worship' happen for you? Talk about an occasion when God showed up at the 'wrong' time!

2. Talk about a time when you met God in a worship setting that was unfamiliar to you – which was outside and maybe even far removed from your own tradition. Discuss both the advantages and the disadvantages of worshipping outside your tradition.

3. One could argue that the moment when 'real worship' happens is just a matter of 'button-pushing' – the right song sequence, the right moment in the liturgy, the right prayer. Is that a fair assessment, or a natural consequence of having a tradition at all? What can worship leaders do to avoid 'manipulating' a group? And how does all this fit with those very few words Jesus said about worshipping God in spirit and in truth?

I Am the Bread

(John 6:1–15, 25–29; Luke 24:13–35)

Introduction

This reading would make a nice introduction to any of the stories it references, or perhaps even an effective Communion meditation.

> **TELLING TIPS: Not much for the crowd to do here. Maybe you could have them 'mumble and grumble' and 'groan and moan' at the appropriate places! Otherwise, it might be best just to read it on your own.**

Verse 1:

There was no bread on the mountain.
On the mountain there was no bread.
Only groaning bellies,
And grumbling tummies,
And one little lad who was willing
To share his McDonalds 'Filet o'Fish Happy Meal'.

So Jesus took the bread rolls.
And Jesus took the fish.

'Here is the bread!' he said.
He said, 'Here is the bread.'
And he spoke a prayer and broke it.
And every belly was full.

Verse 2:

There was no bread at the seaside.
At the seaside there was no bread.
Only moaning crowds,
And mumbling Pharisees,
Who wanted to see
An all-singing, all-dancing miracle show.

'Our fathers ate bread in the desert!' they cried.
'What kind of sign will shine from you?'

So Jesus looked at the crowd.
Then Jesus shook the crowd.

'I am the bread!' he said.
He said, 'I am the bread.
And if you swallow me and follow me,
Then you will live for ever!'

Verse 3:

There was no bread on the road to Emmaus.
On the road, there was no bread.
Just a long sad walk
And a stranger who talked
As if he knew nothing of the death of their friend.

So when Cleopas and his friend
Arrived at last at their home
They urged the stranger to stop and have some tea.

The stranger broke the bread
And he spoke a prayer, as well.

'Thanks for the bread,' the stranger said.
The stranger said, 'Thanks for the bread.'
Their eyes were opened.
They knew who he was!
And like a ghost or a phantom

Or an English summer sun,
He disappeared at once from their sight.

Verse 4:

So here we are – traipsing up life's mountain.
Here we are – simply sailing life's sea.
Here we are – in the middle of life's journey,
A long, long way from home.

Walking and talking,
Groaning and moaning,
Grumbling and mumbling,
And fumbling together for... what?

A bit of sunshine?
A MacDonald's 'Happy Meal'?
An all-singing, all-dancing miracle show?
Or a life that's worth living,
Maybe worth living for ever?

'I am the bread,' says Jesus.
He says, 'I am the bread.
Walk with me. Talk with me.
Swallow Me. Follow me.
Come and taste and live.'

Questions

1. What did Jesus mean when he referred to himself as 'The Bread' in this reading?

2. In what sense is Jesus 'The Bread' for you?

A Walk on the Water

(John 6:16–21)

Introduction

Here's another of those three-line repetition retellings. I think this format works especially well with really active stories, so you need to do it with a lot of enthusiasm. Make the actions really 'big' and just have some fun with this one!

> **TELLING TIPS: Teach your group these sounds and actions before you do the story.**
>
> 'Splash!' (Throw hands up in air, palms out, to represent water splashing up.)
> 'Alas!' (Put the back of your hand to your forehead.)
> 'Crash!' (Make a big and noisy crashing sound.)
> 'Dash!' (Run on the spot.)
> 'Mash!' (Make a potato mashing motion.)
> 'Rash.' (Rub arms like you've got an itchy rash.)
> 'Flash!' (Make a speedy motion with head and body, as if something just flashed past.)
>
> **Do each line three times, so that the story is reinforced and also so that the people have time to catch onto the actions and have more fun with them.**

Jesus' disciples got into a boat.
Jesus' disciples got into a boat.
Jesus' disciples got into a boat.
And set off across the lake. *(Splash!)*
And set off across the lake. *(Splash!)*
And set off across the lake. *(Splash!)*

It turned dark, but Jesus wasn't with them.
It turned dark, but Jesus wasn't with them.
It turned dark, but Jesus wasn't with them.
He missed the boat. (Alas!)
He missed the boat. (Alas!)
He missed the boat. (Alas!)

Then the high winds started to blow.
Then the high winds started to blow.
Then the high winds started to blow.
And the waves fell down with a crash. *(Crash!)*
And the waves fell down with a crash. *(Crash!)*
And the waves fell down with a crash. *(Crash!)*

So they started to row – to get through the storm.
So they started to row – to get through the storm.
So they started to row – to get through the storm.
It was a three-and-a-half-mile dash! *(Dash!)*
It was a three-and-a-half-mile dash! *(Dash!)*
It was a three-and-a-half-mile dash! *(Dash!)*

That's when they saw Jesus – walking on the water!
That's when they saw Jesus – walking on the water!
That's when they saw Jesus – walking on the water!
And their legs turned soft like mash. *(Mash!)*
And their legs turned soft like mash. *(Mash!)*
And their legs turned soft like mash. *(Mash!)*

'Don't be afraid,' said Jesus. 'It's me!'
'Don't be afraid,' said Jesus. 'It's me!'
'Don't be afraid,' said Jesus. 'It's me!'
'Please don't do anything rash.' *(Rash.)*
'Please don't do anything rash.' *(Rash.)*
'Please don't do anything rash.' *(Rash.)*

So they welcomed Jesus into the boat.
So they welcomed Jesus into the boat.
So they welcomed Jesus into the boat.
And they reached the farther shore in a flash. *(Flash!)*

And they reached the farther shore in a flash. *(Flash!)*
And they reached the farther shore in a flash. *(Flash!*

Questions

1. What are the differences between this account of Jesus walking on the water and the one where Peter joins him? Is there a different lesson to be learned from each?

2. Talk about a time when your life got 'stormy' and inviting Jesus into your 'boat' made a difference.

Scribbling in the Sand

(John 8:1–11)

Introduction

What did Jesus write on the ground? That's the question, isn't it? The question that has always accompanied this story. I don't know. I don't suppose anyone does. But there have been lots of guesses. And this is mine.

> **TELLING TIPS: It might be nice to do this reading with a few other people. Someone could stand in for the man, who then slips away at the appropriate moment. A few others could be the religious leaders, who also leave. And then someone could be the woman. At one conference where I did this story, we had a simple red ribbon slung round her shoulder that the reader gently removed at the word 'forgiven'. The participants would all need to be chosen beforehand, I think, and given the time for a little practice, to make the performance most effective. Otherwise, it would also work well if you just told it on your own.**

At dawn Jesus appeared again in the temple courts, where all the people gathered around him, and he sat down to teach them. The teachers of the law and the Pharisees brought in a woman caught in adultery. They made her stand before the group and said to Jesus:

'Teacher, this woman was caught in the act of adultery. In the Law Moses commanded us to stone such women. Now what do you say?' They were using this question as a trap, in order to have a basis for accusing him. But Jesus bent down and started to write on the ground with his finger.

'Forsaken.' That's what he wrote. And much more besides. 'Forsaken. Abandoned. Just a plaything, if you're honest. You told her that you loved her, that you would leave your wife for her, that no one in this world meant more than her. But when push came to shove, when your unfaithfulness was exposed, you ran away and left her to her fate. If you were the man you said you were, the man she thought you were, you would be here now, beside her. But you weren't and you aren't. Because she was just a bit of fun, and this is just a lucky escape.'

At the sight of these words, a man, hiding behind a pillar, slipped away from the crowd and out of the temple courts. But the teachers of the law and the Pharisees refused to let up.

When they kept on questioning him, Jesus straightened up and said to them, 'If any one of you is without sin, let him be the first to throw a stone at her.' Again he stooped down and wrote on the ground.

And what he wrote was 'Forgotten.' 'Forgotten' and so much more. 'You're old, now, I know – respectable religious leaders. But have you forgotten? Forgotten your past? One of you was a stallion, once – spreading yourself all over town. One of you has a mistress, still. One of you is wealthy only because of a shady deal that ruined the business of another one of you! One of you knows and is seeking revenge. One of you spends far too much time with little boys. One of you...'

At this, those who heard began to go away one at a time, the older ones first, until only Jesus was left, with the woman still standing there. Jesus straightened up and asked her, 'Woman, where are they? Has no one condemned you?'

'No one, sir.' She said.

'Then neither do I condemn you,' Jesus declared. 'Go now and leave your life of sin.'

So the woman went. But before she did, she looked again at the ground. And now, somehow, there was only one word. One word and nothing more.

Not 'Forsaken'.

Not 'Forgotten'.

Just 'Forgiven'.

Questions

1. So what do you think of my 'guess'? It's not original, of course, though I'll take a little credit for 'forsaken, forgotten, and forgiven'! But what else might Jesus have written there?

2. Talk about an experience in which you learned something about not casting the first stone.

3. I have this theory that, while everybody wants grace, not everyone is so free when it comes to giving it away. Why do you think that is so?

I Am the Good Shepherd – Three Sheep Stories

(John 10:1–21)

Introduction

This is one of my favourites! It's another reading built around Jesus' 'I Am' sayings in the Gospel of John. You can either do the reading as a whole to introduce a sermon, or weave it into the sermon, commenting on the passage after each section. It could also be the framework for a whole service, with songs and prayers and brief comments between each section.

> **TELLING TIPS: This one is both simple and fun! You say the 'And (all of) the people' line first – 'And all of the people said, "Baa!"'. Say it with as much enthusiasm as you can. And the crowd just repeat 'Baa' after you, in the same way you did it! Practise one of the lines with them, before you start the story – just so it's clear where they come in. But don't give the rest of the lines away. It will spoil the surprise!**

The Sheep Thief

'I've got something to say about sheep,' said Jesus.
And all of the people said, *'Baaa!'*

'Let's start with the sheep thief,' said Jesus. 'That rotten, no-good rustler!'
And all of the people said, *'Boo!'*

'How does the sheep thief get into the pen?' asked Jesus. 'Not through the gate, that's for sure. He creeps over the wall, in the dead of night, when nobody else is looking.'

And all of the people said, '*Sneaky!*'

'And what is he there for?' asked Jesus. 'I'll tell you – he's up to no good. He has knives and shears and lashings of mint sauce. He comes to steal and to kill and to destroy.'
And all of the people said, '*Nasty!*'

'But the shepherd,' said Jesus, 'the shepherd is different!'
And all of the people said, '*How?*'

'He comes through the gate,' said Jesus. 'The right way. The proper way. The honest way. And he comes not to kill, but to lead the sheep to pastures green and gently flowing waters.'
And all of the people said, '*Nice!*'

'I am the Gate of the sheep pen,' said Jesus.
And all of the people said, '*Huh?*'

'I am the Gate!' said Jesus. 'I'll protect you from anything and anyone that sneaks in to steal your joy. And if you go through me, you'll find life and find it to the full.'

The Stranger

'Now let's talk about strangers,' said Jesus.
And the people said, '*You should never talk to strangers!*'

'Exactly!' said Jesus. 'And every sheep knows that. If a stranger calls, the sheep will not follow, because they do not recognize his voice.'
And the people said, '*That's smart!*'

'But the shepherd,' said Jesus, 'the shepherd is different.'
And all of the people said, '*How?*'

'The sheep recognize his voice,' said Jesus. 'And they follow him wherever he goes. And he knows them, too. Knows each of them by name!'
And the people said, '*That's lovely!*'

'I am the Good Shepherd,' said Jesus. 'And I know my sheep, too. There are some of you here, and others I have yet to meet. And I know you all by name.'

The Hired Hand

'And finally,' said Jesus, 'let's talk about the hired hand.'
And all of the people said, *'Show me the money!'*

'That's it!' said Jesus. 'The hired hand is in it only for what he can get. It's not the sheep that are important to him – it's the pay cheque and what he can buy with it.'
And the people said, *'Bling-bling.'*

'So when the wolf comes,' said Jesus, 'what does he do? He runs away, to save his own skin.'
And the people said, *'It's more than his job's worth!'*

'But the shepherd,' said Jesus, 'the shepherd is different.'
And all of the people said, *'How?'*

'The sheep belong to the shepherd,' said Jesus. 'Each and every one of them is special to him. So when the wolf comes, he faces it and fights it off. He risks life and limb. And if he has to, he lays down his life for his sheep.'
And all of the people said, *'Wow!'*

'I am the Good Shepherd,' said Jesus. 'And I lay down my life for you.'

Questions

1. So 'who' or 'what' are the 'sheep thieves'? How does Jesus – the Gate – protect us from them?

2. And who is 'the stranger'? And how do we recognise the Good Shepherd's voice in a world of voices?

3. And, finally, who do you suppose Jesus thought were the 'hired hands'? Do we need to worry about hired hands today?

What a Meal!

(Matthew 26:6–13)

Introduction

This is a short reading, but it's punchy, too – and needs to be delivered that way.

What a meal!

Jesus was eating dinner at the home of a man named Simon. His friends were eating there, too.

What a shock!

Suddenly a woman burst into the room. There were tears in her eyes as she headed straight for Jesus. She might have been someone he'd healed. She might have been someone he'd forgiven. Nobody knows for sure. But whatever the reason, she broke open a little bottle of perfume and let it spill over Jesus' head.

What a smell!

The room was filled with it. And everyone around that table knew that this was expensive perfume. Very expensive, indeed!

'What a waste!' cried Jesus' friends. And his friend Judas, who kept track of all their money, cried loudest of all.

'We could have sold that perfume,' said Jesus' friends, 'and given the money to the poor.' Or kept it for ourselves, thought Judas. But Jesus would have none of it.

'What a gift!' said Jesus. 'What a gift this woman has given. To care for the poor is important – yes. There will always be opportunities for that. But this woman can see that there's not much time left to do something special for me. And because of that – I promise you – her act of generosity will never be forgotten.'

What a promise!

Questions

1. What is the most expensive thing you have ever given to someone? Why did you do it?

2. Is Jesus being dismissive of the needs of the poor? Is he being selfish, thinking about what the woman's gift means to him? Or is Jesus, maybe, just that bit more flexible than we are – looking beyond 'rules' to the needs of a given situation?

3. What costly thing would you give to Jesus – as an honest expression of your gratitude to him?

His Towel

(John 13:1–17)

Introduction

My friend Mark was being ordained into the ministry and asked me to kick off the service with a reading of some kind. This is for him.

TELLING TIPS: Definitely one to just read on your own.

1. The Lord said, 'Go and preach the word.'
   I asked him, 'Tell me how.'
   He reached into his toolbox
   And handed me a Trowel.

   'It's Living Stones you're working with.
   A Living Message, too.
   Be careful not to chip and gouge
   When you cement the two.'

   The Lord said, 'Go and preach the word.'
   I asked him, 'Tell me how.'
   He reached into his toolbox
   And handed me a Trowel.

2. The Lord said, 'Go and preach the word.'
   I asked him, 'Tell me how.'
   He spoke to Carol Vordeman
   And she handed me a Vowel.

   '"I"s the one that you'll prefer.
   "I" want. "I" know. "I" say.

But "U" will make a better choice.
"U" reign. "U" have your way.'

The Lord said, 'Go and preach the word.'
I asked him, 'Tell me how.'
He spoke to Carol Vordeman
And she handed me a Vowel.

3. The Lord said, 'Go and preach the word.'
   I asked him, Tell me how.'
   He placed a basin at my feet.
   And reached for an old Towel.

'I'll wash you, make you clean and new,
I'll serve you best I can.
And then you do the same
For those I place into your hand.'

The Lord said, 'Go and preach the word.'
I asked him, 'Tell me how.'
He washed me, made me clean and new,
Then handed me his Towel.

Questions

1. So what are the dangers of chipping and gouging associated with cementing 'message' and 'stone'?

2. Particularly when it comes to leading a congregation, how do we keep the balance between those two vowels?

3. What does the towel stand for? Talk about a time when you experienced the touch of someone's towel.

Songs in Search of a Tune: God with a Towel

(John 13:1–17)

Introduction

Here's another song looking for a tune. But it would work nicely just as a reading as well – in the midst of a passion-week Communion service or as a response to a sermon on Jesus washing his disciples feet.

TELLING TIPS: One to read on your own.

You are the King of Glory,
You are the Holy One,
You are the promised Messiah,
Jesus the Saviour, God's only Son.
So why did you leave your home in heaven
Where angels and archangels kneel and bow
To wipe clean this dirty mess of a world?
You are the God with a towel!

You are the Lion of Judah,
You are the Bright Morning Star,
You are the First and the Last,
The Living One forever more.
So why are your hands dipped in dirty water?
Why are you kneeling before me now?
Why are you washing the feet of this sinner?
You are the God with a towel!

You are the King of Glory,
You are the Holy One,
You are the promised Messiah,
Jesus the Saviour, God's only Son.
So why does your side drip with blood and water?
Why are you dying before me now?
Wash me and make me clean all over –
You are the God with a towel!

Questions

1. How does the idea of 'a God with a towel' set Jesus apart from the gods of other faiths, old and new?

2. How, on the whole, would you rate Christians as being 'a people of the towel'?

3. What keeps us from picking up Jesus' towel? Talk about someone you know who exemplifies this 'towel' thing. Discuss practical ways in which you could be more of a 'towel' person.

I Am the Way

(John 14)

Introduction

Here's another 'I am' retelling. It would work nicely as an introduction to a sermon on John 14, or even at the start of a 'worship' time.

TELLING TIPS: This is one to read on your own.

'I'm going to my Father,' said Jesus to his friends.
Said Jesus, 'I'm going away.
But there are rooms in his house,
More rooms than you can count,
And I promise to take you there, one day.'

'But how will we get there?' asked Jesus' friend Thomas.
Said Thomas, 'Show us, we pray.
Don't leave us alone.
We don't know where you're going!
So how can we know the way?'

'I am the Way,' said Jesus to his friends.
Said Jesus, 'I am the Way.
The Father's Life
And the Father's Truth
Is in all I do and say.'

'Then show us the Father!' said Jesus' friend Philip.
Said Philip, 'Then all will be well!'
'If you've seen me,' said Jesus,

'You've seen him, too!
We've been together for years, can't you tell?'

'I'm in the Father,' said Jesus to his friends.
Said Jesus, 'He's in me, too.
In the words I say,
In the stories I tell,
In the miracles you've seen me do.'

'You will not be orphans,' said Jesus to his friends.
Said Jesus, 'You won't be alone.
My Father will send you
Another companion
So you will not be on your own.'

'His Spirit will live within you,' said Jesus.
Said Jesus, 'Within you he'll be.
Then we'll all be one,
Father, Spirit, Son –
Together for eternity.'

Questions

1. Why do you think Jesus' disciples were confused about where he was going?

2. In what ways do we see the Father in Jesus?

3. How does Jesus use this very brief coversation to prepare his disciples for his departure? Specifically, what kind of hope is he giving them?

I Am the Vine –
A Communion Meditation

(John 15)

Introduction

One more 'I Am'! And, as the title suggests, this one makes a very nice Communion meditation.

'I am the vine,' said Jesus to his friends.
He said, 'I am the vine.
And my Father? My Father tends the vineyard.
He strims and trims,
He grooms and prunes,
And shapes each grape-bearing branch.'

'I am the vine,' said Jesus to his friends.
He said, 'I am the vine.
And you? You are the branches.
Let me flow in you.
Let me grow in you.
And we will make grapes together.'

'Here is the wine,' said Jesus to his friends.
He said, 'Here is the wine.
It pours out just like blood.
Drink of me – when you come together.
Think of me – and never forget
That love gives up its life for a friend.'

'I am the vine,' said Jesus.
'Here is the wine,' said Jesus.
'I live my life,
I give my life
For you.'

Questions

1. What does Jesus mean when he says that God grooms and prunes and trims the branches? Talk about a time when you believed that God was doing that with you.

2. How do we let Jesus flow and grow in us?

3. What kind of grape do you think Jesus is talking about? What, specifically, is the fruit he wants to bear in us?

Jesus Looks Down

(John 19)

Introduction

A year ago, I was asked to do a retelling of the crucifixion story with a very large group of children and adults. It needed to have a lot of participation and yet communicate the solemnity and sense of that event. There's always the risk, with participation in a serious story, of something unexpected happening, or of giggles at just the wrong time. So I chose four really simple actions and hoped they would keep us all active and together and bring us into the heart of the story. I think it worked.

> **TELLING TIPS: You will need to ask your group to stand and drape their arms over the shoulders of the people standing next to them. You need to stretch your arms out too – as if you were Jesus on the cross. Then simply ask them to look 'up' and 'down' and 'right' and 'left' with you, when you do. When you reach that point in the text, ask them to close their eyes with you as well.**

JESUS LOOKS DOWN (Look down.)

There are people down there who want him dead.

The Roman soldiers who nailed his hands and his feet to this wooden cross, and are gambling for what little he has left in this world.

And the religious leaders too – laughing their heads off and making fun of him.

'You thought you were somebody special.'

'You thought you knew better than us.'

'Well, just look at you now.'

JESUS LOOKS RIGHT (Look right.)

There's a thief hanging on the cross next to him. And his words are filled with hate as well.

'You saved other people – the blind, the sick, the lame. So why can't you save yourself – and me with you?'

JESUS LOOKS LEFT (Look left.)

There's another thief hanging there. But his words are very different.

'Leave him alone!' croaks the second thief to the first. 'We're here because we deserve it. But this man has done nothing wrong.'

And then he looks Jesus in the eye. 'Take me with you, please – to a better place when I die.'

And Jesus looks back. And nods. And says, 'Today you will be with me in Paradise.'

AND THEN JESUS LOOKS DOWN AGAIN (Look down.)

His mum is standing there.
His mum – who talked to an angel
            and had a baby in a stable
            and watched that baby grow into a man
            and turn water into wine
            and talk to thousands at a time
            and now stands there watching him die.
There are tears in her eyes. And so Jesus calls to his friend.

'John,' he says. And it hurts so much to talk. 'Take care of my mum for me, please. Just as if she was your mum too.'

AND FINALLY JESUS LOOKS UP (Look up.)

The sky is dark. The rain is falling. It's as if there are tears in his Father's eyes too.

'I've done what you asked me,' he says to God. 'I've told them about you. I've showed them how to live. And now, with my death, I'm taking away all the bad things anyone will ever do. It's finished. It's over. It's done.'

AND THEN JESUS CLOSES HIS EYES (Close your eyes.)

And, for you and for me, he dies.

Questions

1. What else do you think Jesus saw when he looked down?

2. Have you ever had to say goodbye to someone you loved – someone who was dying? What kinds of thing did you say? What do wish you'd said?

3. Use one word to describe how you think Jesus felt as he hung there on the cross.

Make the Wind Blow

(Acts 2)

Introduction

I don't often do requests, but when a friend asked me if I had a reading for Pentecost that might work in an all-age service, and I didn't – I figured it was time to put something together. I've used it loads of times, ever since. And it always goes down well. So thanks, Tony!

> **TELLING TIPS: You need to teach the chorus before you begin. I have included the actions in the text. At the end, I always repeat the chorus at least twice. Or even three times. And then slow it down for emphasis on the final 'Take the words from your lips and put them on our lips and speak them out to the whole of the world'. I think it just helps to make Pentecost really personal.**

Jesus' friends were watching and praying.
Praying for the present that he had promised.
Praying together in the city of Jerusalem.
Praying on the Feast of Pentecost.

Jesus' friends were watching and praying
When all of a sudden, their prayers were answered.
They heard the roar of a rushing wind.
And tongues of fire licked their heads.

Make the wind blow. (Wave hands like the wind.)
Make the fire glow. (Make shape with hands like fire.)
Take the words from your lips (Pretend to touch God's lips.)
And put them on our lips (Touch own lips.)
And speak them out to the whole of the world. (Make shape of world.)

Jesus' friends were watching and praying
When the Holy Spirit came upon them
Filled them, thrilled them and spilled right out of them
With words they did not know.

'What's going on?' asked the people of Jerusalem.
'What can this possibly mean?
These are plain Galileans, ordinary folk,
Speaking words they could never have learned.'

Make the wind blow.
Make the fire glow.
Take the words from your lips
And put them on our lips
And speak them out to the whole of the world.

'We come from the north, the south, and the east.
We come from all over the world!
Yet we all understand the things that they say
As they tell out the wonders of God.'

But some of the crowd were not so impressed.
Some even said they were drunk!
And that's when Peter, Jesus' friend,
Stood up and put them right.

Make the wind blow.
Make the fire glow.
Take the words from your lips
And put them on our lips
And speak them out to the whole of the world.

'Filled with wine?' he said. 'Not likely!
But we're filled with something else!
Filled with God's own Holy Spirit –
The power the prophets promised.'

'And how did this happen?' asked Peter.
'I'll tell you plain and true.

This is the gift of Jesus, the Messiah,
Whom you killed just six weeks ago!'

Make the wind blow.
Make the fire glow.
Take the words from your lips
And put them on our lips
And speak them out to the whole of the world.

The people were sorry, sad and ashamed.
And they cried, 'What can we do?'
'Repent and be baptized,' said Peter plainly.
And this gift will come to you!'

So the people repented, the people were baptized.
Three thousand people – or so!
And the word spread from there to the rest of Judea
And on to the rest of the world!

Make the wind blow.
Make the fire glow.
Take the words from your lips
And put them on our lips
And speak them out to the whole of the world.

Questions

1. Do you think that Jesus' friends had any idea of what was going to happen when the present he promised them arrived? How do you think you would have reacted if you had been in the room that day?

2. Some people in the crowd that day thought that the disciples were drunk. Talk about a time when you thought you saw God do something amazing, and somebody else just scoffed at it.

3. Talk about your experience of the Holy Spirit.

Barnabas

(Acts 9:1–31)

Introduction

I think I wrote this for a family service on the theme of 'friendship' and 'encouragement'.

TELLING TIPS: Divide your crowd into two groups – one on one side of the room, the other on the other side. One group can be Saul's friends before he became a Christian. The other group can be the Christians. Choose someone to 'play' Saul. And you can be Barnabas!

Start the story with Saul standing among or in front of his non-Christian friends. ('Among' makes the point of the story clearer, but it does make Saul's movement from one side to the other a little trickier. Do what's best in your set-up.) Tell them that they are to pat him on the back (those who can reach him!) and cheer him when they hear the word 'friends' and turn their backs on him and boo when they hear the words 'not his friends'. You will need to lead them in this. When Saul gets rejected by his non-Christian friends, have him move to the 'Christian' side, and then have them cheer and boo on cue as well. When the Christians reject him too, move Saul (who is, of course, Paul by now!) to the middle of the room where he is standing alone. And then you come in as Barnabas (cheering him on and never booing!) and take him back to the Christians.

Saul had lots of friends *(Cheer – pat on back)* in Jerusalem.

He was clever, and well spoken, and very religious.

He didn't like Christians much, though. He thought they were wrong to believe that Jesus was God's own special Son. So he spent a lot of time chasing them, and arresting them and chucking them into prison.

And that made him even more popular with his friends *(Cheer – pat on back)*.

Then, one day, Saul went to Damascus. He was looking to arrest even more Christians. But along the way, he met Jesus in a vision, and his life was changed for ever. Not to mention his name – which turned from Saul to Paul.

He became a Christian himself. He was baptized. And he went round Damascus telling people about Jesus. As you can imagine, his old friends *(Cheer – pat on back)* were not his friends *(Boo – turn away)* any more. In fact, they wanted to kill him.

So Paul went back to Jerusalem, hoping to find some new friends *(Cheer – pat on back)* among the Christians. But the Christians were still afraid of him and did not trust him – so they were not his friends *(Boo – turn away)* either.

Paul was truly alone now. And then a man called Barnabas went to see him. He was a Christian. He was very generous. His name meant 'Son of Encouragement'. And 'encouraging' is exactly what he did.

He went to Paul and said, 'I'll be your friend.' *(Cheer – pat on back)*. Then he took Paul to meet the Christians. He told them how Paul had seen Jesus on the way to Damascus and how much his life had changed. So the Christians agreed to be Paul's friends *(Cheer – pat on back)* too.

And that is how the man with no friends *(Everybody: Boo – turn away)* suddenly had more friends *(Everybody: Cheer – pat on back)* than he could count!

Questions

1. Talk about a time when friends turned their backs on you. Why did it happen? How did it feel? Did it have anything to do with a change of beliefs?

2. Paul had trouble being accepted by the Christian community. Why do you think they were reluctant to accept him? Do you think their reasons were justified? If one of your relatives or friends had been imprisoned by Paul, how

would you have felt about him? And are there any kinds of people that the church has difficulty accepting today?

3. Talk about someone who has been a Barnabas for you. How can we be more like Barnabas in the way that we treat others?

A New Menu

(Acts 10–11)

Introduction

At a conference I attended a couple of years ago, the theme was 'Singing the Lord's song in a foreign land'. In the mornings we looked at Daniel's experience, and in the evenings we examined the way the early church introduced Jesus to a culture that had never heard of him. The readings were all from the book of Acts, and I thought that it would be interesting to retell them as if the early church were literally singing a 'new song' into a world filled with other tunes. This first reading deals with Peter's realisation that the song isn't the only thing that's changed. The 'menu' has, too!

TELLING TIPS: When I did the reading at the conference, I had someone sing the Barbra Streisand lines and would have had someone sing the Dylan lines as well – but I couldn't find anyone with just the right nasal inflection! Ideally, it would be great to have both – sitting off on the side, as a bit of a surprise. But if you don't have the singers, just read the lines, or have someone else do them. Some people also feel more comfortable reading the scripture passage first. I think it depends on how well you think your group will know the story. If they don't, the reading won't make much sense to them, so let that be your guide.

Peter shut his eyes. And the next thing he knew, he was sitting at a table at *The Restaurant of the Holy Ghost*. The waiter looked vaguely familiar – Robert Powell one minute, Jim Caviezel the next, with just a hint of Graham Chapman. But when he picked up one of those little white towels and draped it over his arm, Peter knew for sure.

'We'll talk later,' the waiter winked, as he showed him the wine list and put a bread roll on his plate.

Peter picked up a menu and breathed a relieved sigh. Every item was kosher. This was obviously a good Jewish place. And that's when someone started playing the piano, and Barbra Streisand stepped up to the mike. Peter hoped that she would sing something from *Funny Girl*, but he wasn't disappointed when she chose a tune from another film, instead.

Memories light the corners of my mind.
Misty watercolour memories of the way we were.

The waiter returned and winked at Peter again and then plucked the menu right out of his hands.

'There's been a change,' he explained. And then he set before Peter a simple white sheet of paper, with a new list of entrées scrawled in a hurried hand.

Scattered pictures of the smiles we left behind,
Smiles we gave to one another for the way we were.

Barbra might have been smiling, but Peter wasn't. And even though he was starving, his stomach did somersaults at the sight of his new set of choices.

'Stuffed pork chops on a bed of mustard mash.

Scallops wrapped with bacon.

Rabbit stew.

Curried camel.

Breast of horned owl with a raspberry coulis.'

'Excuse me,' said Peter, waving his hand in the direction of the waiter. 'There's nothing on this menu I can eat.'

'Nonsense,' smiled the waiter. 'I can assure you that everything there has been prepared to the finest standards. Choose. Eat. I'm sure you'll like whatever you have.'

'But you don't understand,' Peter went on. 'I've only ever eaten what's kosher. Nothing unclean or impure has ever entered my mouth.'

'I understand very well,' the waiter answered. 'There's been a change. And if I say that the new menu is good, then you can trust me. Choose. Eat. And you will see.'

And now there was a different song playing in the background. A new song. Barbra was gone, and some stubbly-faced guy named Zimmerman was stabbing at a guitar and croaking out a folk song.

The line it is drawn, the curse it is cast,
The slow one now will later be fast
As the present now will later be past,
The order is rapidly fading,
And the first one now will later be last
For the times they are a-changing.

Peter opened his eyes. There were three men at his door. So he went with them to the house of a Gentile named Cornelius. And when he started to tell him about Jesus, the Holy Spirit came on the whole household, just like it had come on Peter. If God has given them the same gift as he gave us, thought Peter, then who am I to oppose him? So he baptized them there and then in the name of Jesus. And as the family went down into the water, Peter swore he could smell something – roast owl and raspberry coulis. This new menu was going to take some getting used to. And there was no question that he would have some explaining to do – to his friends back in Jerusalem. But as he hummed the new song he'd heard in his dream, Peter was certain of one thing – the waiter would be winking. He'd approve of this choice.

For the times they are a-changing.

_____

Questions

1. What is the biggest change you had to deal with when you became a Christian and started singing a new song? And have there been other changes along the way?

2. Why do you suppose it took a vision to get Peter to see that Gentiles should be able to sing the new song too?

3. Are there any groups that the church treats like 'Gentiles' today – groups that we are reluctant to share the gospel with, either because we are convinced it won't be accepted, or because society doesn't consider it politically correct for us to do so? What can we do about that?

A Visit to Lystra

(Acts 14:8–18)

Introduction

The nice thing about this reading, from a storyteller's point of view, is that it requires you to remember only twelve lines! The repetition and the actions fill up the bulk of the time and make the piece work.

> **TELLING TIPS:** This is one of those stories where you explain the story before you actually tell it! Say that it's about Paul and Barnabas and their first visit to Lystra. They see a lame man, and at that point we all grab our legs and say, 'OW!' The lame man is healed, so we all throw our arms wide and say 'WOW!' The people in the town think Paul and Barnabas are gods, so we all act like ancient Greek gods, throw thunderbolts and shout, 'KAPOW!' The people bring them offerings, so we hold our fingers against our temples like horns and everyone will pretend to be a COW. Paul and Barnabas are horrified by this behaviour. They are not gods, they explain. We join them by stamping our feet and demanding that the people take the gifts away right NOW! And then, as Paul and Barnabas seize the opportunity to talk about their faith, we will join them as they point their audience to the True God, unto whom they should BOW. The repetition in each verse is there both to build some tension (as you say it a bit louder each time) and to give the crowd the chance to really get into the participation.

Paul and Barnabas were preaching in Lystra.
Paul and Barnabas were preaching in Lystra.
Paul and Barnabas were preaching in Lystra.
When they spotted a lame man. (OW!)

When they spotted a lame man. (OW!)
When they spotted a lame man. (OW!)

'You can be healed!' said Paul to the lame man.
'You can be healed!' said Paul to the lame man.
'You can be healed!' said Paul to the lame man.
And the man jumped up and walked. (WOW!)
And the man jumped up and walked. (WOW!)
And the man jumped up and walked. (WOW!)

'These men must be gods!' cried the people of Lystra.
'These men must be gods!' cried the people of Lystra.
'These men must be gods!' cried the people of Lystra.
Gods like Hermes and Zeus. (KAPOW!)
Gods like Hermes and Zeus. (KAPOW!)
Gods like Hermes and Zeus. (KAPOW!)

So they brought them gifts and sacrifices.
So they brought them gifts and sacrifices.
So they brought them gifts and sacrifices.
Fancy wreaths and a COW.
Fancy wreaths and a COW.
Fancy wreaths and a COW.

'We are not gods!' cried Paul and Barnabas.
'We are not gods!' cried Paul and Barnabas.
'We are not gods!' cried Paul and Barnabas.
Take these away right NOW!
Take these away right NOW!
Take these away right NOW!

'We worship the God who made heaven and earth.'
'We worship the God who made heaven and earth.'
'We worship the God who made heaven and earth.'
'Unto him you should BOW.'
'Unto him you should BOW.'
'Unto him you should BOW.'

OW, WOW, KAPOW, COW,
NOW unto him you should BOW.

Questions

1. In what ways, today, do people who minister in God's name run the risk of being mistaken for gods themselves?

2. If you had to tell someone about Jesus, and they had never heard of him at all, where would you start?

Walk and Pray and Listen

(Acts 16:6–10)

Introduction

This reading could be used either as an introduction to the text itself, or in any situation where you want your crowd to reflect on the nature of God's direction.

> **TELLING TIPS: Yes, it's really repetitive, but that's the point.**
> **Walking and praying and listening is what this piece is all about, so**
> **every time you do that line, have the crowd do a walking-in-place**
> **motion, a hands-folded praying motion, and a hand-to-the-ear**
> **listening motion. Don't have them repeat the line with you though,**
> **because at the end of the reading, it changes shape, slightly, and**
> **that will just confuse them.**

Paul and Silas and Timothy
Walked and prayed and listened.
They were looking for a place to talk about Jesus,
So they walked and prayed and listened.

They came to the borders of the province of Asia
As they walked and prayed and listened.
But the Spirit told them to move along
So they walked and prayed and listened.

Day after day, week after week,
They walked and prayed and listened.
Up hill and down hill and across vast plains
They walked and prayed and listened.

They came to the borders of the province of Mysia
As they walked and prayed and listened.
But the spirit of Jesus sent them on
So they walked and prayed and listened.

Week after week, month after month
They walked and prayed and listened.
For 200, 300, 400 miles
They walked and prayed and listened!

Then they came to the sea – to the port of Troas
As they walked and prayed and listened.
And Paul had a dream – a dream of a man
As they walked and prayed and listened.

'Come, talk to us,' the dream man said.
'As you walk and pray and listen.
'Across the sea to Macedonia.
'Come walk, I pray, and we'll listen.'

So Paul and Silas and Timothy
Walked and prayed and listened.
Across the sea to Macedonia
They walked and prayed and listened.

And they talked to the people
And the people believed;
Churches were planted,
The Good News received!

But it wouldn't have happened
If they'd just stayed at home
Or got tired and quit
Or asked a consultant
Or taken a poll
Or made a grand plan
Or just done what they wanted.
No it only happened, only happened at all

Because Paul and Silas and Timothy
Walked and prayed and listened.

Questions

1. Talk about a time when you jumped into something, thinking it was the right thing to do, without asking God first.

2. It takes a lot of patience, and a lot of wandering about, to do what Paul and his companions did. How does one keep focused in the midst of that?

3. Talk about a time when God pointed you in an unexpected direction, against your own preferences, perhaps. Or against your own careful consideration.

A Prison in Philippi

(Acts 16:16–34)

Introduction

One of the most exciting moments in doing a retelling is when you find an idea or set of words that ties a passage together and makes sense of it all in a clear and succinct manner. I think that's what I found here. And, as a result, this particular reading works really well and helps the crowd experience the heart of this passage.

> TELLING TIPS: Before the story begins, teach your crowd the chorus and a set of actions to go with it. If it helps, put the chorus up on a screen.
>
> 'Loose the bonds' – hands as fists, arms crossed, then uncrossed.
> 'Break the chains' – hands still as fists (now in uncrossed position), then pull hands further apart, as if the fists are holding a chain and then breaking it.
> 'Set the prisoner free' – fist in air.
>
> Then do the reading in as dramatic a way as you can, emphasising the fact that the 'prisoners' in the story keep changing. At the end, I usually repeat the chorus three times, making it 'bigger' each time.

Loose the bonds,
Break the chains,
Set the prisoner free.

The girl was enslaved, imprisoned, trapped. Possessed by a demon and by her human masters as well, who used the powers the demon gave her to make themselves a fortune. 'She'll tell your future! Interpret your dreams. Put your money on the table!' they shouted to the crowds in Philippi.

Loose the bonds,
Break the chains,
Set the prisoner free.

Then Paul and Silas came to Philippi to talk about Jesus. And when she saw them, the slave girl shouted, 'These men are the servants of the Most High God.'

Her words were true, but Paul was worried – worried at the poor girl's situation and worried as well that the crowd would confuse his message with the power of the demon.

So Paul told the demon, 'In the name of Jesus,

Loose the bonds,
Break the chains,
Set the prisoner free.'

And the demon came out of the girl!

That should have been that – the end of the story. But the girl had masters, remember? And the men who had made a fortune from her saw their business plan wrecked in a second. Their share prices slipping. Their stocks in free fall. They knew that they had to blame someone, so they got the authorities to arrest Paul and Silas and beat them and throw them in prison. And the men who had set the slave girl free were now trapped and imprisoned themselves!

Loose the bonds,
Break the chains,
Set the prisoner free.

Paul was enslaved, imprisoned, trapped and so was Silas his friend. Their cell door locked. Their feet in stocks. They were stuck in a foreign jail. They might have complained. They might have cursed. They might have rung their solicitor. But instead, they sang, they sang and prayed, prayed and sang praises to God.

Loose the bonds,
Break the chains,
Set the prisoner free.

Shaking and quaking and making such noise, an earthquake broke into their song.

Shaking and quaking and breaking the locks, an earthquake broke open their cell.

Shaking and quaking and taking his sword, the jailer went to kill himself, for the law was clear: if the prisoners escaped, he would have to die in their place.

Loose the bonds,
Break the chains,
Set the prisoner free.

Now the jailer was enslaved, imprisoned, trapped. There was no way out but death. But then Paul cried, 'Don't hurt yourself! Every one of us is still here.'

Shaking and quaking and taking a torch, the jailer went round to see. Paul's word were true. Not one had escaped. And the jailer fell to his knees.

Loose the bonds,
Break the chains,
Set the prisoner free.

'I've heard you sing, I've heard you pray, I've seen the saving power of your God. So tell me,' he said to Paul and Silas, 'what must I do to be saved?'

So Paul and Silas told him about Jesus, told all of his family too. And after he'd washed them and dressed their wounds the jailer was washed and made new. Washed in baptism. Washed clean of his sins. And all of his family too. Washed and set free by the men he'd imprisoned. Washed and set free and made new.

Loose the bonds,
Break the chains,
Set the prisoner free.

Questions

1. The three kinds of 'prisoner' in the story were trapped for different reasons. The girl was possessed by a demon, but also oppressed by her masters. Paul and Silas were imprisoned unjustly for doing something good. And the jailer was trapped by an inflexible judicial system. Which, if any, of these kinds of imprisonment can you relate to? Talk about other kinds of things that trap us.

2. Talk about a time when God set you free from something that had enslaved you.

3. God used Paul and Silas to free both the girl and the jailer. What part can we play in setting others free today?

Paul Waltzed into Athens

(Acts 17:16–34)

Introduction

I had a lot of fun writing this one, but you may find that the songs and singers I have chosen to represent Paul's new musical adventure in Athens are unfamiliar to you or to your group. So please feel free to replace them with whatever works for you.

> **TELLING TIPS: You will need two readers for this one. One person reads the scripture passage. They need to do it really well. And then the other person reads the 'new' text in between. This will need some practice, because the rereading works best when the two texts flow together seamlessly, as if they are one story – which, in a way, they are!**

So Paul waltzed into Athens with a tune on his lips. It was a gospel tune – 'Jesus is the Answer' by Andraé Crouch (or was it The Jesse Dixon Singers?). In any case, it had played well in Derbe and Lystra and Antioch, and even in that 'prison ministry' thing he'd stumbled into at Philippi. But would it play well here? In Athens? The first signs were not encouraging.

While Paul was waiting in Athens, he was greatly distressed to see that the city was full of idols.

So he decided to start with an audience who were at least a little familiar with his tune.

He reasoned in the synagogue with the Jews and the God-fearing Greeks, as well as in the marketplace day by day with those who happened to be there.

And that's where he ran into a crowd who knew an entirely different set of songs.

A group of Epicurean and Stoic philosophers began to dispute with him. Some of them asked, 'What is this babbler trying to say?' Others remarked, 'He seems to be advocating foreign gods.'

The Stoics were playing some sophisticated stuff – a bit of classical, a bit of jazz, the Blue Nile's 'Hats'. But the Epicureans – all they wanted to do was dance! Soul, funk, hip-hop, house – there was always some sort of party going on. And that wasn't all – Athens was buzzing with every other musical style. Heavy metal, alt-country, blues, punk, gangsta rap. How was Paul ever going to be heard in the midst of all this sound? As it happens, however, the Athenians were an eclectic bunch. Or maybe they were just on the lookout for the Next Big Thing.

So they took him and brought him to a meeting of the Areopagus, where they said to him, 'May we know what this new teaching is that you are presenting? You are bringing some strange ideas to our ears, and we want to know what they mean.' (All the Athenians and the foreigners who lived there spent their time doing nothing but talking about and listening to the latest ideas.)

Paul wanted to sing his song, he really did. But it occurred to him that it might be helpful for his audience to know that he understood and appreciated their stuff, too. So he took a chance and launched into a tune that had echoes of gospel, but a bit of what turned them on, as well.

'Men of Athens!' he said. 'I see that in every way you are very religious. For as I walked around and looked carefully at your objects of worship, I even found an altar with this inscription: TO AN UNKNOWN GOD.'

I have climbed the highest mountain
I have run through the fields
Only to be with you
Only to be with you
But I still haven't found what I'm looking for.

They liked the song. They really did. The Athenians were tapping their toes and nodding their heads. Some of them were even mouthing the words and doing that 'Edge' thing on their air guitars. So Paul decided to shift gears and work a little of his own tune into the mix.

> 'Now what you worship as something unknown I am going to proclaim to you. The God who made the world and everything in it is the Lord of heaven and earth and does not live in temples built by hands. And he is not served by human hands, as if he needed anything, because he himself gives all men life and breath and everything else. From one man he made every nation of men, that they should inhabit the whole earth; and he determined the times set for them and the exact places where they should live. God did this so that men would seek him and perhaps reach out for him and find him, though he is not far from each one of us.'

Most of the crowd was still swaying, still moving to Paul's groove. But some on the fringes were losing interest – chatting with their girlfriends, jabbering into their mobile phones. So Paul thought it might be time to switch gears again. He took a chance, a big chance for a rich boy from the posh end of Tarsus – and he broke into a rap. But he was clever, Paul was, and he lifted his lyrics from some of Athens' best – Dirty Ol' Epimenedes the Cretan and DJ Dizzy Aratus.

> '"For in him we live and move and have our being." As some of your own poets have said, "We are his offspring."'

The crowd was with him again, so Paul decided to segue back into his original tune. He took a deep breath and gave it everything he had. He was Marvin Gaye looking for sexual healing. He was Aretha just looking for respect. He was Van the Man looking down at the crowd at the Rainbow Theatre and shouting out that it was simply too late to stop now!

> 'Therefore since we are God's offspring, we should not think that the divine being is like gold or silver or stone – an image made by man's design and skill. In the past God overlooked such ignorance, but now he commands all people everywhere to repent. For he has set a day when he will judge the world with justice by the man he

has appointed. He has given proof of this to all men by raising him from the dead.'

And then, suddenly, Paul felt like a dead man, too. He was Dylan on his English tour in the summer of '66, and even though no one shouted out 'Judas' (largely because he hadn't actually yet told them who Judas was!), the feeling was much the same. The crowd turned on him. Some of them sneered, some of them booed and most of them walked out of the show. But there were a few, just a few, who came up to him after the show was over, their autograph books in their hands.

'We want to hear you again on this subject,' they said.

And there were others, who even started singing Paul's song.

A few men became followers of Paul and believed. Among them was Dionysius, a member of the Areopagus, also a woman named Damaris, and a number of others.

So Paul waltzed out of Athens, still humming his tune. And even though they weren't quite yet Andraé Crouch or even The Jesse Dixon Singers, he managed to leave his own little gospel choir behind.

Questions

1. What 'techniques' did Paul use to introduce his new song to the Athenians? How did he introduce his new song?

2. Have you ever tried to talk about Jesus with someone who had no idea of who he was, or no idea why they should even be interested in him? Who was singing a different song altogether? How did you approach the subject, get the conversation started? Where did it go from there? And is there anything about Paul's experience in Athens that you might have found helpful?

3. The crowd seem to be with Paul while he deals with his faith on a 'philosophical' level, but when he mentions the resurrection, he loses most of them. Are there any aspects of our faith that have the same effect on people

today? That 'turn them off' when they are mentioned. And what should we do? Leave those 'bits' out? Leave them till 'later'?

Paul Walked into Corinth

(Acts 18:1–17)

Introduction

Paul just keeps singing his song! He's in Corinth now, and runs into a slightly different set of musical preferences. Once again, if the musical references don't suit your crowd, or are out of date or obscure by the time you use this reading, feel free to change them.

> **TELLING TIPS: This is one to tell on your own. As with the piece about Peter, you may want to read the scripture passage first. Or – better still, I think – have someone else read it.**

So Paul walked into Corinth, hawking his gospel tunes, and what a shock he had! The city was a living, breathing parental advisory sticker. Marilyn Manson meets Christina Aguilera and The Notorious B.I.G. There wasn't a song he heard that wasn't shot through with violence, perversion and sex.

So Paul decided to start with what seemed like a more sympathetic audience. He hooked up with Aquila and his wife Priscilla, who'd just finished a tour of Italy. And together they formed a little trio. They made tents in the week (Every musician needs a day job!) and at the weekends they busked in the local synagogue, singing their gospel tunes to the Jews and the God-fearing Greeks. It wasn't long before Silas and Timothy joined them, as well. And now they were a five-piece, with Paul on lead vocals, of course!

It seemed like the perfect strategy, except for one thing. It wasn't what God had in mind. And it wasn't long before that became clear to Paul, as well. The Jews started booing in the middle of his sets. And when the beer bottles started to fly, Paul knew it was time to look for another venue.

'I'm singing to the Gentiles from now on!' he vowed. And he marched off stage and booked a gig right next door, at the house of Titius Justus, a

Greek and a worshipper of God. It wasn't long before the place was packed, and even Crispus, who'd been in charge of the synagogue and had secretly been tapping his toes to Paul's tunes, decided to sing the gospel song. There were loads of locals who joined in, as well, in a kind of Corinthian Karaoke. But their old tunes – all those Dirty Dancing numbers they'd grown up with and were cemented in their brains – were so strong that Paul wondered what it would take to make his gospel songs stick. And more than that, he wondered just how long it would be before the Jews shut him down for good.

So God came to him one night, in a dream. And the song God sang was 'You Got to Keep on Keeping On'.

'Do not be afraid; keep on speaking, do not be silent. For I am with you, and no one is going to attack and harm you, because I have many people in this city.'

It didn't take long to find out what the Jews would do. They got together and dragged Paul off to court.

'This man is persuading the people to worship God contrary to our laws,' they told the judge. And they were humming 'Jailhouse Rock', and 'Folsom Prison Blues' and 'Working on the Chain Gang'. But God kept his promise to Paul, and when the judge heard the charges, he dismissed them out of hand.

'This is a religious matter,' he said. 'What's it got to do with me?'

So while the Jews fought among themselves, Paul went back to singing his song. And the Corinthian tour lasted not a week, not a month, but a year and a half!

And the result? Well, not many people know this, but that little five-piece band became the original LCGC. That's right – the Lord's Corinthian Gospel Choir!

Questions

1. Why do you suppose that Paul felt more comfortable in the synagogues intitially? Talk about a time when you felt uncomfortable in a specific place or with a particular group of people. Did you leave or did you 'hang in there'? And what made the difference?

2. Ironically, Paul leaves what looks like a difficult situation and finds an even more difficult one in the synagogue. Talk about an experience in your own life where God led you out of something that looked easy into something that looked hard.

3. I can think of several people I know whose 'parental-advisory-sticker' lives were transformed by the power of God. And I'm sure you can, too. But the idea of transforming a whole culture seems so much more difficult. Not to mention the challenge of helping people who have been transformed to live obediently in a culture that questions their new found faith. This was the challenge that confronted Paul in Corinth. Can you think of a culture that was changed by God? And, if you live in a culture that wars against your faith, what are you doing practically so that you can continue singing the Lord's song in that culture, while still being close enough to it and understanding enough of it to make a difference?

'I'm Different'

(Romans 1:26–27)

Introduction

Some of you are going to like this piece and some of you aren't. That's the nature of this issue. It divides people. And now it threatens to divide the church.

I don't think it needs to be that way, however. And my hope is that this reading reflects that. Yes, as you will see, it takes one 'side', but only to make the point that 'stereotyping' and 'name-calling' is never going to settle this issue. To call someone a 'homophobe' is exactly the same thing as calling someone a 'fag'. Neither word is an accurate description of the person. Both are intended to belittle and dehumanise. 'You're a pervert!' You're a bigot!' That conversation has been going on for too long now. And it won't solve a thing. What is needed, as I hope the reading suggests, is tolerance. Not 'assent' masquerading as tolerance – as in 'I will only admit that you are tolerant if you agree with me.' Because when there is agreement, there's no need for tolerance! But real tolerance – as in 'I don't like your position, but I will continue to respect you as a person, try to understand you, and love you like Jesus does.' Given the unlikelihood of agreement over this issue, that kind of tolerance seems to me to be the only way forward.

TELLING TIPS: This is one to tell on your own. Start with the Bible passage at the beginning and then move right into the reading.

I'm different from you. That's all.
We worship the same God.
We read the same passage of scripture.
But we arrive at opposite conclusions.

I'm different from you. That's all.
I'm not asking you to agree with me.
I only ask that you tolerate my point of view.
But with you it seems that only assent will do.

I'm different from you. That's all.
I have tried to understand you. I really have.
But I see little evidence of that, in return.
Only stereotypes and labels and slogans.

I'm different from you. That's all.
So why do you think I'm a monster?
Why do you call my faith into question?
My ethics? My morality?

I'm different from you. That's all.
So why do you call me names?
Heaven knows, you don't like it.
And I don't do it. Never have.

I'm different from you. That's all.
So why do you judge me?
And why do you mock me?
And why do you call me
A homophobe?

Questions

1. So where do you stand on this issue? Which 'side' are you on? And why?

2. How does it feel when someone calls you 'names'? Reflect on some experience from your childhood. Or perhaps you have felt the pain of that with regard to this very issue. Do people on both sides of this issue have something to repent of with regard to the way they have treated those on the other side? Do you?

3. What do you think it means for one person to be tolerant of another?

Songs in Search of a Tune: We Belong to the Day

(1 Thessalonians 4:13 – 5:11)

Introduction

Just a little poem/song thing about the 1 Thessalonians passage.

> **TELLING TIPS: Again, one to read on your own. Or sing, if you can come up with that elusive tune!**

Verse 1:

Watching,
Ever patiently watching,
Watching for Jesus,
We look to the sky.

Waiting,
Ever faithfully waiting,
Waiting for Jesus,
To come back from on high.

Bridge:

Jesus comes to meet us in the air.
Death and sin all drowned in night's despair.
Light and love forevermore to share.
And we'll be right there.

Chorus:

We belong to the day,
We belong to the day,
Daughters so bright,
Sons of the light,
We belong to the day.

We belong to the day,
We belong to the day,
Leaving the night,
Right out of sight,
We belong to the day.

Verse 2:

Sleeping,
Our loved ones are sleeping,
It hurts when they leave us,
When we must say goodbye.

Keeping,
They're in your safe keeping,
Just waiting to greet us,
Just waiting to fly.

Bridge:

Jesus comes...

Chorus:

We belong to the day...

Questions

1. What do you think it means to 'belong to the day'?

2. Is the promised return of Jesus something that you regularly consider, or is it stuck way in the back of your mind? Are you waiting for Jesus' return or is it

something you don't bother about because you reckon it's not going to happen anytime soon, anyway? What are the real, day-to-day effects of taking the imminent return of Jesus seriously?

Location! Location! Location!

(Hebrews 3:1–11)

Introduction

This reading was based originally on a British home-improvement show of the same name, which tries to help its 'contestants' find a more desirable place in which to live. Even if you haven't seen the show, you've got to admit it's not a bad way of talking about the differences between the old and the new covenants!

> **TELLING TIPS: This is one piece where you should definitely begin by reading the scripture passage first. Or have someone else do it (and do it well!) and then you follow with this reading. If you like, you can divide your crowd into three groups and have each group shout 'Location!' in succession at the appropriate points in the text. Have each group get a little bit louder than the one before.**

Location! Location! Location!

Let's be honest here, shall we? The Israel House was adequate at the time. It was sturdy. It was functional. It was, after all, God, himself, who built it. But it was only a starter home. The first step on the property ladder that leads to our heavenly mansion. And Moses was a faithful servant in that house. He didn't own it. He didn't even rent. He was more like a live-in handyman. Laying down the law, and the tiles on the kitchen floor. Taking up our cause to God with the old linoleum in the hall. Paving the way to the promised land and the path to the garden shed. His job was to fix the place up. Get it ready to sell. So all of us could move on.

Location! Location! Location!

Now we live in the Jesus house. And you've got to admit – it's a much better proposition, all round. Bigger rooms, so more of us can squeeze in. More doors to enter. More windows, more light. And not so many rules. We can tidy up on Saturday if we like. And make whatever we want in the kitchen. It's a gracious, spacious place to live. And that's because Jesus doesn't just work here. He's not just a handyman. He owns the place.

Oh, the jobs are much the same. Revealing God's will and his plans for the place. Cementing our relationship with him and the cracks that come between us. And installing the odd skylight so we can look to heaven as well. But because the house is his, he has far more invested in it than any workman could ever have. Just think what it cost him in the first place.

Location! Location! Location!

So let's live in the Jesus house. Let's trust in the one who owns it and follow his household rules. And let's not make the mistake they made in the Israel house. They rebelled against the builder – remember? They disbelieved, they disobeyed, they gave up and tried to tear the place down. And what happened? They ended up with negative equity on a rundown property in an unfashionable desert district, sandwiched between a camel factory and a neighbour with a rusting Ford in his front yard. It took them forty years to sell that place. And I'd hate to see the same thing happen to us. Because we want to keep moving up that property ladder, don't we? And there's a mansion waiting for us. One that Jesus himself has prepared. So let's fix our eyes on him, the apostle and high priest we confess. And let's follow him up that ladder. Because it's all about...

Location! Location! Location!

Questions

1. The author of Hebrews is trying hard to demonstrate the superiority of the new covenant over the old. Which of the differences seems most important to you? And why?

2. As you look around your church, what redecorating needs to be done so that it looks more like Jesus' house?

3. The reading ends with a warning – so that we don't make the same mistakes the children of Israel did. Have we heeded that warning, or do we sometimes fall into the same errors? Offer examples to make your case.

Now That's What I Call Music!

(Hebrews 8)

Introduction

We continue the Hebrews theme in this reading, but the imagery moves from property to popular music! Again, the emphasis is on the difference between the two covenants.

> **Telling tips: As in the first Hebrews piece, it's important to read the scripture passage first. You can get the crowd involved by having them all shout 'Now That's What I Call Music!' in the appropriate places.**

Now that's what I call music!

Let's be honest here, shall we? 'Moses and the Twelve Tribes' was a great band. Memorable tunes. Solid vocals. First-class musicians. And the gigs they played at The Tabernacle deserve their place in history.

But when it comes down to it, Moses and the Twelve Tribes was really just a tribute band. The Rolling Clones, The Illegal Eagles, The Karaoke Covenant, if you like. Nothing more than a copy of a better band, on a bigger stage, with a belting lead singer – the true Godfather of Soul.

And that's the problem with tribute bands. The lyrics have to be memorized. The posturing imitated. The guitar solos practiced to perfection. And the costumes and hair recreated exactly. Everything according to pattern – from the outside in. Which is fine as far as it goes. Until the real band comes to town.

Now that's what I call music!

They know the words. They wrote them. They've been singing them for years. The performance is like second nature. The hair and the clothes are their own. They fit them. And the solos spring to the fingers from somewhere deep inside.

> After that time, declares the Lord, I will put my laws in their minds and write them on their hearts. I will be their God, and they will be my people. No longer will a man teach his neighbour, or a man his brother, saying, 'Know the Lord,' because they will all know me.

Or to borrow a lyric: 'Jesus put this song into our hearts.'

Now that's what I call music!

Questions

1. So what exactly is the advantage of having laws written on one's heart as opposed to written down in a book or a scroll? How does that work in practice?

2. In what respect is the old covenant a shadow or an imitation of the new?

A Dying Dream

(Hebrews 9, Revelation 15)

Introduction

Here is another reading from Hebrews – a more serious reading – that attempts to take the imagery from chapter 9 and link it directly to Jesus' death on the cross. There is obviously a lot of speculation here, and you might find that uncomfortable. But I do think that, by personalising the connection, it helps the reader to better understand the link between Jesus' death and the sacrificial system in the old covenant.

> **TELLING TIPS: You need to read this one alone, although you could have someone else read the passage from Revelation at the end. As with the other Hebrews pieces, it will also help to open the reading with a passage from Hebrews itself – in this case, verses 1–14, or, if that seems too long, verses 11–14.**

He slipped into a stupor, a daze, a dream. And, suddenly, he was no longer suspended in the air. He was walking slowly through the tent. The light from the lampstand sent his shadow trembling across the walls. He bumped into a table and picked some bread up off a plate. This is my body, he thought.

And then he saw the curtain and the altar and heard the voices of the beasts. The bleating of goats. The calves crying for their mothers. Millions upon millions of them. And the knives raised and the throats slit and the blood. The blood everywhere, over everything. The blood upon the altar. This is my blood, he thought.

And now the knife was in his hand. He was the High Priest Aaron. He was Abraham on the mountain. And he was the goat bleating for mercy as well. The calf crying for its mother. And Isaac asking his father, 'Why?'

So he cried for his mother, 'Take care of her, John!'

And he cried to his father, 'Why? Why have you forsaken me?'

And he drew the knife across his wrists and feet and across his head and plunged it into his side. And the blood poured out. Everywhere, over everything. Everywhere, over everyone. The blood upon the altar. And that's when the curtain opened. Not drawn open. Not pulled open. But torn open. Curtain rails wrecked. Fabric on the floor. Never to be shut again.

Then he walked through the place where the curtain had been, into the place beyond. And like Isaac skipping down the mountain, that's where he found the answer to his question. For there was his Father. All that smelled and felt and tasted of him. The fresh manna of his provision. The chiselled words of his will. The budding staff of his beauty and power. And the soft beaten gold at the seat of his mercy.

Above that seat the angels sang. But they did not sing alone. For there were other voices too. The voices of everyone who had slipped into that place behind him. Behind him and because of him. Through the blood, across the rags of the curtain and into the presence of the Father. Millions upon millions of them. Swelling the place with their bodies and with their song. Not the bleating of goats, nor the cry of calves, but the grateful praise of the forgiven, mixing with the incense and rising to the Father.

> **Great and marvellous are your deeds, Lord God Almighty. Just and true are your ways, King of the ages. Who will not fear you, O Lord, and bring glory to your name? For you alone are holy. All nations will come and worship before you. For your righteous acts have been revealed.**

'It is finished,' he said, with the song ringing in his ears. 'It is finished.' And the dream faded. And the stupor cleared. And he closed his eyes and died.

Questions

1. What do you think of the idea of having to slaughter an animal to take away your sin? In the long term, do you think it would make you more or less likely to sin?

2. Does the quantity of blood in the reading help you to better appreciate Jesus' sacrifice? And why so much blood, do you think?

314

3. There have been lots of theories about the 'atonement' through the ages – the purpose behind Jesus' sacrifice. How do you think that 'works'?

Clouds and Crowds and Witnesses

(Hebrews 11, 12)

Introduction

I know that, strictly speaking, the idea of the 'cloud of witnesses' in Hebrews is not that they should be watching us, but that we should be looking to them as our examples of faith and sacrifice and steadfastness. Having said that, I think that, by pushing the *Chariots of Fire* racing imagery, this reading does what the author of Hebrews intends. It uses the lives of the 'saints' who have gone before us as an encouragement for us to 'stay the course' as well.

> **TELLING TIPS:** The cheering is obviously the key participation device here. I usually just bring the crowd in with a cheer after each time I say 'They're cheering (BIG CHEER!). Can you hear them?'. It's as simple as that, though it might help to warm them up with a few practice cheers ahead of time – and to tell them that the cheers need to get a little bit bigger each time. When you get to the part where Jesus throws his arms open in the shape of a cross, do that, just as if you're crossing the finishing line! And, yes, if you want to get someone to play the theme from *Chariots of Fire* in the background, it probably won't be all that cheesy – and just might work!

They're cheering. Can you hear them?
Like a cloud, they surround us.
The ones who've run the race before.

Abel and Enoch,
Noah and Abraham,
Isaac and Jacob and Joseph and Moses.

Look at them training.
Take note of their technique.
They'll teach us how to run the race.

They're cheering. Can you hear them?
Like a cloud, they surround us.
The ones who've run the race before.

Rahab and Gideon,
Barak and Samson,
Jephthah and David and Samuel and the prophets

Throw off everything that holds you back.
Like Noah threw off his doubt,
Like Abraham threw off his homeland,
Like Enoch threw off the weight of the world and went to walk
    with God.

Throw off whatever is wrong as well – whatever tempts and tangles
    and trips you up.
Like Rahab threw off her idols,
Like Jacob threw off his deceit,
Like Moses threw off the pleasures of sin and chose the plight of
    his people.

Then run with perseverance. Run the whole course and never give up.
Like Joseph waiting for his dreams to come true,
Like Samuel's search for a king,
Like Gideon watching his army weaken to the point he could
    claim God's victory.

They're cheering. Can you hear them?
Like a cloud, they surround us.
The ones who've run the race before.

And out in front, out in front of us all
Is the one on whom we fix our eyes.
He's setting the pace. He's leading the race.
The author and perfecter of our faith.

He hurdles the shame,
He fights through the pain.
It looks as if the race will be lost.
But in spite of his foes
He endures, wins, then throws
His arms wide in the shape of a cross.

So let's run the race.
Run and not grow weary.
Run for the prize that's set before us.

And when we get run down,
Let's look and let's listen.
For we don't run this race alone.

They're cheering. Can you hear them?
Like a cloud, they surround us.
The ones who've run the race before.

Questions

1. Whom would you put in your 'cloud of witnesses'? Which people, living or dead, have inspired you to keep running the race?

2. Which of the biblical figures listed in the reading do you find most inspiring?

3. What kinds of thing make you want to stop running? What discourages you?

A Choosy People

(1 Peter 2:9–10)

Introduction

I have pastored three churches over the past twenty-five years – one in the States and two in the UK. And during that time I have heard an amazing variety of reasons why the Lord calls Christians to move from one church to another! And no, before you think it, I'm not a complete loser! Yes, sometimes the Lord had his reasons for calling people away from the churches I pastored, and sometimes (just to keep things even, I guess) he had his reasons for calling them *to* the churches I pastored, as well. As you have probably guessed by now, I have strong suspicions about whether the Lord was actually involved in this process at all. And that is partly where this reading comes from. 'Chosen' or 'Choosy'? – that's the question. And I'm not sure the contemporary church has benefited much from choosing one answer over the other.

> **TELLING TIPS: This is a reading for two to do. Have one person read the scripture passages (keep this quite serious) and the other the lines in between. You might want to change names and references to suit your own situation.**

But you are a chosen people, a royal priesthood, a holy nation, a people belonging to God, that you may declare the praises of him who called you out of darkness into his wonderful light.

When we first moved to town, we had a pretty clear idea of the kind of church we were looking for.
The worship had to be right, for a start.

But you are a chosen people, a royal priesthood, a holy nation, a people belonging to God.

Post-Kendrick. Pre-Redman. A touch of Taizé. That's what we had in mind. And we thought we'd found it. But when the organist at the first church we joined played the chorus of 'Shine, Jesus, shine' while the offering was being collected, we knew there and then that the Lord was telling us to leave.

That you may declare the praises of him who called you out of darkness into his wonderful light.

The next church was better. Yes, they seemed to love God and love one another. But they weren't really in touch with the Spirit. They weren't 'moving on'. If you know what I mean.

But you are a holy nation, a royal priesthood.

So we tried a church on the other side of town. Sadly, the pastor was entirely too legalistic. He wouldn't let women pray!

A holy nation, a people belonging to God.

While the vicar at the next place was entirely too loose. He wanted women priests!

That you may declare the praises of him

So God called us on. What could we do?

Who called you out of darkness into his wonderful light.

But everywhere we went it was the same story.

But you are a chosen people,

The paintwork was too bright.

A royal priesthood,

The drums were too loud.

A holy nation,

The incense made me sneeze.

A people belonging to God.

The woman sitting next to me had a funny nose.

That you may declare the praises of him who called you out of darkness into his wonderful light.

I think the church is like a supermarket! If you don't like the quality of the produce at Tesco's, you can always pop down to Sainsbury's. Or ASDA. Or even the corner shop. Choice – that's the important thing. Keeping the customer satisfied. And I'm sure that's true of church as well.

But you are a chosen people.

Questions

1. If you're a pastor or a leader in a small church, you can't help taking it just a little bit personally when someone leaves – even if their leaving has nothing to do with you. Is this true in big churches as well, do you think? Are church leaders just too possessive or sensitive on this matter?

2. In what circumstances does God call people from one church to another? How do you know when he's the one who's doing the calling?

3. What effect does a lot of movement from one church to another have on the individual who does the moving? What effect does it have on the churches?

Let's Hear it for the Church!

Introduction

I have to confess – sometimes I get a little tired of the self-flagellating routine that the church regularly puts itself through. A couple of years ago there were several high profile books about how awful the authors' church experience was and how the church really needed to get its act together if it was going to be an adequate representative of Jesus in the modern world. I have two responses to that. The first is, 'When did the church ever really have its act together – in the modern world or any other?' Not among Jesus' disciples, as far as I can tell. And not among most of the churches referred to in the New Testament, either! Oh, there are a few brief shining moments mentioned here and there. And I'll bet you could pick a few of those out from your experience of the church, as well. But the rest of the time, the church was and continues to be more a 'work in progress' than a 'masterpiece'. And that brings me to my second response. I'm not at all sure that Jesus ever intended it to be any more than that. I'm not saying that Christians ought to be satisfied with hypocrisy and scandal and manipulation and apathy (see, there I go, too!), but that we ought, at the very least, to get a little less satisfaction from beating ourselves up!

I heard a sermon once where the speaker observed that in some Christian traditions the congregation believed that it hadn't been adequately preached to until it could feel the bruises of its own imperfection. But what does that say about grace? If I can't even talk about our church experience without pointing the finger of blame at the elder who shunned me, or the group leader who oppressed me, or the minister who disagreed with me, or the Sunday-school teacher who passed heresy on to me, then how am I ever going to live in grace with the rest of the world? The church isn't perfect. It's never going to be, not this side of heaven. That's why it's the place for grace. Because we need it there, sometimes more than anywhere. And when we find it, well… that's what this reading is about.

Let's hear if for the Church!

OK, so it's had some negative press recently.

Like the Simpsons' Reverend Lovejoy:

'Thank you, Marge, for showing me that there's more to being a pastor than not caring about other people's problems.'

But where did we get the idea that it would be perfect?

Not from the Bible – that's for sure!

The church in Corinth was dirty with division and immorality.

But Paul thanked God for it.

And I want to thank God for my church, too – the church I grew up in.

For Kathy Miller and the indescribably delicious cookies she baked for every wedding and funeral and bridal shower these last 30 years.

For my dear departed and ever-so-slightly-insane grandmother, who taught the Junior Boys' Class like she was directing a B-grade horror film.

'That's right; it was the firstborn who died in the final Egyptian plague. And which of you boys are the firstborn in your families?'

And for the whole lot of them, who held us and cried with us when my dad passed away a few years ago.

There are more that I could name – and plenty that you could name, too – who were there just when you needed them.

So let's hear it – let's hear it for the Church!

And let's hear it for the Bride!

OK, so she gets shot down sometimes.

Like Uma Thurman before she slipped into that bright yellow jumpsuit.

But where did we get the idea that following Jesus would make us popular?

Not from Jesus – that's for sure!

'If they persecuted me,' he said, 'can you expect anything better?'

No, he dresses us up and prepares us and makes us beautiful – not for the world – but for his eyes only. And that's a different kind of beauty.

It's the beauty of a church in pain – arrested and beaten and imprisoned –
in China and Africa and across the Middle East.

It's the beauty of a church with principles – that knows right from wrong
and will not bend with the changing winds of social and political
convention.

And it's the beauty of the person sitting next to you, as well. Who hangs in
there, believing and praying and trying to do what's best when much of
the rest of the population laughs and makes fun and scratches its head
and simply doesn't 'get it'.

So let's hear it – let's hear it for the Bride!

And let's hear it for the Body!

OK, so it's a little out of shape.

Like the 'before' pictures in the latest diet-fad ad.

But where did we get the idea that it would be 'pumped'?

Not from Paul, that's for sure.

Most of the churches he wrote to were '97-pound weaklings'.

But that's the point. It's only by God's grace and God's power that we
become what we never could have been on our own.

And the horror is not that we mess up sometimes. That's to be expected.

That's what grace is for.

No, the miracle is that we sometimes get it right!

And the poor get fed.

And kids find a place where they are accepted.

And the sick get healed.

And marriages get saved.

And the grieving are comforted.

And folk just like you and me find God.

People often say to me – and I know what they mean – 'I love Jesus, but I
just can't stand the church.'

And what I want to say, and what I ought to say, and what I'm saying right
now is this:

'How? How can you say you love Jesus and not love his Body?'

So let's hear it for the Body!

All fingers and thumbs sometimes, but the Body of Christ nonetheless.

And let's hear it for the Bride!

Beautiful and broken and unbowed.

And let's hear it
Let's hear it
Let's hear it for the Church!

Questions

1. Talk about a really positive experience you have had of the church. And, yeah, all right then, talk about a negative one, too.

2. Why do you think that when Christians talk negatively about the church, it often sounds as if they are talking about someone else, over there, and not themselves?

3. What do you think of the statement 'I love Jesus, but I can't stand the church'? Why do people say that? Is it possible to love the one and not the other? Can you be a Christian 'on your own'?

Songs in Search of a Tune: Mercy

Introduction

Yeah, one last poem – to sum up everything that's gone before.

TELLING TIPS: One to read on your own. The temperature is in celcius, to convert to fahrenheit: F = (1.8C) + 32.

It should have been freezing.
There should have been snow.
Thermometers should have read thirteen below.
But the sun stretched its arms out
And wouldn't let go,
In the middle of March
It was thirty or so.

And that's just how you are.
And that's just like you.

She should have ignored me.
She should have said no.
I had the wrong shoes on,
She wore all the right clothes.
But the girl stretched her hand out,
She wouldn't let go.
And behind her blue eyes
Something more than blood flowed.

And that's just how you are.
And that's just like you.

And that's just how you are.
And that's just like you.
Wind blowing, wings beating,
You go where you go.
And I can't explain or deserve or demand,
I just know that grace pours from the palm of your hand
When you touch me.

I should have been happy
To recite my own lines.
I should have been left
To pay my own fines.
But you stretched your arms out,
You wouldn't let go.
It's not mercy you earn,
It's Mercy you know.

And that's just how you are.
And that's just like you.

And that's just how you are.
And that's just like you.
Wind blowing, wings beating,
You go where you go.
And I can't explain or deserve or demand,
I just know that grace pours from the palm of your hand
When you touch me.

Questions

1. Talk about a time when you surprised yourself by showing mercy to someone.

2. Why do we feel we have to pay our own fines? Where does that come from?

3. Talk about a time when you were genuinely surprised and amazed by someone else's grace.

Three Days of the Dragon

Introduction

This is obviously not a Bible story at all! But it does contain certain themes – sacrifice, peacemaking, stereotyping – that I think are inherently biblical. It first appeared in the *Lion Storyteller Book of Animal Tales*, and I then expanded it into four short chapters so that I could tell it over four days at a Christian conference. That is the version that appears here. You can either break it into parts, like I did, or just tell it in one go. I have included 'Telling tips' for each 'chapter'.

Chapter One

> **TELLING TIPS:** Divide the crowd into three groups – 'women', 'children' and 'men'. But do it by section and not by gender or age – so you have everyone playing everyone, if you see what I mean. Teach each group their actions. The women chat (yeah, sorry!), the children play (sing la-la-la-la-la), and the men laugh and wave pretend mugs and make carousing noises! Lead each group in its action at the appropriate place. And then later, as well, when the actions turn to something more menacing.

Once upon a time, there was a river. It flowed through the middle of a dry and mountainous land. And it flowed between two tribes – the Tiana and the Aroman.

When the river flowed fast and full, both tribes drank from it and watered their cattle and washed their clothes. Their women chatted, their children played, and their men laughed and drank and traded goods.

But when, one summer, the water flowed slow and shallow – and when that summer stretched to a year and then two – the chatting turned to argument, the playing turned to name-calling, and the laughing and the trading turned to war.

Men on both sides died. Just a few at first – then more and many more. And that is when Tiana-Rom, chief of the Tiana tribe, came to his elders with an idea.

'The legends say there is a dragon who lives in the Far Mountains. A dragon that will come to the aid of any tribe that is willing to pay the price.'

'We don't need any help!' argued one of the elders. 'We are strong. We can do this ourselves!'

'It's a risk,' said another. 'And what if the legends are wrong? I say we stick to what we know and keep on fighting.'

'We need time to think,' said a third elder. 'We've never done it this way before.'

'And besides,' said the oldest elder of them all. 'You haven't yet told us what price this dragon demands.'

Tiana-Rom looked solemnly around the room. 'A life,' he whispered. 'The life of a brave young girl.' Then he nodded to a servant by the door, and into the room walked the chief's own daughter, Tiana-Mori.

'No!' cried the elders as one. 'Never!'

'But I have already agreed,' said Tiana-Mori. 'And I will go whether you permit me to or not. We do need help. We have run out of time. And each day more of our people die. This is a great risk, yes. But surely it is better to lose just one more life, than for all of us to perish.'

The elders looked at one another. This was indeed the bravest girl in the village. And that made their decision doubly hard. But their people needed water. The tribes were evenly matched. And the dragon would give them the advantage they required.

And so, sadly, they agreed.

Tiana-Mori left the very next morning. She walked for a day and a night and another day. And finally, at the foot of the tallest mountain, she came to the mouth of the dragon's cave. Bones were scattered everywhere. Tree branches rattled, bare and burned. And the dragon lay sleeping. His scales shimmered green and gold, and atop his head – like a cockerel's comb – ran a ridge of bright red horns. He was both the most frightening and the most beautiful creature that Tiana-Mori had ever seen.

For a second, just a second, Tiana-Mori thought about running. But at that very same second, the dragon stirred. He opened one green eye. He stared right at her. And then, to her amazement, the dragon spoke!

Chapter Two

'Is there something you want?' the dragon muttered. 'Something important enough to wake a dragon from his sleep?'

'There is,' said Tiana-Mori. 'I have come from the tribe of Tiana. I am the bravest girl in the village. And I am here to sacrifice myself so that you will help us defeat our enemy, the Aroman.'

'The bravest girl?' said the dragon, both eyes open now. 'Really? Well, why don't you climb onto my head, and we'll see about that.'

Tiana-Mori walked slowly towards the dragon. Past his sharp teeth and his shiny split tongue. Onto his paw and up his long foreleg. Over his mountain of a shoulder and finally up onto his head.

Was he playing with her? she wondered. Like a big cat, waiting for just the right moment to strike? Why didn't he just eat her and get it over with!

'Now sit down between the horns,' said the dragon. 'And hold on tight!'

And without another word, up the dragon flew – out of the mouth of the cave and high above the mountains, so quickly that Tiana-Mori could hardly catch her breath.

Up they flew, up towards the clouds – the dragon twisting and turning, and Tiana-Mori hanging on for dear life.

'Afraid yet, brave girl?' roared the dragon.

'Yes!' shouted Tiana-Mori, her eyes shut tight. 'But I will not let go, no matter how hard you try and shake me loose. For my people need me and I will do what I must do.'

'Very well, then,' the dragon replied. And he stopped his twisting and his turning and floated gently back towards the ground.

Tiana-Mori opened her eyes, relieved. But her relief did not last long.

For the dragon was not returning to his mountain cave. No, he was doing something far worse. There, ahead, lay her village. And there, beyond it, the

330

dry river. The dragon was doing the most awful thing of all. Her mission unfinished, the dragon was taking her home!

They landed just outside the village, and as the tribe ran to meet them, Tiana-Mori pleaded with the dragon.

'Eat me now!' she cried. 'Spare my father and my friends from the sight of the thing you must do!'

'Eat you?' said the dragon. 'Wherever did you get that idea?'

'The legends,' answered Tiana-Mori.

'The legends?' snorted the dragon. 'The legends? Well, let me tell you this, young lady. I don't care what the legends say. There is more than one way to win the help of a dragon. And you have done so with your bravery and your selflessness. There is no doubt in my mind that you love your people and would do whatever it takes to save them. So go! Go and tell them that the dragon will come to their aid!'

Chapter Three

TELLING TIPS: This is my favourite section, because we all get to play dragons! You can get everyone to take their jumpers or jackets or fleeces and wear them on their heads. (If you take the neck-hole and jam it on your head like a hat, then the sleeves hang down beside your face and look like great big floppy ears!) Then get everyone to shake their heads about when the dragons play (leap, soar, turn, roar...) near the end of this section.

Tiana-Mori scrambled down from the dragon's head and ran to meet her father. She told him everything that had happened, and he hugged her and thanked her and gathered the elders together to make their war plans.

'Come, Dragon!' he said. 'Come meet with our council. It is good to have you on our side.'

'I will meet with you later,' the dragon shrugged. 'I have something more important to do right now.' And he turned to walk away.

'But, the legends...' said Tiana-Rom.

'The legends!' snorted the dragon. 'Don't talk to me about the legends.' And with a flap of his wings and a puff of smoke, he was gone.

'He's not what I expected, Father,' said Tiana-Mori.

'No,' grunted Tiana-Rom. 'Just as long as we can count on him. That's the important thing.' And they walked home, hand in hand.

As a reward for her bravery, Tiana-Mori was invited to the meeting as well. She sat in the corner of the hut. She listened carefully to the plans. She was fascinated by every detail. She was certain that her people would win. And when the meeting was over, she went to find the dragon and tell him everything that she had heard.

The dragon, however, was still not interested. Not interested at all. He was lying on his back, at the edge of the village. And the Tiana children were bouncing on his belly, and hanging off his tail, while their mothers watched and laughed.

'Dragon!' cried Tiana-Mori. 'You said you were on our side! You said you were loyal to us! Don't you care what the war plans are? Don't you know that you and you alone can strengthen the hearts of our people!'

The dragon picked the children, one by one, from his belly and gently set them down. Then he rolled over and looked straight into Tiana-Mori's eyes.

'There is more than one way to win the heart of a people,' he said. 'Listen to their laughter. And then go and ask your elders if they really want to turn that laughter into tears. For that is what their war will do.'

'I don't understand!' shouted Tiana-Mori. 'What about the legends?'

'The legends,' the dragon sighed. Then he picked up Tiana-Mori, and set her, once again, on his head. He tore off into the evening sky, blowing pinwheels of fire to the cheers of the children below. He flew straight for the ceiling of clouds. He burst straight through. And when he did, Tiana-Mori just stared and gasped.

The sun stood at one end of the sky, setting in a sea of blazing orange and pink. The moon stood high at the other end, like a ghost in the advancing blue of night. And between them, over a soft white floor of cloud, soared more dragons than Tiana-Mori could count.

There were giant purple ones, bigger than whales. Tiny red ones, smaller than hummingbirds. And every size between. Some had wings like bats. Some had wings like fairies. Some had no wings at all, but still somehow managed to fly.

They leaped.

They soared.

They turned.

They roared.

They shook their dragon heads.

'What are they doing?' asked Tiana-Mori. 'Are they going to have a fight?'

'A fight?' snorted the dragon. 'Heavens, no! They're playing! It's what they do every night. I bet your legends don't tell you that!'

'But I thought dragons were...'

'Vicious? Fierce? Likely to gobble up brave little girls? Is that what you were going to say?' asked the dragon.

'Yes,' whispered Tiana-Mori. And then she fell silent.

'We were that way once,' the dragon admitted. 'But then, then we discovered this. This beauty. This joy. This play. This peace. And that is our only loyalty now.'

'But what about us?' asked Tiana-Mori. 'What about being loyal to us? You promised you would come! You promised you would help! Are you saying you no longer want to defeat our enemy?'

'I have come. And I will help,' the dragon grinned. 'And if all goes well, when I am finished the Aroman will no longer be your enemy. And perhaps then you will finally understand.'

Then he waved goodbye to the other dragons, dropped through the clouds and carried Tiana-Mori back to her home.

Chapter Four

> **TELLING TIPS: In this section get everyone to stomp and breathe fire and shake the earth (beat feet on ground).**

The next morning dawned drizzling and grey, and the dragon sat like an enormous dog and listened patiently to Tiana-Rom.

'The plan is quite simple,' he explained. 'Go before us. Blow fire, shake the earth. Terrify our enemy. Then be the bridge that we cross to crush them!'

Everything went well, at first. The dragon stomped out in front of the Tiana warriors, breathing fire and shaking the earth. And the Aroman army shook as well. But when the dragon reached the middle of the riverbed, he stopped and he stood between the two tribes. And he spoke.

'People of Tiana! People of Aroman! Once you lived in peace. You can live that way again! And I have come to show you how.'

'Peace?' cried Tiana-Rom. 'When we are so close to victory? Never!'

And in his rage, Tiana-Rom let one arrow fly – an arrow that struck the Aroman chief and killed him where he stood.

'See!' he shouted to the dragon. 'The legends were right! This is what you have come for – not for peace, but to help us defeat the enemy!'

And so pleased was Tiana-Rom with his shot that he did not see the arrow shot in return – the arrow that would surely have pierced his own heart, had someone not leaped in the way.

'Tiana-Mori!' cried the chief. But it was already too late. His only daughter lay dying in his arms.

'The legends! The legends!' roared the dragon. 'The sacrifice of a brave young girl. A dragon's aid. Now I will show you what the legends really mean!'

And as the arrows flew thick and fast, and as many more warriors fell, the dragon tore into the sky. High and higher he soared, till he was but a bright speck among the dark clouds. Then he dived straight towards the earth, faster than the driving rain – down, down, down, until he struck the riverbed with a mighty crash!

The force of the landing knocked the warriors from their feet. And when they rose, and when they looked, the dragon was gone. But the river was flowing fast and full!

Green and gold the water shimmered. And a voice called out from the deep.

'You must hurry. The time will soon be past. Come together to the river. Wash your dead in the water. And they will live.'

So that is what the two tribes did. Tiana-Rom went first, carrying Tiana-Mori. And the Aroman followed, with their fallen chief. They dragged the rest of the dead in as well. And there, in the river, the warriors of Tiana and the warriors of Aroman came back to life!

And that was not all. As they waded and splashed, as they shared their grief and their joy, the people of Tiana and Aroman looked into each other's faces for the first time in a long time. And they remembered. They remembered the chatting and the playing and the laughing and the days when the river was full. And so, something else came back to life as well. And the two tribes agreed to be friends, once again.

Washed and wet, they embraced one another, and so caught up were they in their reunion, that they did not notice the bridge – a ridge of bright red horns, like a cockerel's comb – that grew from one side of the river to the other.

That evening, as the tribes ate and drank and celebrated their peace, Tiana-Mori sat on the bridge and stared into the water.

'I'll miss you,' she said. 'And I'm sorry. I'm sorry that I did not trust you. But I understand now. I really do. There's more than one way to do everything. To win the help of a dragon. To win the heart of a people.'

'Yes,' rose a voice from the river. 'And there's more than one way to win a battle too.'

And then a shadow rose from the river as well – green and gold so that only Tiana-Mori could see. High and higher still. Past the setting sun and the rising moon. To a place where dragons play.

Questions

1. Everyone had an idea of what the dragon would/should be like. He was, of course, nothing of the sort. Talk about a time when you had made your mind up about someone and they turned out to be very different. What are the dangers of stereotyping?

2. The dragons discovered something that transformed them – something they loved better than fighting. Consider the conflicts in the world today. Is there anything that we or our enemies might find that could take our attention away from war?

3. Is the solution in the story – the dragon's sacrifice for both sides in the conflict – a constructive or realistic solution to the conflicts we face today?

Made in the USA
Middletown, DE
13 November 2021